MODERNITY AND WAR

Also by Philip K. Lawrence

PREPARING FOR ARMAGEDDON

DEMOCRACY AND THE LIBERAL STATE

KNOWLEDGE AND POWER

Modernity and War

The Creed of Absolute Violence

Philip K. Lawrence
Professor of International Politics
University of the West of England
Bristol

First published in Great Britain 1997 by
MACMILLAN PRESS LTD
Houndmills, Basingstoke, Hampshire RG21 6XS and London
Companies and representatives throughout the world

A catalogue record for this book is available from the British Library.

ISBN 0–333–67026–4

First published in the United States of America 1997 by
ST. MARTIN'S PRESS, INC.,
Scholarly and Reference Division,
175 Fifth Avenue, New York, N.Y. 10010

ISBN 0–312–17402–0

Library of Congress Cataloging-in-Publication Data
Lawrence, Philip K.
Modernity and war : the creed of absolute violence / Philip K.
Lawrence.
p. cm.
Includes bibliographical references and index.
ISBN 0–312–17402–0 (cloth)
1. Military history, Modern.   2. War and society.   3. Air warfare–
–Social aspects.   I. Title.
U39.L38 1997
355.02'09'04—dc21   96–52561
                                                        CIP

This book is printed on paper suitable for recycling and made from fully managed and
sustained forest sources.

10   9   8   7   6   5   4   3   2   1
06   05   04   03   02   01   00   99   98   97

Printed and bound in Great Britain by
Antony Rowe Ltd, Chippenham, Wiltshire

to Benita

Contents

Acknowledgements

In writing this book my chief debts are owed to other authors whose work in the last decade has transformed the way in which war has been interpreted and theorized. This is not to say that the traditional genre of military history has been supplanted. Orthodox military history remains as a rewarding and insightful approach to military affairs. But in recent times this approach has been supplemented by a perspective which links military developments to wider aspects of the social totality, particularly that of culture. My work would have been impossible without the insights I have gained from Christopher Coker, Tom Engelhardt, H. Bruce Franklin, Daniel Pick, Michael S. Sherry and Spencer Weart. On occasion I criticize their ideas, but I could never hope to match their efforts in this field.

I would also like to thank my new colleagues at the University of the West of England, Bristol, for the enthusiasm and encouragement they have shown towards my work. It has been an uplifting experience to work amongst academics who are genuinely supportive of each other's intellectual endeavours. I owe a particular debt to Gerry Crawley, who read the manuscript and made many suggestions as to how it might be improved. I also owe a debt to the eminent physicist Dr Anders Hansson who helped to clarify my thinking on certain technical issues. Needless to say, I remain solely responsible for the book's weaknesses and faults.

On a personal note I thank my sons James and Michael, who have been very patient while the computer has been off-limits to them for much of the last year. They have also been very stoical about their father's grumpiness during what has been a year of fairly intense writing. Finally I owe an immense debt to my wife, Benita. While writing a doctorate and holding down a high-powered job, she has given me enormous support and help with this project. This book is dedicated to her.

Introduction

SELF-DELUSIONS

The modern period, by which is normally meant the era after the French Revolution, has been one of extreme violence. Beginning with the Revolutionary and Napoleonic wars, a radically new form of war was practised by Western countries. Napoleon introduced new tactics and strategy into warfare, and had at his disposal a new means of motivating men to fight each other. After Napoleon these innovations were supplemented with the radically more destructive means of warfare created by the application of systematic scientific research to industrial production. Thus throughout the nineteenth century invention after invention, coupled with new rational forms of mass production and standardization, gave armies the tools for unprecedented levels of slaughter.

In the nineteenth century these novel tools of violence did not dent the prevailing spirit of the age, which was one of optimism. Preceding industrialization, the philosophers of the Enlightenment had laid down a manifesto of change for the coming era which envisaged the perfectibility of man. Beginning with Locke, and running on through the French and Scottish Enlightenment, a new age was proclaimed where the inherent contradictions of the past would be overcome. Man would emerge more rational, more free, more productive and more just. Intellectual tools which could shape and mould nature could also engineer a better society.

The Enlightenment rooted its credo of progress in an ontology of the individual and reason. This has been the conception of modernity advocated and enacted by the dominant classes of Western liberal societies. But modernity has also sprung from the beliefs of philosophers with a more organic notion of the self. In the tradition of German idealism the West also saw the development of conceptions of utopian political forms created when a historical force of reason became immanent to man. Hegel called this reason 'spirit', and he believed that it was being revealed to man in the modern period. Marx adopted the same view of progress, but replaced the metaphysical idea of spirit with a materialist notion of creative, sensuous human beings. Both anticipated a future utopia.

In the nineteenth century both these traditions and their derivatives imparted a powerful ideological framework for the self-understanding of Western social development. Neither saw apocalyptic dangers in the radically more powerful technical means produced by industrialization. As Western social and economic practices spread across the globe behind the cutting edge of colonial conquest, the creed of modernity showed no remorse for the forms of life it destroyed. The universalization of modernity seemed a natural consequence of its inherent superiority. Although painful and destructive, modernity would bring a better future; modernization was worth the price.

In the liberal countries the creed of modernization conceived the new order as peaceful. Liberal thinkers, such as Cobden, saw war as a symptom of absolutism and mercantilism. In this view Europe was expansive, but this was the result of the spread of trade.

The conception of capitalist industrial society as peaceful was possible because in the nineteenth century European powers largely eschewed war. But as I show in Chapter 1 the new tools of war were having their first work-out in the colonial campaigns of the late nineteenth century. The scene of this violence was thousands of miles away from the metropolitan countries, and it did not penetrate the self-understanding of the West as peaceful and progressive. But, more importantly, the victims of this violence were not white or Christian. The Enlightenment had promised a new age for man, conceived as a universal figure. But, as Bauman has argued, this was not empirical man in the real world.[1] This was man as envisaged in an idealization of the bourgeois self. In this image the lower orders were excluded as an irrelevant 'other'; non-whites did not even enter the picture at all. It is no accident that the Enlightenment's precursor, Locke, could offer a blasé justification of slavery. In the nineteenth century the victims of the West's new tools of war did not appear at all on the canvas of human authenticity.

The lacuna which lead the advocates of the Enlightenment to see no victims and no costs in the process of modernization lay in the concept of a trans-historical idea of reason. From Descartes onwards a tendency had been established to conceive reason as utterly removed from concrete cultural embodiment. Traditions and cultures could be swept away by modernity because modernity stood above all tradition and culture; it was a configuration of pure reason. But the truth was that modernity was itself a tradition and a culture born in a particular corner of Western Europe. Of necessity it absorbed all the prejudices and biases which that part of Europe exhibited at that specific conjuncture. But these were swept underneath a carpet called 'reason'. Modernity was blind to its own historical specificity.

THE CULTURE OF MODERNITY

This book attempts to lay bare some of the concrete elements of the culture of modernity. One of my central contentions is that these have been pivotal in the form of war practised by modern states. A central element in the real culture of modern societies has been racism, and in warfare racism has been crucial to generating images of the enemy which justify acute forms of violence. My experience is that this fact is one that is still found to be discomforting and shocking. The real racist and imperialist history of Western countries is inconvenient to current forms of self-satisfaction. In the United States the history of the oppression of African-Americans is still largely absent in the official histories and narratives of US development. But the evidence of the role of a populist and racist culture in justifying forms of military slaughter is incontravertible. From the wars against American Indians, through the Pacific War and up to Vietnam, racism has been used to explain why the enemy got his just deserts. It was a staple in what Engelhardt terms 'victory culture'.[2]

Racism is not the only concrete cultural form which has generated images of the 'other' which are critical to war. As I reveal in Chapter 2, in the late nineteenth century nationalism and eugenics paved the way for the narrative defence of the slaughter on the Western front between 1914 and 1918. But coupled with social Darwinism nationalism was close to a racist conception of nationality. Despite this, the horrors of the 1914–18 war overpowered the available forms of discursive legitimation. Too many soldiers brought back their own image of the war for the official narrative to remain in tact. For many the Great War exposed the myths of modernity's progressive intentions. In the liberal West intellectuals turned their back on war and adopted a sour and disconsolate view of the twentieth century. The trenches seemed to deny all claims that Western society was a force for moderation and reason. Man's technical powers had outgrown his moral capacity.

After 1918 those still committed to the tenets of modernity found a way of rescuing war in the theory of strategic air warfare. The problem with the First World War was not the slaughter *per se*, but rather the fact that white Europeans had turned their war machines on each other. Also the grotesque form that the violence took mocked any self-understanding based on notions of civilization and reason. But as I show in Chapter 3, with air war it was thought that it might be possible to deliver mayhem and destruction on the enemy with minimal losses to one's own side. In addition, the slaughter would be over quickly, as terror would prompt rapid surrender. Finally, another benefit of air war was that it would distance Westerners from the consequences of their own side's violence. It would be less damaging to a progressivist sense of self-righteousness.

The attachment to a concept of strategic air warfare was evident in the democracies in the Second World War. Britain and America rained down death and destruction on Germany and Japan. The German blitz was much publicized in accounts of Britain's stoical defiance, but few wanted to concede that individual raids on Germany killed more individuals than the whole of the *Luftwaffe*'s campaign. US raids on Japan were even more merciless, yet no sense of moral ambiguity attached to reflection on these acts. Societies committed to a modernist self-understanding had found a means of vanquishing their enemies which detached them from the effects of their acts. Even now individuals in the West are demanding apologies for Japanese actions, while Hiroshima and Nagasaki remain unproblematic.

The atomic blasts which concluded the Second World War seemed like a Godsend at the time. But in reality the atomic bomb was highly problematical for a modernist understanding of war. In Chapter 4, I suggest that the fundamental paradox of nuclear weapons was that they represented a staggering scientific achievement, but also threatened to undermine a modernist conception of the future. Post-1945 the United States spearheaded a new Enlightenment with a global system of free trade and an American guaranteed peace. Yet Soviet nuclear weapons cast a dark shadow over the very future of the USA and the West. Needless to say, Western nuclear forces also raised difficult questions for Marxist-Leninist assumptions about the ultimate triumph of socialism. Bearing this in mind, I portray nuclear strategy as essentially a means of neutralizing the emotional anxiety inherent in nuclear vulnerability. Intellectuals gave the security state a sterile taxonomy for strategic calculations. They held the line against nuclear anxiety.

The semantic control of the discourse of nuclear rationality was ultimately bound to fail. After the acute anxiety of the Cuban missile crisis, détente and arms control pushed the issues to one side, but acute alarm over nuclear weapons resurfaced in the 1980s, thanks to the policies of the Reagan administration. Western culture became saturated with gloomy prognoses about the effects of nuclear war and the drift of the arms race towards confrontation. Culture began to imagine the end of the world.

The renewed nuclear fear of the 1980s triggered a counter-offensive that had paradoxical consequences. As I show in Chapter 5, it was not the intention of the far right strategic planners to bring peace. But the collapse of the USSR has brought at least a temporary lifting of the curse of nuclear war and allowed those committed to a massive arms buildup to claim the credit. Supposedly this ushered in a new world order built on the end of history, where only liberal democracy existed as a viable political form. However, the post-1991 period has given us a surfeit of history, with war crimes in Europe and new techno-violence against developing countries. Conversely, anti-Westernism increasingly takes the form of an unpredictable and unjustifiable terrorism.

In the final chapter I show that in this context postmodern thinkers have emphasized the uncertainty, undecidability, contingency and indeterminacy which is our lot in the age of the postmodern.[3] Bosnia represents the age of 'universal victimhood' and the world's cruelties spread across our TV screens as entertainment. There is something to this, but not as much as Derrida, Baudrillard and others suggest. There is nothing new about victimhood. The difference now is that our field of vision has widened after the end of the Cold War, and TV leaves few stones unturned. There is certainly a pronounced narcissism in the West, such that when Iraq was being liquidated, the chief concern in the USA was how American children would handle the psychological effects of the war. No one should have worried, as the conflict materialized on US television as a form of entertainment. At the end of the slaughter, when the Marsh Arabs and Kurds rose against Saddam Hussein, no one remembered that the West had encouraged them to fight. Modernity still revealed its disinterest in the other.

As this century draws to a close, it seems to me that many of the archetypal syndromes of modernity have resurfaced. At the current time a hundred million individuals have perished in twentieth-century war. There is still the possibility that through the combination of self-righteousness and power the advanced countries will continue to impose their will through absolute violence. But there is also a chance that the powerful will tread more warily in the world. Hope is not an entirely implausible emotion.

1 Enlightenment, Modernity and War

REFLECTIONS ON MODERNITY AND POSTMODERNITY

The modern is not just the preserve of modernity. Even in the fifth century A.D. Latin moderns celebrated and emphasized the rupture between their new Christian era and what had gone before. But arguably our sense of being modern, of being carried along by the trajectory of modernity, is unique. My justification for this observation is largely sociological. The position taken here, and throughout this book, is that the philosophical representations of modernity, which are now usually referred to as 'Enlightenment narratives', mask and disguise a concrete socio-economic cultural form. Thus, here modernity is viewed essentially as a structural organization of state, economy, society and culture; a power complex and a mode of consciousness. Its historical significance results from the manner in which it self-consciously cut its links with all that had gone before and its generation of novel technical powers, which it constantly sought to upgrade. Modernity unleashed forces which were able to vanquish the past and the horizontal present in the form of less technologically powerful cultures.

The form of social organization which concretely articulates the order of consciousness of modernity most clearly has been and continues to be capitalism. Its political embodiment has been the modern state, but this is changing. The values and practices of modernity are today increasingly disseminated by non-state organizations, and are manifested now in a globalization of capitalist culture. But this does not mean the triumph of the era of liberal democracy, or the ludicrous notion of the end of history. Here I follow Meštrović in arguing that the West's self-conscious celebration of the era of liberal democracy and the hegemony of reason is essentially a symptom of narcissism.[1] Further, I endorse the position of critics such as Bauman who conceive the past trajectory of modernity as one of destruction for all forms of life which stood in the way of forces of modernization.[2]

In case my remarks above imply that we shall tread a now familiar path, let me emphasize that this book is not a treatise in the style of postmodernism. I shall argue that in some respects the grandiose posturings of certain postmodern theorists represent an ideal veil for the destructive forces of modernity to hide behind. Today the iconoclasm of theories allegedly based on deconstruction and difference are invariably substituted for real historical and empirical analysis of the costs of modernity.

A classic case of the syndrome I described above was Baudrillard's bizarre claim in the *Manchester Guardian* that the Gulf War would never happen and subsequent argument that it did not happen. As Norris has argued, this was a byplay on the now fashionable idea that the global media has instituted a new 'hyper reality' which cannot be distinguished from the domain of real lived experience. Thus, according to Baudrillard, we cannot distinguish truth from its simulated counterpart;[3] the media now write the text that constitutes the phenomenal world.

Conversely I maintain here that the phenomena studied by historians and social scientists are not indistinguishable from simulated reality; truth is not reducible to pure textuality. This is not a plea for a naive ontological primacy; the facts do not speak for themselves. The interpretation of historical and social events is only possible within a textual framework. But the framework does not provide the standards of critical evaluation which determine if the framework itself is valid. The community of researchers share epistemic, normative and operational criteria which delineate legitimate and illegitimate forms of inquiry. These shared assumptions are the guarantee that intellectual work has an ethical dimension.

In recent times it seems to me that the ethical commitment to endeavour to pursue truth has been undermined. But this is not the result of a lack of integrity; it derives from the near hegemony of the latest academic fad. This is particularly the case with a second and third generation of post-modern theorists who have not wrestled with the philosophical difficulties confronted by the originators of the tradition. Armed with a general theory, the third-generation legatees of Foucault and Derrida go forth to investigate anything and everything. In the discipline of international relations, young scholars now apply the blandishments of postmodern method to a welter of empirical and historical issues with scant regard for the established scholarship in the area. Reluctantly I find myself in accord with the following lament of Bogdan Denitch:

> History unfortunately involves dull and specific facts, sometimes even dates. History and facts are unfashionable in advanced academic circles nowadays. ... Deconstruction and postmodernism have apparently convinced an entire generation that it is sufficient to be acquainted with a powerful and, above all, fashionable and contemporary general theory ... These overarching abstract theories enable their adherents to generalize glibly about almost ... everything, including politics in lands they know nothing about.[4]

In some respects my comments above are churlish. The operational concepts of some postmodern analyses have invigorated the intellectual investigation of modernity. I share the view that modernity misrepresents itself by articulating the essence of modern civilization through a discourse of liberation. However, rather than tying myself up in the intellectual knots of the virtually incomprehensible discourse of French poststructuralism, I suggest that the true costs of modernity and its fundamentally unattractive character are best probed by assessing it through a sociological analysis of the concrete processes of social organization and culture. Rather than a postmodern approach, this, tentatively, is more one of anti-modernism. It seeks to spell out the destructive consequences of modernity. In particular these becomes clear when we focus on the relationship between modernity and war. This relationship is not accidental; it is fundamental. As Coker correctly asserts, 'War has been the accredited theme of modern life.'[5] The same author continues, 'For much of the modern era war and the West were synonymous, if only because war was a medium of modernisation.'[6] But before we investigate modernity's appetite for destruction, let us first review some of its more optimistic claims.

VARIANTS OF MODERNITY

The roots of much of the political creed of modernity were first articulated theoretically by Hobbes. But Hobbes's absolutism was undercut by the assorted liberalisms of the Enlightenment, which championed a politics designed to enhance and protect the powers of free individuals. Such free individuals are the ontological foundation of liberalism, although at least two versions exist of what such individuals comprise. One view, which is evident in Hobbes's writings, construes the individual as a bundle of appetites. In left-wing versions of liberal political theory Hobbes has been seen as the founder of the bourgeois conception of human nature, as the appetites are believed to centre on accumulation. But Hobbes's idea of appetite pre-dates the mundaneness of the capitalist enterprise. Appetite, construed as the search for economic utility, is more accurately located in the writings of Jeremy Bentham, whom Marx lampooned as 'the leather-tongued oracle of the bourgeoisie', and other later English and American liberals. Essentially this form of liberalism amounts to utilitarianism.

The other major liberal variant of the theory of the individual is one that characterizes the person as a bearer of rights. Rights liberalism is at the heart of Enlightenment narratives concerning human emancipation and progress. In the early liberalism of Locke, rights are derived from theories of natural law which posit God as the ontological foundation of inalienable rights. But Locke's epistemology, contained in *An Essay Concerning Human Understanding*, was always likely to undermine a theological ontology, especially as Locke attacked metaphysics and revelation with his insistence that the human mind was a 'tabula rasa'.[7]

The secular character of rights liberalism was confirmed in the liberalism of the French Enlightenment, although not all its proponents were atheists. Building on the pleas of Locke for an enlightened, rational society, thinkers such as Diderot, Alembert and Voltaire sought 'an empire of natural rights' where privilege, superstition and ignorance would be vanquished.[8]

Rights liberalism is also grounded in Kant's presupposition of a transcendental ego governed by universal reason. Here freedom is attainable because the ego achieves autonomy by following the dictates of a universal morality. Kant's essential moral imperative is, 'act according to a maxim you might will to be a universal law'.[9]

If we assume that Enlightenment narratives are not mere fables or fictions, then we must see them as intellectual traditions which help us to think about the development of the modern state. At the very least they can be viewed as a discourse which defines some of the major terms of debate of modern politics. This debate charts a process wherein political authority shifts from an anchor in divine ontology to a foundation in humanism. Discursively the original rupture was highly traumatic. Machiavelli's stark revelation of the role of force in politics and his recommendation that effective rule might depend on immoral acts were a violent and shocking beginning for the new politics. As Meinecke noted, 'Machiavelli's theory was a sword which was plunged into the flank of the body politik of western humanity, causing it to shriek and rear up.'[10] This iconoclastic assault on the moral foundation of authority was modified in Hobbes's theory of the state, which devised a logical means for competing, hostile egos to enjoy the fruits of 'commodious living'. Fearing death more than any other peril, Hobbes's individuals contract to surrender sovereignty to an absolute authority which institutes the rule of law.[11]

Although Hobbes's state is not founded on pure force, his ideas were regarded as highly controversial, and he was accused of atheism and immorality. But Hobbes was a bridge between the old and the new politics. His role in establishing the intellectual edifice of modernity lies in his decisive break with tradition, whereby he reduces society to a mere means for the realization of self-interest.[12] This assault on tradition was complemented by an attack on culture in the philosophy of Descartes. Here the ego is its own presupposition, and is removed from any absorbtion in culture or other forms of particularity.[13]

Hobbes could not be absorbed into the Enlightenment because of his psychological pessimism and his endorsement of monarchal absolutism. From Locke onwards Enlightenment narratives enshrined a legal and constitutional form of state, where the power complex of sovereignty is transformed into a system of authority strong enough to protect the rights of individuals, but not so strong as to be able to destroy them. This transformation is possible because the Enlightenment posits an optimistic theory of human nature, although not one based on the real character of existing individuals.[14] Moreover, these narratives conceive the rational power of intellectual tools as means which can make and remake both man and society. The source of the view that regards intellectuals as social engineers is the Enlightenment.

The Enlightenment and its legacy stipulated the social form which would embody the values of reason, freedom and emancipation. Building on the ideas of Locke, Anglo-Saxon liberalism celebrated a form of state that limits or minimalizes central political power. The liberal state, in contradistinction to absolutism, was to provide a framework for the workings of a free society and rational economy. But *laissez-faire* did not mean non-intervention, because a liberal state had to sweep away the impediments to a rationally constituted social order, particularly the corporatist debris inherited from absolutism and feudalism. Liberalism constituted an ongoing reform programme. In England this was a piecemeal process, but in the United States the Constitution congealed a single, fundamentalist liberal framework for the conduct of politics based very much on the ideas of Locke. The division of powers, the separation of state and society, and the safeguarding of essential human rights have been at the centre of American contributions to the discourse of modernity.

In total opposition to the liberal view of society established by the decisive social, economic and cultural changes of the seventeenth and eighteenth centuries, which culminated in the French and Industrial Revolutions, Marx advanced his own modernist charter. For Marx the political solutions offered by liberalism to the question of emancipation were illusory. Marx regarded the economic relations established by capitalism as a heightened form of alienation. The explicit egoism of bourgeois economics and the institution of private property had created a society which denied individuals their 'species essence'. Marx defined this, with heavy Rennaisance overtones, in terms of creativity and a capacity for free co-operation between rational and self-conscious beings. The central contradiction of capitalism was that it created an economic order premissed on conflictual relations between classes; in its simplest dichotomous form the enrichment of one class caused the impoverishment of the other. Hegel had noted the contradictions in civil society, which was the realm of egoism; but he believed that these could be resolved in the state, and in the Prussian state of the eighteenth century he saw the most advanced institution that man had so far evolved.

In the writings of both Hegel and Marx there is an alternative charter for modernity to that profferred by French and Anglo-Saxon liberalism. But the key point to note here is that Enlightenment liberalism, German idealism and historical materialism all offered a vision of human progress culminating in assorted utopias. Similarly, all three traditions showed no pity for the social and cultural forms that progress must sweep aside. Come what may, 'Gesellschaft' would replace 'Gemeinschaft'.

I have mentioned these other variants of modernist narratives to indicate the complexity of the concept. But the main focus of interest here is the version of modernity presented in liberal narratives of progress. The central question I want to probe is how the pretensions of Enlightenment narratives match up to the practical results of the building of the civilization of Western liberal society? In particular, I wish to question the positive self-image of our civilization, given the record of Western states in their dealings with the rest of the world. The phenomenon under scrutiny is war. The central problematic which this book addresses is the relationship of war to modernity.

THE CREED OF HUMAN PROGRESS

Modernity as mood – *Stimmung* – celebrates a political-theoretic vision of progress encapsulated in ideas of liberty, rights and emancipation. It is a clearly optimistic view, especially in relation to the past. As Connolly notes, 'it defines itself by contrast to earlier periods which are darker, more superstitious, less free, less rational, less productive, less civilized, less comfortable, less democratic'.[15] As Unger has argued, the critique of the past is essentially an attack on the metaphysical systems of thought of antiquity and the Middle Ages.[16] In particular, the Enlightenment rejected the ideas of divine revelation and intelligible essences. In the more radical philosophers the link between religion, error and oppression is central. Thus d'Holbach wrote:

To error we owe the oppressive chains, which despots and priests everywhere forge for the people. To error we owe the slavery in which people languish in almost all countries. To error we owe the religious terrors which freeze human beings in fear and make them slaughter each other for the sake of figments of the mind.[17]

Essentially the Enlightenment championed the proposition that if the falsehoods of the *ancien régime* were exposed, the oppression which they justified could be overturned. Instead of a fixed world in which the human place was pre-ordained and subordinate, humans could refashion the globe to suit human ends and establish freedom. But what of ethics and social norms? What particular form of life would the new order enshrine?

Medieval ethics derived from the *lex naturae*, Christian natural law based on the Sermon on the Mount and, since Thomas Aquinas, suffused with Aristotelian metaphysics. But sometimes consciously and sometimes not, the Enlightenment was destroying the presuppositions of revelation and metaphysics. The significance of the problem was not lost on Voltaire, who remarked that, 'If God did not exist one would have to invent him'.[18]

The intellectual ferment which swept through the eighteenth century was not, of course, just an expression of ideas. The change in philosophical consciousness was accompanied by institutional changes in economy and society and a general shift in the human orientation towards nature. The perception that science could be used to systematically manipulate nature for the fulfilment of human ends was growing in plausibility. Arguably the first real general fruits of this process were seen in a series of agricultural revolutions and also in some gains made in the treatment of certain diseases. Before the eighteenth century Europe was plagued by epidemics and famine. In Braudel's words, 'they were incorporated into man's biological regime and built into his everyday life'.[19] After 1750 population growth indicated that a fundamental change was taking place in European demography, with rising birth rates and declining death rates. This was a process that would supply a work force for industrial capitalism and manpower for the new mass armies of the modern era. But it was also symptomatic of 'progress'. The broader canvas of progress was seen with industrialization and the conscious application of the results of scientific invention to the economy. Thus the character of social and economic organizations began to reflect the intentions of human actors. As Coker observes, this was utterly novel: 'Before the late eighteenth century the major transformations of human life never corresponded to the consciously held objectives of the historical participants.'[20]

With the benefit of much hindsight the surge forward in the technical powers of men and women at the dawn of the industrial age has been seen in many quarters as a quantum leap in only the means available to humankind. Modernity was the age of instrumental reason. However, the original architects of the new order conceived the intellectual dynamics of the new era as the basis for improvement, not just in human beings' technical powers, but in human life *per se*. The social and political order would also be perfected through the medium of reason; new ethics and new norms would emerge. But this implies a moral/practical revolution as well as a technical one. In order to effect this – and it was essential that they did – Enlightenment philosophers and their disciples required a foundation for a normative framework. But this could not be based on either divine revelation or essentialist ethics. But what could ground ethics, given that the foundations of revelation and essentialism had been demolished?

The basis of the new social and political ethics would, in fact, be mankind itself. But this raised an enormous problem. As Jacques Domenech has argued, the *philosophes* had nothing but contempt for the real empirical men and women they found in their midst.[21] How could it be otherwise? 'Le menu peuple' were the children of the *ancien régime*. Their heads were full of the superstitions and metaphysics spouted by clerics.[22] Thus d'Alembert thought the multitude 'ignorant and stupified ... incapable of strong and generous action'.[23] As Bauman shows, the solution to this dilemma could not exist in the character of real men and women.[24]

The answer to the problem lay in projecting human perfection into the future. Today's contradictions, through colonizing the future, would be overcome tomorrow. The philosophers of the Enlightenment based their foundation for morality on what men and women could become at some point over the temporal horizon. But, as in the Marxist variant of enlightenment, this future would not happen spontaneously. The future was scripted by the philosophers, who would provide the blueprint for the educators and the legislators.[25] In other words, this was an intensely elitist programme for social and political engineering. It was also coercive, for the dynamics of reason and freedom would triumph, come what may. In cultural terms it was a recipe for a masked imperialism. The particularity of any specific *Gemeinschaft* whether at home or abroad, would be swept away by progress.

The points of contact between a philosophy and lived experience are often not as close as intellectuals might believe. However, it seems to me that the creed of human progress exemplified in Enlightenment philosophy can be seen in the real belief systems of the liberal bourgeoisie and in much of Europe's middle classes in the early nineteenth century. Belief in rationality, individualism and a scientific vision of progress were real, socially constituted values. In France it is obvious that the ideologists of

Modernity and War

the Revolution, articulated, albeit in corrupted form, many of the impulses of the Enlightenment and modernity. These individuals spearheaded a cultural transformation, even if, ultimately, Napoleon preferred his intellectuals safely closeted in the university. The Enlightenment focused the beam of reason on a radically new future which was being made by real men and women in a variety of institutional settings. But as these changes were intellectually congealed in a narrative of progress, hardly anyone seemed to notice their implications for war. Hegel and Marx recognized that history had become proactive, but neither conceived of the possibility of man's alienation before forces of total destruction.

Two of the decisive attributes of this transformation were that it was future-oriented and highly rigorous in the discipline it advocated for ordinary people. Giddens associates the following 'institutional clusterings' with modernity: heightened surveillance, capitalist enterprise, industrial production and increased centralization of the means of coercion.[26] This, I believe, makes the disciplinary programme of modernity clear. But Giddens fails to explore what Hans Fabian has called 'chronopolitics', the colonization of the future in order to resolve today's contradictions.[27] Chronopolitics means that cultures which are static or not geared to modernization must be destroyed. From the point of view of modernity, progress is compulsory.

A typical spokesperson for the chronopolitics of modernity is Condorcet. In his *Sketch for a Historical Picture of the Human Mind* (1794) Condorcet laid down the following credo of progress: 'the perfectibility of man is truly indefinite; and ... the progress of this perfectibility ... has no other limit than the nature of the globe upon which nature has cast us'.[28] For the masses, this 'perfectibility' was evident in the new forms of economic organization embodied in capitalist production and new legislation designed to build institutions around the principles of self-interest. In other words, the construction of what Theodore Lowi has called the 'automatic society'. From a sociological point of view, the new order is best described through Weber's concept of rationalization – in Kumar's words, 'the embodiment of the method and substance of science in the institutions, practices and beliefs of society'.[29]

In the early nineteenth century the philosophical creed of progress was supplemented by a more explicitly industrial doctrine. I am thinking here of Comte's positivism and Saint-Simon's vision of industrial society. Thus Enlightenment liberalism, English reformist liberalism and progressivist visions of industrial society fused together to create a powerful ideology built around ideas of liberty, productivity, rationality and science. This amalgam represented perfectly the chronopolitics of modernity; the future would always be brighter: 'The logic of industrialisation would drive societies forward to a new point of stability: to a new plateau, on a higher plane, where all the dynamic contradictions of the past would be resolved.'[30]

THE CONSERVATIVE CRITIQUE

There were, of course, voices crying out against the images of the new utopia. Burke and his fellow conservatives in Europe detested everything about the French Revolution and the currents it had unleashed. They were also fearful of the alienation characteristic of urban and industrial society. Burke felt that in the coming era man would be rootless, and he viewed the consequences of the death of tradition as particularly devastating: 'When ancient opinions and rules of life are taken away, the loss cannot properly be estimated. From that moment we have no compass to govern us; nor can we know to what port we steer.'[31] French conservatives, such as de Bonald and de Maistre were more extreme. In their massive rhetorical overkill, it seemed as though the greatest loss caused by the passing of the *ancien régime* was that of the gallows and the hangman.

The essence of the conservative critique was that old forms of authority and social control had been taken away, and that those who knew how to rule by custom and practice were being replaced by rulers inspired by theory and ideas. From Burke's point of view, much of the French Revolutionary terror resulted from the use of metaphysics to justify political rule rather than sentiment and prudence. In my opinion, Burke's perspective had much to commend it. As we shall see, a key aspect of modernity's impact on war was the clinical linking of means and ends. War became the ruthless application of means–ends rationality to the business of overcoming an enemy. In modernity abstraction and cruelty went hand in hand.

The negative response of conservatives to the Enlightenment and its legacy was but a straw in the wind. As the Faustian legend implied, nothing would stand in the way of the new era. While conservatives lamented the social consequences of modernity and romantic poets attacked its spiritual poverty, virtually no thinker sensed the destructive military potential of the new civilization, or at least not from a critical perspective. So far from fearing the military consequences of the new period, the dominant ideologies of the post-Napoleonic age offered little reflection on war at all. Europe was regarded as the cradle of peace, as Gallie notes: 'Nineteenth century speculation and rhetoric had created the myth of a new pacific, although commercially expansive Europe.'[32] But what of Napoleonic warfare? What did it reveal about modernity?

MODERNITY AND WAR

The wars of European absolutism were relatively controlled affairs fought according to the principles of manoeuvre. Both limited ends and limited means reduced the scale of destruction, as did the cost of model armies, such as the Prussian army of Frederick the Great, which made them too valuable to be exposed to annihilation. What was tactically possible was often the result of the degree of direct supervision that was needed to ensure discipline. As de Landa comments, the armies of this period were essentially 'clockwork' – that is, simple machines controlled by external inputs.[33] Desertion was an ongoing problem: if direct control was not maintained, men and weapons could simply 'melt away'.[34] From the end of the Thirty Years War until the French Revolution, war in Europe had the quality of an aristocratic hobby. Armies were the expensive toys of monarchs playing a game of inter-state diplomacy according to commonly agreed rules. However, all of this changed decisively with Napoleon.

The key changes in French military thinking in the late eighteenth century resulted from general intellectual developments, as well as from the reaction in France to their poor performance in the Seven Years War and particularly the disastrous defeat at Rossbach in 1757. Indeed, Napoleon regarded Frederick's generalship at Rossbach as 'a master-piece'.[35] In the wake of this defeat, where Prussian mobility had been decisive, and aided by the theoretical writings of Comte Jacques de Guibert, the Secretary of War, the Duc de Choiseul, reformed the French infantry into battalion-strength units based on eight companies of musketeers and one of grenadiers.[36] Infantry men were to be armed with the relatively new bayonet, which meant the use of a single-shock weapon. More importantly, the new French thinking emphasized a more mobile, dynamic battlefield. Instead of the relatively static lines of the absolutist era, Guibert recommended a mixture – an *ordre mixte* – of lines and columns, depending on the circumstances of battle.[37] Columns could concentrate force more decisively than the long thin line, and organized into battalion-strength units, the column would be more mobile.

Guibert's thinking helped to move tactics away from the geometric conception of manoeuvre, aimed at either double envelopment or Frederick's 'oblique order', to a more dynamic vision of battle. Implicit here was a new and looser notion of discipline. The battalion and its companies would have more autonomy, and fighting henceforth would often take the form of the skirmish line rather than the fixed order of volley fire from the line. Mobility was also sought for artillery, and here the pioneering work of Jean Baptiste de Gribeauval was fundamental.

De Gribeauval was a military engineer and inspector of artillery. His work reveals how central ingredients in the system of factory production came originally from the military. This point deserves emphasis. Some commentators have seen the growth in the military potential of modern societies as a by-product of the enhanced powers of the civil sectors of industrial production. This is a false conception. Many of the critical features of systematic industrial production began life in the field of munitions manufacture. Reflection reveals that this was implicit in the lineage of the modern state.

Absolutism brought together the powers of governance into a unified centre. A critical element in this power complex was military munitions. As absolutism understood economic welfare through the categories of mercantilism, the military capacity of the state was seen as the essential prerequisite for economic success. Enhanced military performance meant a stronger state, an even more unified centre, and the pre-conditions for yet more success. Thus the military was central to the political form from which the modern state evolved. Military-oriented research was thus intertwined with the application of science to industry right from the beginning of the capitalist era.

De Gribeauval sought to bring standardization to the production of French munitions. He standardized parts for guns, carriages and ammunition.[38] Particularly significant was the creation of cartridges where shot and powder were combined. This was an essential prerequisite for Napoleonic warfare, which demanded more mobile field artillery. Without seeking to exaggerate the point, de Gribeauville's work shows how modernity could expand the scope of destruction by applying new criteria of organization to military production. Before the modern era, weapons were produced by artisans who had a sensual relationship with the materials they worked.[39] Individual swords and muskets were made by craftsmen, which limited the volume of production and made weapons expensive. By way of contrast, de Gribeauville's work began a trend leading to the mass production of weapons, which meant lower price, higher volumes and interchangeability. It is essential to realize that this was a key prerequisite for the wars of attrition of the modern period.

If standardization and mass production were features of a modernist outlook, so too were other pre-conditions for Napoleonic warfare. A key element in the new thinking was the complete destruction of the enemy's forces: 'Another part of the the new French tactical formula was an insistence on all out pursuit to decisive victory.'[40] The mobility of armies and the pursuit of the defeated demanded better communications. This was made possible in the eighteenth century because Europe's roads and bridges were substantially improved.[41] Within the mind-set of the disciples of the Enlightenment, improvements in communications were regarded as one of the ingredients in the spread of reason and liberty. In 1796 Robert Fulton's *A Treatise on the Improvement of Canal Navigation* was liberally sprinkled with optimistic assumptions about how better communication would obliterate 'local prejudices' and promote 'international harmony'.[42] What Fulton, himself a military inventor, revealed was the naivety of the dominant view of progress at this time. Better communications meant that military assets could be moved around more extensively and more rapidly. Thus military operations could unfold on a wider canvas. The scope and potential of forces of destruction was growing.

In general terms, in the period immediately prior to the Revolutionary and Napoleonic wars, economy, state and society were becoming equipped with the capacity to allow more extensive forms of military operation. As Ropp comments, 'During the eighteenth century Western Europe's military potential had greatly increased. There were more men, more food, more metals and better transportation.'[43]

These new assets bore fruit in the Revolutionary and Napoleonic wars. In the civil war and the disastrous campaign against Austria in 1792 the future potential of the 'Grande Armée' was not yet apparent. Yet, in the confused character of the early Revolutionary campaigns, something new was clearly evident. Clausewitz remarked on the end of 'the restricted, shrivelled up form of war', and already larger and more violent military operations were in evidence. At Valmy in 1793 the French fired 20,000 artillery rounds in the largest bombardment Europe had yet seen.[44] Also in the same year, the *Levée en masse* was introduced, which ultimately raised 1,200,000 men. Possibly this was the most profound change of all. Previously, European armies had recruited mercenaries, adventurers and vagabonds whose loyalty was always in doubt. However, the new Revolutionary army was one of citizens who swore an oath to the nation. For the first time Europe witnessed the ideological effects of nationalism as a military instrument. Wars of manoeuvre, fought according to civilized rules, were replaced by wars of ideological zeal. From the point of view of Europe's old order, this was a terrifying prospect. French military forces were engaged on a propaganda mission to spread the creed of the new order. Schiller summed up the maxim of the French thus:

> Und willst Du nicht mein Bruder sein,
> so schlag Ich Dir den Schädel ein.[45]

In the new military code, the officers were to have daring and vision to match the zeal of the citizen-soldier. After a French force pursued and defeated an English army at Dunkerque in 1793, the French commander was arrested and executed for not routing the opposition. This execution and that of 25 other generals was meant, in Napoleon's quaint phrase, 'to encourage the others'.[46] Lazare Carnot, who was elected to the Committee of Public Safety in 1793, outlined the new military philosophy. French forces were 'to act offensively and in masses. Use the bayonet at every opportunity. Fight great battles and pursue the enemy until he is utterly destroyed.'[47]

Carnot's bloodthirsty recommendations were enacted by the armies that Napoleon assembled in the first years of the nineteenth century. Through utilizing the manpower generated by the *Levée en masse* and the economic assets created by the special Revolutionary committees set up to orchestrate military production, by 1805 Napoleon had the most formidable military force Europe had ever seen. At Valmy in 1792 Goethe believed he had seen something radically new when what appeared to be a mere rabble defeated the best army in Europe, but in 1806 at Jena Hegel knew that Napoleon's armies were the historical instrument of a new world spirit, that of liberalism.[48]

What was lacking in the reflections of Goethe and Hegel was any sense that the new form of war was a glimpse of a future that was frightening – a possible dis-utopia of total destruction. By focusing on the political element, the capacity of war to effect decisive change and sweep away the old order, the negative aspects of war were ignored. To be fair, this was not entirely surprising. If we divide the business of war into its subcomponents of weapons, tactics, strategy and logistics, then we can see that the Napoleonic method was revolutionary in the final three, but not in weapons. In the early nineteenth century the contribution that industrialization was going to make to the business of destruction was still not apparent, despite the fact that inventors like Fulton were eagerly seeking new weapons.

Following Koch, we can sum up the changes Napoleon effected as follows: first, the use of mass conscription; second, the ease of securing manpower; third, the pursuit of total victory through the tactic of annihilation; and finally, the use of propaganda.[49] Despite the use of traditional weapons, the scale of the transformation was immense. In Prussia in 1807 Napoleon had an army of approximately 600,000 men. More typically his forces numbered 250,000 to 300,000. Remembering that the French policy was to reduce supply chains by living off the land, we can glimpse the impact such forces would have had on local populations by assessing the supplies that were required. Assuming a force of a quarter of a million, the French would have had 100,000 horses, which would generate the following daily needs: 225 tons of bread, 550 tons of oats and hay, 450 tons of straw, and 2,800 tons of animal foods.[50] What was remarkable was that for Napoleon these men and materials were utterly expendable. At the end of the Russian campaign of 1812, the Grand Armée had lost 400,000 dead and 100,000 wounded. The remnants of the French forces under Murat numbered a mere 30,000.[51] But the following year another army of 300,000 was raised, which was also destroyed. At the end of the Napoleonic wars in 1815, combat fatalities numbered two million, with another two to eight million civilian deaths. All of this was made possible by new forms of state, economy and society – in short, by modernity. But this was a mere glimpse of what was to come.

REFLECTIONS

The historical and military significance of Napoleonic warfare was encapsulated and disseminated in the nineteenth century through the work of Carl von Clausewitz (1780–1831) and Henri Antoine de Jomini (1779–1869). Clausewitz was born in Burg, 70 miles south-west of Berlin, to bourgeois parents, and was allowed to become an officer cadet in the Prussian army only because of the relaxation in the conditions of entry occasioned by the death of Frederick the Great.[52] He entered the Berlin Military School in 1801, and graduated top of his class in 1804. He then served as adjutant to Prince August of Prussia, and later as a colonel in the Russian army. Significantly, he spent some months as a prisoner in Paris in 1807, which allowed him to gain first-hand experience of French intellectual culture. His *magnum opus On War* (1831) was published by his wife after his death.

Jomini was born in Switzerland, and in his late teens began a career in banking. As a child, his passions had been aroused by the French Revolution, and when revolution broke out in Switzerland in 1798, he abandoned his banking career in Paris and began to study war. Nothing if not determined, Jomini found a route to Napoleon, and in 1805 was appointed to his staff. But Jomini's intellectual ideas and his vainglorious personality did not appeal to the professionals around Napoleon, and after the armistice of 1813 he became a general in the Russian army, a rank he retained for the next 56 years.[53] His major work, *Summary of the Art of War*, was published in 1837.

By introducing the ideas of Jomini and Clausewitz together, it is possible to note and emphasize an extraordinary paradox. Until very recently, it was widely assumed that Clausewitz had had an enormous impact on nineteenth-century military thinking, and that his ideas strongly influenced the German General Staff's plans for the First World War.[54] In intellectual circles Clausewitz's name is well known, and most students of strategy are familiar with at least some of his maxims. Jomini, on the other hand, is much less well known, and many students of strategy have never heard of him. In short, there has been very little intellectual interest in his work. For those seeking an intellectual culprit for the carnage of 1914–18, Clausewitz has always been the likeliest candidate, because of the assumption of his impact on military doctrine. Liddell-Hart, for example, in his critique of the 'suicidal obsession with the Great Battle', labelled Clausewitz the 'Mahdi of Mass'.[55] In a recent book John Keegan doesn't go as far, but he still credits Clausewitz with setting the agenda for 1914:

> By an irresistible process of osmosis, they then percolated throughout the whole European military establishment; by 1914, it is true to say that its outlook was as Clauswitzian as the continent's coalition of socialist and revolutiory movements was Marxist.[56]

Keegan maintains that *On War* was a 'slow fuse' – that is, influence gradually increased as the nineteenth century wore on.[57] Supposedly this influence was enhanced by the Prussian victories of 1866 and 1870. But this is not the case. What Keegan overlooks is that the senior commanders in the Prussian army were ardent supporters of Jomini long before Clausewitz became popular in Berlin. As Shy observes, 'By the time the German military appeared to be Clausewitzian, they had long been Jominians.'[58] The key here is both the legacy of Clausewitz's reputation and the difficulty of *On War*. During the Napoleonic wars Clausewitz was highly critical of Prussian conduct, and he supported the reformist programme of von Scharnhorst. So complete was his alienation from the military establishment that in 1813 he was refused entry into the Prussian army.[59] In 1818 Clausewitz was appointed to the post of Director of the Berlin War College, but, as Ropp emphasizes, he was not allowed to lecture.[60] Thus Clausewitz's radicalism diminished his impact. In addition, the text of *On War* was unlikely to appeal to the military mind: 'The truth is that most German students of war found Clausewitz no less difficult, obscure, and of doubtful utility than did non-Germans.'[61] As Shy notes emphatically, 'The idea of Clausewitz as the bible of the Prussian army is a joke.'[62]

Jomini's influence on the European military imagination after 1815 resulted primarily from the match between his ideas and the general tenor of Enlightenment thinking. It was Jomini and not Clausewitz who understood strategy as a 'science'. Thus it is Jomini who is the true founder of the deracinated strategic conceptions we associate with the nuclear era: 'Jomini, more than Clausewitz deserves the dubious title of founder of modern strategy.'[63]

Jomini sought to isolate timeless features of warfare which would be known only to great commanders. In his words, 'all strategy is controlled by invariable scientific principles'.[64] He applied a Platonic notion of essence to the business of war in order to strip away all peripheral detail such as history, culture and the character of the soldiers who fought. As de Landa observes, 'In the hands of Jomini (and his successors in general staffs and think tanks), war became a game in which friction, morale and even the independent will of the enemy disappeared.'[65] When scrutinized closely, Jomini's precepts actually appear mundane. His observation of Napoleonic warfare led him to recommend that 'massed forces' should be applied at the 'decisive point' against 'weaker enemy forces', and that an army should operate along 'strong interior lines'.[66]

Jomini's influence resulted not from the incisiveness of his analysis of war, but from his fit with the prevailing post-Enlightenment mood of the times. In addition, he was a prolific writer who lived nearly 40 years longer than his great rival. Building on the mechanistic theories of General Henry Lloyd and von Bülow, Jomini reduced war to a geometric calculus, which meshed with the post-Enlightenment sentiments of early nineteenth-century philosophy. Jomini also helped to ossify and hypostatize the Napoleonic legend, by revealing the last of the 'Great Captains' as 'the leader of genius'. In many respects he simultaneously mystified and normalized the Napoleonic legacy. By concentrating on Napoleon as an individual, Jomini ignored the really revolutionary aspects of Napoleonic warfare and the dramatic consequences of nationalism for the conduct of war. As a legatee of the Enlightenment, he shows clearly how the naive scientific optimism of the time occluded any appreciation of the new scale of destruction that would soon be possible. It is surely no accident that it is the Jominian paradigm that dominated the war-gaming mentality of the post-war US think-tanks.[67] As I shall indicate below, the psychological and emotional trauma associated with nuclear weapons was a major threat to a modernist understanding of war; but this potential maelstrom was safely locked away behind the veil of a rationalistic calculus that owes much to the Jominian inheritance.

As I have suggested above, Jominians move in the circles of a Platonist epistemology which seeks to isolate a true and timeless model of war. In Clausewitz's *On War*, on the other hand, we find the clear influence of the dialectical method of German idealism. Gallie, and more recently Klein, have identified this influence as predominantly Kantian.

In particular, they emphasize the impact on Clausewitz of Kant's distinction between 'noumena', the true 'thing in itself', and 'phenomena', reality as it appears to human cognition.[68] I am not interested here in the detail of Clausewitz's intellectual inheritance; but it still seems worth noting that Clausewitz expresses the general spirit of German idealism, including a strong whiff of Hegelianism, and not just elements of the Kantian tradition. The central message of Clausewitz is that we may seek to know the pure or ideal form of a phenomenon, but that what we really find in the world of experience will always be removed from this ideal type. Thus war has an ideal or absolute form and a real form which we confront in our historical experience.[69] Clausewitz identified the ideal form of war as 'absolute violence'. Its purpose was to 'overthrow the enemy' or leave him 'militarily impotent'.[70] In historical settings this absolute is tempered by two other fundamenmtal aspects of war: chance and politics. The effects of chance are seen in Clausewitz's concept of friction. Friction refers to the unanticipated and unforeseen factors that throw plans off course. In command terms friction indicates the inability of any system to override accidents, errors and technical difficulties. Any commander who understands the notion of friction will never expect a blueprint or battle plan to match what actually happens. Politics, for Clausewitz, is what makes war meaningful. War is 'the continuation of policy with other means'.[71] Thus war is not an end in itself; nor is it a game. The purpose of war is to further the achievement of political ends. War without political direction is pointless.

Comparing Clausewitz with Jomini, it is interesting to note that it is the latter who provides a rationale for an independent military free of political interference. By contrast, Clausewitz espouses the subordination of military institutions to political ones. This was always a controversial view in Germany, and is another reason why claims concerning Clausewitz's impact on German military thought are exaggerated: 'Until the late 1930s, his most significant German readers were either unwilling or unable to accept his thesis of the close integration of politics and war and the primacy of political considerations even during the fighting.'[72]

If we look at the historical assessments of Clausewitz and Jomini in relation to Napoleon, the descriptions of the campaigns are very similar. The difference is in the method and the emphasis. Clausewitz highlights the historical and specific features of these conflicts. To be sure, he believes that Napoleon may have brought absolute war to virtual fruition, but he sees this in Hegelian terms. History is revealing the hand of spirit in the world, in this case in the shape of the revolutionary fervour of the

French troops. So far from being complacent about this, Clausewitz is sensitive to its potential:

> Since the time of Bonaparte, war ... had approached more nearly to its real nature, to its absolute perfection. ... The cause was the participation of the people in this great affair of state, and this participation arose partly from the effects of the French Revolution on the internal affairs of countries, partly from the threatening attitude of the French toward all nations. Now, whether this will always be the case ... would be a difficult point to settle. ... but everyone will agree ... that bounds, when once thrown down, are not easily built up again; and that, at least, whenever great interests are in question, mutual hostility will discharge itself ... as it has done in our time.[73]

Neither Clausewitz nor Jomini was sensitive to the real potential of war in the nineteenth century. Clausewitz, who died in 1831, had no chance to witness the decisive changes in munitions wrought by industrialization, or the revolution in military education in his native Prussia. However, he did sense the decisive consequences of nationalism in the dynamics of inter-state enmity. What I would like to note in passing is that some of the charges that have been laid at Clausewitz's door, most recently by Keegan,[74] are ludicrous. The truth is that we have no idea how he would have reacted to the slaughter of 1914–18 or the dilemmas thrown up by nuclear weapons. If we seek to find a theorist who laid the basis for some of the more bizarre notions of the nuclear era, it is Jomini, precisely because of his belief that strategy could be conceived and articulated independently of notions of history and culture. It is Jomini rather than Clausewitz who reveals the self-delusions of a modernist theory of war.

WAR AND INDUSTRIALIZATION

The Revolutionary and Napoleonic wars revealed to the world a new carelessness in the waste of armies and a new source of motivation for fighting in the form of nationalism. But they did not utilize the new technologies which would revolutionize war in the nineteenth century. Many of the new inventions were, of course, not available by 1815. But it is also important to realize that armies were conservative, and that the new technologies of the Industrial Revolution appealed first to naval forces.[75] In Britain the adoption of new technologies in the Royal Navy was linked to the class composition of the two services. While the army remained the preserve of the gentry and lads from the countryside, the Navy was more closely connected to the new middle classes.[76] In general terms the commercial middle classes were not interested in the army, but the growth of powerful private shipyards meant a significant lobby in Parliament for spending on naval forces. Both the army and the navy were deluged with ideas from private inventors showing how science could transform war, but it was the Navy which benefited first from the fruits of industrialization. As Ropp observes, 'Mechanization was devastatingly rapid in naval warfare.'[77]

The key change in naval warfare was the development of steamships and vessels made of iron and (later) steel (ironclads). Inventors such as David Bushnell, John Holland and Robert Fulton had been working on a variety of new naval technologies, including submarines, steamships and torpedoes, and it was Fulton who successfully designed the first steamship in the early nineteenth century. The first steam-powered warship made its début in 1812.[78] Fulton, a disciple of Francis Bacon, had also built and tested a submarine – the *Nautilus* – in the Seine in 1800. Although the American Civil War was predominantly a land war fought between infantry units, the new naval technology played a key role in the blockade that put a stranglehold on the Confederacy. In the Civil War the implications of naval innovation were plain to see: ironclads would defeat wooden vessels, small ships could sink large ones, and ships of iron and steel could be sunk only by torpedoes (used to some effect by the South) which would strike below the water-line. The submarine was not a great success, but its potential and, critically, its stealth were clear. In less than a hundred years a boat named after Fulton's experimental vessel would threaten America's enemies with nuclear annihilation. Fulton's *Torpedo War and Submarine Explosions*, published in 1810, was truly a testament to human progress.[79]

Robert Fulton's work, as I have already indicated, was replete with naive assumptions about science, enlightenment and human progress. In an important study Bruce Franklin links the mentality of Fulton and other inventors to a fundamental malaise in American culture resulting from a deep fascination, if not obsession, with technological means of destruction.[80] While Franklin sees the issue primarily in American terms, I seek to broaden its implications to a general critique of modernity. Indeed, I follow the analysis of Toynbee, and more recently Baudrillard, in conceiving America as the most essentially modernist society.[81] This is the result of two interrelated factors. First, the culture of scientific industrial capitalism was constructed in America on a virtually empty canvas; certainly, as Ambrose notes, the indigenous Indians were not allowed to stand in the way: 'American leaders and America's white population have allowed nothing to stand in the way of progress. Not a tree, not a desert, not a river, nothing. Most certainly not Indians, regrettable as it may have been to destroy such a noble and romantic people.'[82] Secondly, as the passage from Ambrose indicates, the main values of American society reveal the clear hegemony of a modernist creed of progress. Thus, from my perspective, Franklin's critique of the USA is *ipso facto* a critique of modernity. Franklin, an ex-SAC pilot, attempts to explore how the contemporary tyranny of super-weapons has evolved. His explanation is unequivocal: 'it is American culture of the past century that has most clearly shaped the imagination of a human destiny dominated by superweapons'.[83] He continues, 'As the creator of awesome weapons America has surpassed all rivals, becoming the great pioneer nation of modern warfare, especially in the oceans and skies.'[84]

In the nineteenth century, America's role in shaping the causal trajectory of modern warfare was evident as early as 1812. I have already noted the innovations of the French engineer de Gribeauval in standardizing munitions components. Because of a crisis in munitions supply during the war of 1812, the American Army's Corps of Engineers and its Ordnance Department sought to standardize component parts and routinize their manufacture. This was the beginning of a novel industrial process which culminated in the mechanistic productive techniques of Taylorism. According to Merrit Smith, it was a fundamental revolution:

Much has been written about the Topographical Bureau and the Corps of Engineers, whose extensive explorations, geodetic surveys, and construction activities resulted in an impressive fund of scientific data as well as in a wide variety of civil works. A good deal less is known about the exploits of the Ordinance Department, specially its involvement in one of the great technological achievements of the nineteenth century, popularly known as the 'American system' of manufacture ... [This system involved specific patterns of] division of labor and application of machinery in the production of firearms with interchangeable parts.[85]

This process was developed in the years leading up to the American Civil War, and shows clearly how the business of war was becoming rationalized. Again it is worth making the point that innovative productive processes were not shifting across from the civil to the military sector, but rather the other way around; de Landa notes, 'The standards set in these monitoring practices were later transmitted to the civilian industry via the contract system.'[86]

The problem of the control of the supply of parts in the military sector was linked to the development of the technology which made the greatest impact on nineteenth-century warfare; namely, the railway. The train revolutionized the logistics of warfare. With the advent of the railway, armies could be mobilized more rapidly; large numbers of troops could be rapidly deployed over vast distances; and large supply dumps could be established at railheads. In the American Civil War the railway was essential in bringing the North's industrial supremacy to bear decisively on the conflict. In 1864 Sherman's advance on Atlanta would have been impossible without the logistical support provided by the train. Supplies for his army of 100,000 men and their 35,000 animals were easily moved by rail. Sherman later calculated that without the railway he would have required nearly 37,000 wagons to provide his men with supplies.[87] The distances traversed by the train also necessitated a process of monitoring and control beyond anything required in the civil sector. Monitoring the flow of goods over huge geographical distances was thus another innovation pioneered in the military sector which prefigured the command systems of industrial networks.

The North's victory also showed the significance of the revolution in engineering which the American army had enacted. At the beginning of the conflict no West Point graduates held senior commands. However, the West Point system, which was based on the technical and engineering schools set up in France after the Revolution, dominated the thinking of the Northern commanders who emerged victorious in 1865. While the Confederacy may have had more daring and imaginative generals, those of the North were well equipped to bring the Union's massive industrial superiority to bear on the fighting. In the advance on Atlanta, Northern engineers were able to build a bridge over the Chattahoochie river which was 800 feet long and 100 feet high in four and a half days.[88] Against such feats, daring and elan might fire the imagination, but were scant defence against a mechanistic war machine. Henderson wrote that Grant used his army 'as if it was a battering ram, without consciousness and without feeling. It was a machine, perhaps unskillfully used, but challenging admiration by the manner in which it answered every touch of the manipulator'.[89]

In the Civil War another new technology which transformed logistics and strategy, although not tactics, was the telegraph. The railway revolutionized the mobilization and transportation of armies, but without the telegraph a command system which could use these forces intelligently would not have been forthcoming. Thus, as the new technologies of rail and telegraph criss-crossed countries and continents, new possibilties arose for co-ordinating mass military action. By the end of the nineteenth century the Schlieffen Plan to catch France off guard and win a dramatic victory presupposed the most detailed and precise use of rail and tele-graph. But in Europe, even in the 1860s, rail and telegraph were helping to transform Prussia's military potential in the innovative mission-oriented plans of von Moltke. The key communication technology of the Industrial Revolution, the 'step-child of war' as Martin van Creveld has called it,[90] was already preparing the ground for the greatest military slaughter the world had yet seen.

As we have seen, land war was revolutionized by the railway and the telegraph. It was also transformed by the gradual absorption of new weapons into battlefield practice, although with conservative armies this was not as dramatic as in naval warfare. The nineteenth century saw the development of the breech-loading rifle, the conoidal bullet, breech-loading artillery, the machine-gun and smokeless gunpowder. The weapon which wrought the most decisive change was the humble rifle. Breech-loaders came in gradually, and eased the problem of reloading, which could now be done when a soldier was running; breech-loading also increased the rate of fire. However, the devastating change came with the increased range and accuracy of the conoidal bullet, which had a brass casing which spun in the grooves of the 'rifled' barrel. The spinning action resulted in the projectile attaining coherence in flight, thus extending range and increasing accuracy. In tactical terms this new weapon made the concentrated artillery of the Napoleonic battlefield vulnerable and, in effect, changed the whole relationship between artillery and infantry. Trevor Dupuy sees its effects as utterly dramatic:

> No other technological change in weaponry, before or since, has had a comparable, directly discernible, immediate effect on the battlefield ... During the French revolutionary and Napoleonic wars ... artillery was responsible for 50% or more of battle casualties ... In the principal nineteenth century wars after 1860 ... artillery was responsible for barely 10% of the casualties ... This was because the conoidal bullet so vastly increased the range and accuracy of the rifle that infantry-men could fire as far and as accurately as could artillery.[91]

The consequences of the new rifle technology were already clear in the American Civil War. As Ropp clearly shows, the rifle gave a clear advant-age to the tactical defensive. Now a few men who were dug into strong fortifications could hold vastly superior numbers at bay.[92] Concurrently, while it was still sensible to concentrate artillery fire, it was no longer advisable to have artillery platforms too close together. Another feature of the Civil War prefigured a glimpse of US tactics a hundred years later in South-east Asia. With mass production replacing the artisan, supplies of weapons and ammunition were more plentiful: 'Most foreign observers noted the tremendous waste of ammunition. American soldiers preferred to save lives by spraying bullets at every suspicious object, no matter what the cost to the taxpayer.'[93] This is surely a key point. The efficiency of military production was beginning to offer a virtually limitless supply of munitions. Marx had noted that in factories 'Masses of workers crowded into the factory were organised like soldiers.'[94] As a result of just such organization, the Woolwich Arsenal in London was producing 250,000 bullets a day by 1860.[95] The irony of this is that the prevailing mentality of the time saw nineteenth-century society as turning away from its mercantile, militarist past towards an identity anchored in trade and commerce – whereas, in reality, the means of destruction were becoming cheaper and more extensive.

OUT OF SIGHT, OUT OF MIND

A constant theme of this book is that the destructive potential of the material instruments of modernity was occluded from the mind-set of dominant post-Enlightenment ideologies. Certainly in Britain and America a liberal theory of state and society had not grasped the military implications of the new age. As Pick observes, 'the military implications of industrialisation had not been substantially explored ... in the first half of the nineteenth century'.[96] Why, though, were the new technologies of destruction given such a benign gloss?

After the Congress of Vienna the dominant sense in Europe was of an unparalleled period of peace lasting nearly a hundred years. Away from the technical discussions of the military academy, the legacy of Napoleon was seen chiefly in its revolutionary implications for European domestic order. As Ropp comments, the energies of Europe's governing classes after 1815 went into the business of securing order at home.[97] Liberal thinkers, such as Cobden, saw war as the proclivity of a corrupt aristocracy.[98] As Waltz shows, nineteenth-century liberalism adopted the individualism of Hobbes, but tamed it so that neither internal order nor external relations were problematic.[99]

As we saw above, the liberal Enlightenment turned the seeming weakness of man, his self-interest, into the presupposition of a rational order in which rational self-interests interact to produce a harmonious society.

If war was the hobby of the old ruling families, who had now been displaced, then the problem of war would go away. J. S. Mill asserted that war was bad because it stopped production and destroyed resources. Only states seeking to raise taxes, to extend bureaucracy and increase control over their populations would seek to make war.

In the nineteenth century this Panglossian naivety was possible because the first real victims of the military technology of the Industrial Revolution were non-Europeans and non-whites. Thus, while Europe appeared to be enjoying a period of peace, its armies were refining their art against the peoples of less technically advanced societies. In the British case Giddens notes that 'British troops, for example, were more or less continually fighting colonial campaigns in the nineteenth century'.[100] In fact, in the 40 years after 1860 British forces were involved in fifty colonial wars.[101] Ropp paints a more detailed picture: 'That army pacified India and carried on "small wars" to protect the advance of white settlement.'[102]

In Britain the mid-nineteenth century was the era of 'scientific racism'; colonial conquest was viewed as a right bestowed because of the civilizing norms of the white man. But what of the 'other', the outsiders whose history and culture were simply disregarded? Where did these people fit in the grand narrative schemes of post-Enlightenment modernity?

In the official narratives of colonialism, military conquest was given the normative gloss of spreading civilized behaviour. Modernity had taken charge of Western Europe, and was now pointing the beam of reason at the dark places on the globe. But could Africans and Asians be moulded to the design of instrumental reason and rational self-interest? In fact, it didn't matter whether they could or not. As Coker suggests, 'A people who could not be improved or reformed ... were ruthlessly excluded.'[103] In Africa, in particular, the white European simply swept all obstacles to commercial development out of the way. People were cleared from the scene as if they were just part of the natural environment. This was not just because the hard men at the front end of colonization were let off the leash; on the contrary, it was implicit in the dominant cultures of the European, and evident in their literature and philosophy. At the beginning of the Enlightenment Locke had provided a racist justification for slavery in the Two Treatises; a century later Hegel could speak of Africa as a 'country without history'; and another hundred years later Weber spoke of Africa as 'kulturlos'.[104] If a country had no history or culture, then it mattered little what was done to it. In fact, the Africa of the nineteenth century was an invention of the European imagination. In the mid-nineteenth century the remnants of a highly complex civilization were discovered in what is now Zimbabwe. What was impossible for Europeans to believe was that this had been an authentic African civilization. Various bizarre notions were put forward to explain its existence, including the idea that it was an unknown example of a Phoenician settlement. But it was not African.

In general terms, in the nineteenth century the global hegemony of West Europe was established through the superiority of Europe's new industrial tools of war. In global military terms, Westerners had had the edge since the invention of gunpowder weapons, which underscored the global reach of the fifteenth- and sixteenth-century voyages of discovery. As early as the 1520s Cortez could reap havoc amongst the Aztecs because of Spain's military superiority. When the Spanish arrived in Mexico in 1520, the indigenous population stood at something between 9 and 25 million. Thirty years on it was less than 2 million.[105] This virtual extinction was, of course, not just the result of military defeat. The Europeans' way of life and, critically, the viruses he brought with him were the greatest threat to the indigenous people. In essence, contact with Europeans was fatal.

In the nineteenth century, though, the military imbalance was greater and more devastating in its implications. The issue is seen clearly by Giddens: 'It would be hard to exaggerate the significance for global history of the "armaments gap" which existed between the Western countries and the rest of the World throughout the nineteenth and early twentieth centuries.'[106] This 'armaments gap' was the cutting edge of colonialism. The military products of industrialization allowed the West to hold much of the rest of the globe in subjugation. It was also the prerequisite for genocide committed in the name of modernization. As Bauman grimly observes, 'The modern era has been founded on genocide, and has proceeded through more genocide.'[107]

As I have suggested above, the reality of modernity as the grim reaper was hidden from the gaze of nineteenth-century doctrines of enlightenment because the victims were far away in lands that were considered strange and alien. Moreover, these victims were not considered real human beings; the death of non-Europeans was of no moral consequence. In my view, this aspect of modernity is not tangential, but fundamental. In abstract terms, what Westerners were in possession of was a quantum leap in the powers of technical means; what was missing was any sense of restraint in the ends to which these means were put. It is surely no accident that Clausewitz, a child of modernity, should see the essence of war as 'absolute violence'. In pre-modern societies war was invariably subject to ritualized forms of restraint. But in industrial societies the use of new inanimate forms of energy applied to industrial production and the frenzied search for ever more potent technologies gave the potential for unrestricted slaughter. The historical record shows that no ends or ultimate values have restricted the use of the technology of death. With the emergence of airpower in the twentieth century, campaigns have been waged where hundreds of thousands of civilians have perished. Absolute violence now amounts to the potential for complete global destruction. Is modernity, then, the age of nihilism? Bauman, for one, would seem to believe that it is. As technical means have grown in power under the central direction of key values of modernity, the realm of ends, as Nietzsche predicted, has shrunk to the residual. 'The "modern movement" pulverized any ground on which moral commandments can be conceivably founded – it undermined morality as such: responsibilities which go beyond contractual obligations, ... values interfering with the supreme precept of maximum efficiency, ends which forbid the use of potent means.'[108]

This hegemony of instrumental reason has been clearly displayed in the West's behaviour towards less technically powerful cultures. In the United States the imperatives of economic development entailed that any temporary cessation in the slaughter or forced migration of Amerindians would be vetoed by the next economic opportunity which an Indian settlement stood in the way of. The net result was that 3 million Indians died in forced marches, random massacres and resettlement programmes.[109] Ultimately, the remnants of these people 'without history' were offered a classically utilitarian possibility for mere physical survival on wildernesses referred to as 'reservations'. In a sense they became a museum piece frozen in a time and space chosen by their conquerors.

The plight of the Amerindian is now well known, and yet it does not prevent the continuing proclivity of members of the US political and intellectual elite to parade before the world as the guardians of human rights and the judicial overseers of global justice for humanity. I would not go quite as far as the stinging criticism of Meštrović in his recent book *The Balkanization of the West*; but the narcissism and ethnocentrism of the USA does imply a stunning lack of reflection concerning American culture and history. According to Tom Engelhardt, the destruction of the Indian was a staple ingredient in a central cultural narrative of American triumphalism, where the slaughter of Indians merely confirmed the white population's sense of supreme superiority.[110] He also makes the key point that this narrative disguised the real moral dilemma of US history: 'Although a racially grounded tale, it deflected attention from the racial horror story most central to the country's development – the African American.'[111]

As Coker notes, 15 million Africans were taken from their country and sold into bondage. But long after slavery was illegal, the white man was exterminating Africans. As the race for colonies hotted up after 1870, the treatment of the victims of colonization beggars belief. In the Belgian Congo under Leopold II the population was reduced from 22 million to 10 million in a policy that has become known as 'administrative massacres'.[112] At the same time the German policy towards the Herero people was one of complete extermination. In the German Cameroons the bodies of dead slaves were recycled as fertilizer, while in South Africa the Boers persecuted the Hottentots to the point of extinction. In Australia white men went on 'culls' to reduce the Aboriginal population. Everywhere the new military instruments in the hands of white men proved irresistible. The most deadly of all was the machine-gun. Gunsmiths had long since sought a weapon that would provide automatic mass fire. In 1870 the French perfected the *mitrailleuse*, but this was only semi-automatic, and it was heavy and cumbersome. In 1884 the first real automatic fire gun was invented by the American Hiram Maxim. This weapon truly altered the calculus of slaughter. Using a mechanism powered merely by the energy released by the previous detonation, bullets could be unleashed at a rate of 600 per minute.[113] Here military skill had been made redundant, as the operator of a machine-gun was really just an industrial operator in uniform.[114] The machine-gun reaped havoc in the First World War. But what is harder to imagine is the effect it exerted in colonial settings. In one notorious incident two soldiers in German South-west Africa mowed down 2,000 Herero in a period of one hour. Thus well before the dawn of 1914, Europeans knew the implications of the new military technology. But the victims lay outside the domain of European Christendom.

CONCLUSIONS

The modern age has been a period of total and global transformation based on the application of rapidly evolving technologies to industrial production. The net effect of this process has been a massive increase in the technical means available to human societies. In the West this material revolution in the economic circumstances of society was accompanied by an intellectual transformation based on a variety of Enlightenment and post-Enlightenment narratives of progress. This intellectual rupture had antecedents going back centuries, but was only plausible as a hegemonic ideology when nature and society appeared as objects malleable to intentional directives of instrumental reason. In the congealed narratives of modernity these directives provided a charter for a process of wholesale and continuous modernization, where tomorrow would always be better than today.

The contention of this chapter is that the dominant understanding of these processes of change neglected the destructive aspects of the new machine culture of industrial society. Instead of the West's military prowess being a by-product of industrial manufacture, it can be shown that many of the key innovations in manufacturing had their roots in the drive to improve and perfect military instruments. Thus, as Franklin argues, the cultural basis for the constant upgrading of weapons technology was present right at the beginning of the industrial age.[115] Particularly in countries where liberalism was the dominant political ideology, the militarization of society was misunderstood, because it appeared that military institutions had declined in significance. Thus, in the nineteenth century, America seemed to be a completely demilitarized society, yet many of the most deadly military innovations of the period originated in the United States. The sleight of hand which disguised the significance of a militarized culture was reinforced by the fact that the main victims of munitions innovation were the peoples of colonies, and in the US case Amerindians. In the nineteenth century, armaments ascendancy was the cutting edge of colonization and modernization, but its victims were mute.

2 Rumours of War

INTRODUCTION

The previous chapter assessed developments in war in the nineteenth century against the background of post-Enlightenment assumptions concerning human progress. The central argument was that the destructive military potential of the new civilization was not evident in the dominant narratives of modernity, and that modernity, in the mode of modernization, was highly destructive. The analysis also revealed how many of the new productive techniques of industrialization came originally from a military environment. But this was not meant to imply a form of technological determinism. On the contrary, this book advances the proposition that the essential driving force of war lies in society's culture. By this I mean key norms and values, patterns of social organization, and, even without a conscious use of propaganda, popular culture.

With regard to weapons technology, Franklin makes the point that weapons must be imagined before they are invented.[1] This construction of imagination is the role of culture. The presupposition here is that the creation of our artefacts of war represents and reflects fundamental elements in the culture of modernity. It would be extraordinary if a society self-consciously developed technologies that it deplored or deprecated. The technologies of war, as we shall see, reflect deeply embedded values within Western culture. They also represent a powerful ideology of progress. Within the general environment of scientific activity it has been assumed that nothing should stand in the way of further innovation and upgrading. We have sought ever more powerful technical means. In the civil sector of industry this results from the constant search for more economic efficiency; in the military sector the competitive dynamic is the need to stay ahead in producing the means of destruction; to maintain an edge on the field of battle and to compete in the global arms market.

The drive to maintain an edge in military affairs is also rooted in an image of enemies. As Keen notes, 'In the beginning we create the enemy. Before the weapon comes the image.'[2] In the modern period the increasing scope and pervasiveness of war have pushed this culture of enmity to the point where the enemy is the whole society of the adversary. I call this process 'strategic anthropology'. By this I mean the systematic construction and development of a culture and narrative of struggle and conflict with other nations and peoples through the articulation of powerful images of threat and danger. Clearly this has been pivotal in establishing patterns of identity in society conducive to mobilization for war and in securing integration and consensus. The war story encodes a collective past in forms which frame and establish in-group, out-group identities. It has been a staple ingredient in nationalism, and it was critical in the cultural and emotional preparation for the First World War.

The creation of a consensual strategic anthropology has occurred in all the Western countries in different periods. In America in the 1950s integration and consensus were built around a potent discourse of anti-communism which secured social harmony, despite the troubling spectre of nuclear war. Mass culture revealed a mobilized and militarized society. To some extent today, and especially after the end of the Cold War, this element of representational culture has been masked in Western countries, as it clashes with self-images built around a narrative of care and responsibility and a mission to secure a new world order based on law and morality. Yet a reflective analysis of our popular culture reveals that an aesthetic of violence and a fascination with the means of destruction persists, despite the fact that the image of the enemy may have changed. Having been an ally of Saddam Hussein in the 1980s, the West showed in the Gulf War of 1991 how quickly it could articulate a new culture of threat and enmity. In the USA representational culture rapidly reconstituted Saddam as a Satanic figure in the Hitler mode. I shall pursue this in detail in Chapter 6, my point here is merely to remind us briefly of the strategic discourse of the recent past. Current assumptions in the West still tend to stress the peaceful character of liberal democracy. But the Falklands, Grenada, Panama and the Gulf are hardly events from prehistory.

CULTURE AND WAR

In this chapter I want to explore how certain cultural representations shaped the view of war that developed in the late nineteenth century and how this was affected by the 1914–18 War. I also want to introduce the idea that war has an explicitly aesthetic dimension which substantially complicates the way it is evaluated. To put it very simply, what may appear utterly atrocious from a moral point of view can seem attractive and desirable when the frame of reference is aesthetic. Death and mass destruction have an aesthetic appeal, particularly when the one doing the judging is not likely to be a victim of the violence under scrutiny. If this is in any doubt, then a moment's reflection about modern popular culture would seem to confirm the point. Popular computer and video arcade games simulate individual and mass acts of gross violence. Recent popular films, such as *Casino* (1995), show the most horrendous interpersonal violence. Yet this is regarded as an acceptable form of entertainment. Thus societies which are ostensibly demilitarized can still reproduce cultures where an aesthetic of violence is deeply engrained.

Significant here are the instruments of destruction themselves. The technology of death is aesthetically attractive to many who value the power and design rationale of military machines. Gallie notes, 'on many minds the gadgetry of war in any age exercises a powerful imagination'.[3] As we shall see, this has been particularly powerful in the sphere of air power, where the symmetry and physical power of planes and missiles attracts adulation. But even a humble hand gun like the Magnum .44 calibre can be a cultural icon. More controversially, this technology can be seen to have a sexual appeal linked to deeply embedded emotions rooted in images of male potency and power. Psychologically, as the means of destruction have grown in power, this concentration on the machine, and not its effects, has been very useful in displacing feelings of concern for victims and making state-enacted violence legitimate. Today death is often delivered 'over the horizon', not just geographically, but cognitively as well. Westerners simply cannot visualize the long-range effects of their military technology, while the technology itself is often subject to adulation.

The aesthetic appreciation of mass violence is also coupled to the way in which the victims of such violence are conceived and culturally represented in domestic society. In the nineteenth and twentieth centuries racism helped to justify forms of war against non-whites that would have been problematic had the victims been white and Christian. In *War and the Twentieth Century* Coker describes how the captain of the *USS Texas* exhorted his men to pity those dying on the Spanish ship *Vizcayo* because they were white and European. But when the victims were Asian, there was no such concern.[4] In ontological terms, the further away any group is deemed to be from those who draw the map of human authenticity, the less need there is to worry about what becomes of them. In the nineteenth century the unrestricted use of new military instruments against the peoples of colonies and the destruction of the Amerindians did nothing to dent a self-righteous image of spreading civilization. As Kiernan observes, 'colonizing countries did their best to cling to the conviction that they were spreading through the world not merely order, but civilization'.[5] But as we shall see, this confidence in the project of building Western civilization was jolted by the First World War, because the new industrial war machine turned inward on Europe.

In terms of the major *leitmotif* of this book, the First World War was the first major shock for those who were convinced of the progress implicit in the project of modernity. The Great War shattered many illusions, not least in the cultural edifice of military heroism. As Daniel Pick suggests in his study *War Machine*, from which I have gained many insights, two contradictory narratives are at work in nineteenth-century reflection on war.[6] One seeks to capture war as a child of rationality, a rational political instrument, *pace* Clausewitz. The other conceives war as a machine which has gone out of control, a symptom of alienation. I contend that the latter image was much enhanced by the experience of 1914–18. In 1914 European culture had to come to terms with the fact that the military instruments derived from industrial progress were turned inwards for use in intra-European war. In the countdown to the war, nationalism, xenophobia, romanticism and social Darwinism had fuelled enthusiasm for the coming conflagration. Indeed, culture served to blind strategists and commanders to the likely consequences of the use of the new military technology. As we have seen, the key lesson of the American Civil War was the superiority of the tactical defensive because of the new power and accuracy of the rifle. But this highly significant fact was ignored in the cultural climate leading up to 1914. To reiterate, culture could override and refashion arguments rooted in science. Culture was anchored in powerful belief systems which transcended factual or rational grounds. Indeed, in the areas of evolutionary theory, eugenics and anthropology, so-called science was no more than populist 'hot air'.

VARIETIES OF SOCIAL DARWINISM, EVOLUTIONISM AND ROMANTICISM

Major elements in British nineteenth-century social and political culture derived from the impact of liberalism and utilitarianism. However, not all social commentators and critics were happy with a vision of society conceived through the categories of trade, commerce and economic improvement. This unease about a society geared merely to welfare and social betterment increased rapidly after 1871.

For many centuries France had been the preponderant military power in Europe and also Britian's traditional enemy. But after the Franco-Prussian War of 1870–71 this changed. In the campaign against France, von Moltke showed how the educational reforms associated with the new *Kriegsakademie* had borne fruit. The training of Prussian officers had led to a fundamental superiority in this sphere.[7] Similarly, although Prussia and France were equally endowed with railways, it was the Prussians with their superior organization who were able to harness them to better use.

In Britain these events signalled a cultural focus on Prussia which was fundamentally ambiguous. On the one hand was a fear and respect for Prussian militarism, on the other a contempt for a state that was seen as degenerate. In fact, as Pick shows, 1870 triggered a series of neurotic pseudo-scientific accounts of Prussian and German history and personality which continued right up to the Second World War.[8] This process was far from simple, as it revealed the rise of numerous new perspectives on war from biology, anthropology and evolution theory. These were interwoven with cultural currents which revealed anxiety, not just about external enemies, but also about bogeymen at home associated with urbanism and mass society. It is worth noting that the late nineteenth century was the period when polite society began to attain some systematic knowledge of the previously off-limits world of the urban, industrial working class. Coker notes a link between this process and the exploration of strange, alien lands in the shape of colonies, the street urchins of London being just as much an unknown quantity as the peoples of far-off lands.[9] Thus there seemed to be much to be anxious about both at home and abroad.

Broadly speaking, if anything brought these strands together in a manner of some coherence, it was social Darwinism. After mid-century the cultural representation of the competition between European nations and their imperial rivalry was increasingly refracted through the prism of evolutionary theory and the dictum of the survival of the fittest. The struggle between individuals was replicated by the competition amongst nations to be top of the evolutionary tree. In simple terms, a theory of war developed showing that war was vital to national health, and that victory in war revealed racial superiority. As Pick observes, 'Evolutionary theory was increasingly invoked in later nineteenth-century accounts of the necessity of war.'[10]

In England a significant spokesman for the new bio-evolutionary perspective on war was the eugenicist Karl Pearson. In *The Scope and Importance to the State of the Science of National Eugenics* we find the following:

Permanence and dominance in the world passes to and from nations even with the rise and fall in mental and bodily fitness. No success will attend our attempts to understand past history, to cast light on present racial changes, or to predict future development, if we leave out of account biological factors. Statistics as to the prevalence of disease in the army of a defeated nation may tell us more than any dissertation on the genius of the commanders and the cleverness of the statesmen of its victorious foe.[11]

Somewhat earlier, in the 1850s, a pre-Darwinian French text which ultimately had a major impact in this field was Arthur de Gobineau's *Essay on the Inequality of the Human Races* (1853–5). Gobineau, an explicit racist, saw the issue essentially in terms of the purity of blood.

> Societies perish because they are degenerate ... The word degenerate when applied to a people means ... that the people had no longer the same intrinsic value as it had before, because it has no longer the same blood in its veins, continual adulterations having gradually affected the quality of that blood.[12]

The greatness of France, he believed, stemmed from the infusion of Teutonic blood in the north of the country. But this had been weakened by Celtic and Latin stock in the south. Military decline stemmed from this degeneration.

In Germany the impact of social Darwinism was strong, but its reception was shaped by the strong legacy of philosophical idealism and the theory of the *Machtstaat*. From Hegel and Fichte, German thought had inherited a powerful emphasis on the state as the institution of human inclusiveness, where social and economic contradictions were resolved. Also Hegel's *Philosophy of Right* appeared to both idealize the Prussian state and interpret war as the means whereby superior civilizations spread their influence by absorbing and liquidating inferior ones. In war, Hegel believed, the ethical calibre of society was put to the ultimate test. In particular, the capacity of the individual to rise above egoism and identify with the whole was vital. In war, 'the power of the association of all with the whole is in evidence'.[13]

The fusion of idealism and Darwinism could be found in many texts, but the writings of General Friederich von Bernhardi represent an ideal example of the genre. Bernhardi thought war to be one of civilization's great gifts. In *Germany and the Next War* he argued that 'The inevitableness, the idealism, and the blessings of wars' should be 'repeatedly emphasized to every citizen'.[14] Similar sentiments can be found in his *On War of Today* and in General Colmer von der Goltz's *Nation in Arms* (1887), which had an enormous impact on young officers such as Erich Luddendorf.[15]

Many commentators have accorded Germany the prime role in fashioning a militarized social Darwinism. As a number of historians have subsequently noted, Germany did not tread the path of development of other Western states. As Bracher emphasizes in *The German Dictatorship,* the Enlightenment legacy and liberalism in general were largely absent from German historical consciousness.[16] Indeed, Bracher cites these factors as critical elements in the causation of Nazism. However, in the case of nineteenth-century cultural discourse on war, it would be wrong to see the German contribution as unique. While the status of the army and its officer class of *Junker* was high in Germany, this does not mean that Prussian militarism was the sole driving force for late nineteenth-century militarism. Nor was the Prussian *Kriegsakademie* the only institution to radically rethink military operations. The social Darwinist twist to thinking on war was a general trend amongst the Western societies that were shaping up to confront each other as the end of the century approached. If the advocacy of war was stronger in Germany, it may well have had more to do with Germany coming late to statehood, and the historical experience of being the victim of French military power for several hundred years, than to any deep structure of militarism. In many ways 1870 settled a score going back centuries, but it did not exhaust the full extent of German military ambition. Nor did it obviate the sense of vulnerability felt by being a *mittel-Europa* civilization, sandwiched between East and West.

In Britain the image of Germany as the rogue state in Europe and as the culprit for the new militarism was an important element in the festering racism and biologism which attained a significant hold on the popular imagination as the century drew to a close. In British culture figures such as Hegel, Fichte, Bernhardi and, not least, Bismarck represented an easy target for satirists and propagandists. But it was not just the popularizers who sought to build a narrative around the cliché of German malfeasance. Locating an essential German psyche, rooted in megalomania and aggression, was sport for serious science. As Pick recounts, the anthropologist J. W. Jackson presented a paper to the Anthropological Institute in March 1871 detailing the racial and cultural characteristics of different European nations.[17] As in the theories of de Gobineau, Jackson locates the Teutons as the dynamic and aggressive force in European history. To some extent this was to be welcomed, as more effete peoples such as the Celts had benefited from the energy infused by the Teutons. But ultimately Jackson conceives the Teutons as a negative force. They could destroy, but not build up.[18]

In Jackson's paper there is an appreciation of some positive aspects of German culture. However, as the clock ticked on towards 1914, the discursive representation of a Prussianized Germany became cruder and uglier: 'Prussia was at once the machine and the spanner in the European works, emerging as a deranged, aberrant freewheeling creature, a spanner in the general peculiarity of German history.'[19] But as I suggested above, this was not without its ironies. On the one hand, Prussia had bequeathed a legacy of militarism and expansionism; but on the other, these were the very qualities that some critics wanted replicated in Britian. As a militarist mentality developed, the classic virtues of British liberal capitalism and the alleged nature of the British personality came in for criticism. Bourgeois values such as making money, increasing social comfort, and emphasizing domestic life came under attack. But further, the so-called classic British virtues of individualism and freedom were seen as counter-productive. If the enemy was irrational and barbaric, then decency could backfire. In some quarters there was a strong feeling that society was becoming 'feminized', too soft and prone to sentimentality. Also it was suggested that commercial and domestic life offered no real challenges, whereas war offered excitement, romance and comradeship. As Kipling made clear, the Germans would be a dastardly foe: 'The Hun has been educated by the state from birth to look upon assassination and robbery ... as a perfectly legitimate means to the national ends of his country.'[20] To defeat them, Britain would have to stir itself, and perhaps adopt alien forms of institution. Pick notes the contradiction: 'But, ironically, some-thing of the Hegelian vision of war often underpinned the models of the Allied propagandists who denounced him together with much else of German culture and philosophy.'[21]

In France a social Darwinist vision of war was evident in the work of the major military theorist of the time, Ferdinand Foch. Foch, a key parti-cipant in the new French War College, copied and admired many of the Darwinist themes evident in von der Goltz and Bernhardi. The result was the building of a consensus about the next war determined by positive normative assumptions. In short, war was seen to be good for human progress. As Ropp emphasizes, the daunting nature of the new military technology was regarded as less significant than morale and the spirit of the troops. Foch quoted de Maistre's maxim that 'A battle lost is a battle one thinks one has lost ... for a battle cannot be lost physically'.[22]

This Panglossian optimism was part of a cultural mood which allowed millions of young men to march cheerfully off to war in 1914. With social Darwinism as the anchor of culture, it was inevitable that the commanders of 1914 would see the offensive as the key to military success. All the European General Staffs believed that the lessons of 1870 would be repeated, and that the defender would never recover from a massive assault early in the conflict. The ranks were led to believe that the war would not only be short, but also glorious. Ropp comments, 'Consciously and unconsciously, the men in the ranks in 1914 had been led to believe that the coming war would be short and glorious.'[23] Perhaps never before or since has the expectation about a phenomenon and its subsequent reality been so discrepant.

CULTURE, NATIONALISM AND RACISM

In the context of colonial war and the slaughter of the American Indians, a classic form of racism had absolved many Westerners of any need to regret what had transpired. In the late nineteenth century a new form of racial distinction, based on the pseudo-science of eugenics, allowed a refined racism to emerge, premissed on utterly bogus distinctions between different European peoples. When coupled with the mystical nonsense spouted by writers such as de Gobineau, this made possible the construction of imaginary racial types such as the Aryan. In essence, national and ethnic distinctions were wrapped up in racist language. In this evolutionist fantasy, competition was taking place to determine who and what was the superior race and culture in Europe and America.

In Britain and the USA this racially encoded nationalism expressed itself in a popular culture which focused on the military conflicts to come in the struggle for preponderance. In Britain it was clearly manifested in a genre of invasion scare stories and a bizarre fixation with the dangers posed by a channel tunnel. In the USA, as Franklin has argued, it led to a specific genre of 'future war' novels.[24] Both reveal much about the Anglo-Saxon image of enemies and the belief in the efficacy of certain military instruments. More generally, this popular culture was reflective of more serious ideas concerning the role of war in society and the manner in which it could be conducted. It was the cornerstone of strategic anthropology.

Franklin sees the war-oriented cultural output of the USA in the late nineteenth century as indicative of a deep fascination with 'techno war' and also a fundamental racism in American society. It also revealed anxieties about domestic weakness and the possibility of invasion and conquest by alien powers such as China, Spain, Britain, Japan, Italy, France, Germany and Russia. The most virulent forms of racism were still reserved for black and Asian peoples, but as I have indicated, the new notions of eugenics and evolutionary theory led to the construction of racial hierarchies, with US and British writers often placing the Anglo-Saxons at the top.

A writer typical of this genre was the militarist adventurer General Homer Lea. His widely read *The Valor of Ignorance* (1909) predicts an inevitable future war with Japan, a country Lea regards as a major threat because the Japanese are racially pure. Lea also reveals how the Darwinist encoding of culture leads to fear of an enemy within. Echoing the concerns expressed in England, he is anxious about the domestic effects of feminism and commercialism, which may weaken the will to resist.[25] He fears 'the heterogeneous masses that now riot and revel'.[26] Lea wanted to school his countrymen in the lessons of national development and survival. The following passage from another of his texts is instructive:

> The brutality of all national development is apparent, and we make no excuse for it. To conceal it would be a denial of fact; to glamour it over, an apology to truth. There is little in life that is not brutal except our ideal. As we increase the aggregate of individuals and their collective activities, we increase proportionately their brutality.[27]

The concern about not meeting international challenges in the field of war was also frequently expressed by Theodore Roosevelt: 'In this world the nation that has trained itself to a career of un-warlike and isolated ease is bound, in the end, to go down before other nations which have not lost the manly and adventurous spirit.'[28] These ideas were at the more 'serious' end of the continuum; but much out-and-out fantasy was evident in the cultural speculation of the time. Key texts here were M. P. Shiel's *The Yellow Danger* (1899), J. H. Palmer's *The Invasion of New York* (1897), Frank Stockton's *The Great War* (1889), Samuel Barton's *The Battle of the Swash and the Capture of Canada* (1888), Stanley Waterloo's *Armageddon* (1898) and Jack London's *Unparalleled Invasion* (1908). London, an avowed racist, was concerned about the threat posed by Japan, and in 1904 published an article in the *San Francisco Examiner* to try and alert his countrymen to the danger posed by Japanese expansion.[29]

Established scholarly opinion in the USA has been inclined to see the outburst of imperialist racial *angst* at the turn of the century as something of an aberration within America's anti-militarist culture, occasioned by the emergence of the USA as an imperial power. But the lack of regard for formal military institutions in America compared to European countries disguised a deep strain of cultural militarism which the works cited above clearly reveal. In a recent study Engelhardt traces the role of the war story in what he regards as the dominant narrative of American historical development.[30] He argues that the power of this narrative may have been overlooked because it was interwoven with what seemed to be such an ordinary and natural story: 'The American war story was so effective as a builder of national consciousness because it seemed so natural, so innocent, so nearly childlike, and was so little contradicted by the realities of invasion or defeat.'[31] Following this line of argument, I would suggest that the role of the military in the USA in the nineteenth century allowed for a more casual appreciation of military power than in Europe. War did not need to be given such a formal locus in political thought, because the USA's military experience was less significant in issues of national survival: 'In a country uninvaded since 1812 and, after 1865, opposed at home only by a small population of native Indians, most Americans encountered war as a print, theatre, screen, or playtime experience.'[32]

The importance and relevance of the cultural output on war can be seen if it is linked to real issues of policy which were confronted by the US state. I am not suggesting here a mechanical model of culture as a simple reflection of constellations of power. But it must be noted that it is not just in totalitarian environments that popular culture attains a propaganda function. The position adopted here is that popular culture is part of a process in society in which ideas are elements in a contest to establish a persuasive discourse linked to the struggle for hegemony. What is deemed to be entertainment is not removed from wider issues concerning the key values which groups struggle to establish as the framework of societal identity. But again, let me reiterate, this is not a mechanical model. The aim may be to establish consensus, to make one view dominant and indispensable to national identity, where a cognitive line is drawn defining self and other, us and them. Arguably this was achieved in the USA in the 1950s, as a hegemonic model of identity was constructed around the core ideology of anti-communism. However, the search for hegemony can fail, as it did at the time of the Vietnam War. At the turn of the century there were voices opposed to the imperial discourse of racist nationalism, but they were not the dominant ones. A partial hegemony was attained around the themes discussed here, and the output of popular culture played a key role in that process.

The connection between popular culture and policy is evident if we analyse the historical shift in America's global position at the end of the nineteenth century. The most significant academic theorization of the changing global circumstances of the USA was Captain Alfred Thayer Mahan's *The Influence of Sea Power on History* (1890). In the early nineteenth century the US Navy's role had been defined by Jefferson as coastal defence. Mahan, sensing America's coming global mission, wanted to move to a more active and interventionist policy, with the US Navy able to protect the vital shipping lanes to the United States and police a global system of trade.[33] Mahan's originality, as Klein has argued, lay in his linking of sea power to issues of commerce, national character and geopolitics.[34] In an era when America had no tradition of grand strategy, Mahan was able to link conceptions of US interests to a vision of global order beneficial to the United States. Less interesting was Mahan's uncritical social Darwinism and his belief that what Jomini had done for theories of land warfare, he would achieve for sea power.[35] He himself acknowledged a debt to Bacon and Raleigh, but he was convinced of the originality of his focus on naval power. Again, it should be emphasized for those who believe in the anti-militarist thrust of American thought that although the great naval arms race was going on in Europe, it was an American who was the most important theorist of sea power at the end of the nineteenth century. In the 1890 publication and in *The Interest of America in Sea Power* (1897), Mahan was spelling out a message that was listened to by senior American politicians, such as Under-secretary of the Navy Theodore Roosevelt and Secretary of State John Hay. While navalism in Europe sparked a fairly meaningless competition between Britain and Germany to build navies that were largely sidelined during the First World War, Mahan's ideas actually helped shape a policy that was of much use to the United States. In the history of the evolution of strategic doctrine Mahan should not be underestimated.

Regarding policy, let us remember that after a period of confrontation with the Spanish, the USA disposed of the Spanish threat in the three-month war of 1898. It then promptly relieved Spain of the Philippines, and formally annexed the islands of Hawaii. In 1899 the USA took control of part of the Samoan Islands by agreement with Germany, and henceforth expressed its policy towards China as one of the 'Open Door'. In 1900 American troops helped to suppress the Boxer rebellion in China, and by 1902 US forces had won a bloody civil war in the Philippines.[36] Thus, from nowhere, America had established a powerful global presence in four years. In this process the requirements which Mahan had laid down for a successful global maritime strategy were largely achieved. Earlier he had demanded a network of bases to support a global navy:

> Having therefore no foreign establishments, either colonial or military, the ships of war of the United States, in war, will be like land birds unable to fly far from their own shores. To provide resting places for them, where they can coal and repair, would be one of the first duties of a government proposing to itself the development of the power of the nation at sea.[37]

Mahan's precepts were thus adopted in naval policy. As Klein notes, this foregrounds the contradiction inherent in America's self-image and the reality of its strategic power:

> The result was a fleet flung out far into the Pacific, and a growing fleet in the North Atlantic, which less than a generation later would turn the tide against the Central powers. This strange concatenation, of liberal America and global power, was to intensify its presence among the

nations of the world. The exceptional trading nation designed by the Founding Fathers became, just over a century later, a growing industrial power with worldwide strategic outposts.[38]

Mahan's work shows how serious intellectual inquiry shadowed the needs of policy, but the popular diet of novels and stories was also linked to real historical processes. The fear of invasion by Asians, the domestic anxiety in California over immigration, and the sudden emergence of metropolitan America created anxieties that were reflected in popular culture. Franklin notes a virtual synergy in the perception of foreign policy issues and the form that racist war literature took. The national and racial targets in the novels and stories were the same as those identified as a threat by the state. This linkage is evident in the focus on Japan after 1905 and the Japanese victory in the Russo-Japanese War. After 1905 a welter of literature after the style of Lea homed in on Japan as the major threat to the USA, with Japan eclipsing China as the focus of the 'yellow peril' syndrome. Stories abounded concerning Japanese atrocities, and in 1906 California legislated to segregate Japanese schoolchildren.[39] Much of this literature was unrelentingly crude, and it frequently depicted the USA utilizing its superior technology to annihilate the 'Asian hordes'. As Franklin comments, 'And yet much of this literature advocates and enthusiastically describes total genocide, down to the extermination of the last person, of Black and Asian peoples.'[40]

The fit between the focus of popular literature and issues of *realpolitik* was also evident in the case of Germany. Before 1914 the popular future-war novel paid little or no attention to Germany. But with the outbreak of war, the cultural gaze shifted accordingly: 'Before 1914, virtually no American fiction projected Germany as an invader or likely enemy ... but in the wave of future-war novels published between 1914 and 1917, all of America's earlier imagined enemies disappeared beneath torrents of anti-German images.'[41]

As I have already mentioned, this cultural output in the USA was not unique. In Britain prior to 1914 the invasion scare story was also a popular genre. As in the USA the targets of this literature varied, with Germany not emerging as the unified focus until after the turn of the century. What the literature as a whole reveals is a deep anxiety about aliens, foreigners and assorted 'others' who may have designs on British wealth and power: 'Popular invasion stories swapped one enemy for another, drawing on an extensive reportoire of hostile images and stereotypes.'[42] As in the case of the USA, the anxiety is not just about external enemies, but is rooted in fears of 'others' inside the citadel. In essence, the more the middle and upper-middle classes learned about the hidden corners of the metropolis, the more anxious they became. Internal and external threats were linked: 'It also speaks to a specific ensemble of late Victorian and Edwardian fears about metropolitan degeneration.'[43]

A point of difference between the USA and Britain's cultural output on these themes concerns technology. The British *angst* reflected racial concerns and the proximity of traditional British enemies in Europe. But the core of stories such as Childers's *Riddle of the Sands* (1903) and Saki's *When William Came* (1913) is rooted in issues of class and national character. Here I am more interested in the American literature, because it speaks of an ideology which I maintain is at the centre of a modernist conception of war.

In the US case the popular literature I have cited shows how technical genius and Yankee inventiveness resolved the problems posed by being outnumbered by alien hordes. Repeatedly this literature reveals how technology was at the forefront of military thinking in the USA. In my opinion it prefigures the emergence of America as the world's pre-eminent arms manufacturer and superpower. Here it should be noted again that accounts which emphasize the anti-militarist thrust of American philosophy miss the point. In the United States a culture of militarization was subordinate to a narrative of progress encoded in a discourse of scientific advance and technological superiority suffused with racism. In terms of social philosophy the oppressive character of this discourse was hidden behind a political-theoretic narrative which articulated America's global role through the mission of the spread of free trade, liberalism and democracy. Klein refers to this as 'millenial liberalism', which he sees as coming to fruition after 1945, with America's explicit grasping of global dominance.[44] However, I trace its cultural roots to the literature exemplified in the future-war novel. This literature was uncritically premised on the idea of America as a unique and superior civilization with a right to spread its culture and way of life across the globe. In the twentieth century the spread of this culture has been given a less aggressive and racist hue through defining its essence as modernization. If the creed could be spread peacefully, then all well and good; if not, the values of liberalism and democracy would be driven forward through the mechanism of extreme violence. Thus the liberal surface of the modernist credo disguised a more violent core: 'Janus-headed liberalism shows its other face. This one is unpleasant and impersonal, unsympathetic and aggressive. In a word, violent. This other face is capable of showing the most profound intolerance and aggression.'[45] This account of double-headed liberalism epitomizes the central argument of this book: that a political-theoretic representation of modernity masks the violent nature of its more concrete social processes. More bluntly, it can be said that the liberal interpretation of liberal society is simply wrong. Regarding more recent times, Connolly notes, 'how the doctrine draws a veil of ignorance across the most disturbing features of contemporary life'.[46]

END-GAME: THE FIRST WORLD WAR

The cultural representations discussed above show how Western states developed a doctrine of war rooted in a Darwinist synthesis of historical, scientific and nationalist elements in the countdown to 1914. The romantic and heroic aspects of this culture helped to promote arguments in favour of offensive military operations. Foch, for one, was convinced that the revolution in firepower would favour the offence, as a massed force on the attack could bring a much heavier weight of fire to bear. He argued that the army must surge forward 'with all the means it possesses: guns, rifles, bayonets, swords ... *as one whole on one objective*'.[47] But the key was spirit, the will to win. According to Foch, and to a slightly lesser extent his German equivalents, success would derive from idealism, a triumph of will over material circumstances. Following McInnes, this view can be termed the theory of the 'psychological battlefield'.[48] While this theory was most strongly held in France, it is important to realize that the 'cult of the offensive' was a general belief amongst commanders in the years prior to 1914. In 1910, Lieutenant-General Sir Ian Hamilton, who later commanded allied forces at Gallipoli, offered the following observation:

Blindness to moral forces and worship of material forces inevitably lead in war to destruction. All that exaggerated reliance placed upon *chassepots* and *mitrailleuses* by France before '70; all that trash written by M. Bloch before 1904 about zones of fire across which no living thing could pass, heralded nothing but disaster. War is essentially the triumph, not of a *chassepot* over a needle-gun, not of a line of men entrenched behind wire entanglements and fireswept zones over men exposing themselves in the open, *but of one will over another weaker will*.[49]

In the quotation Hamilton refers to the work of Ivan S. Bloch, a self-made banker from Warsaw, who published a five-volume study of war at the end of the nineteenth century called *The Future of War*.[50] If we take Marshall Foch's views as one end of a continuum on the issue of the nature of future wars, then Bloch's view can be clearly seen as the other end. Bloch, whose incursion into military science was not welcomed by the military, believed that the nature of modern armaments would make the battlefield an environment too hostile for soldiers, and that the new military technology clearly favoured the defence. His conclusions about the nature of wars to come were as follows: (1) the opening of battle from greater distances; (2) the use of loose formations in attack; (3) the strengthening of defence; (4) the increase in the size of the battlefield; and (5) a large increase in casualties.[51]

It seems to me that Bloch had glimpsed very acutely the consequences of modernity for war. His view of war was not coloured by social Darwinism or any romantic nonsense about heroism. But Bloch underestimated the irrationality of human behaviour and the coercive discipline that made it possible to drive men forward towards mass death. The following image of battle is horrific, yet does not capture the grim truth of what was to come:

> At first there will be increased slaughter – increased slaughter on so terrible a scale as to render it impossible to get troops to push the battle to a decisive issue. They will try to do, thinking they are fighting under the old conditions, and they will learn such a lesson that they will abandon the attempt for ever.[52]

Bloch's ultimate conclusion was that 'War has become impossible ... except at the price of suicide.'[53] But mass suicide turned out to be possible, as the horror of the reality of the industrialized battlefield was masked by the cult of the offensive. A cultural edifice built on social Darwinism, romanticism, nationalism and super-patriotism was not to be undermined by a clinical assessment of the pragmatic and utilitarian nature of war. The war of attrition, where the firepower produced by mass industrial systems would be the ultimate arbiter, did not fit a heroic or romantic conception of war. Theory and practice were poles apart.

The First World War began in July 1914 with the declaration of war by Austria–Hungary on Serbia. By early August, Britain, France, Belgium, Russia and Serbia were pitted against Austria-Hungary and Germany. On 3 August the great battles of the Western front began with Germany's invasion of Belgium. The German strategic plan was based on the famous Schlieffen Plan which had been refined over many years. The plan was rooted in a dilemma which continued up until the Second World War. For decades German commanders had had to grapple with the prospect of a two-front war. Thus, at least on one front, victory would have to be rapid and decisive in order that two protracted campaigns would not have to be fought. In particular, the Schlieffen Plan envisaged a quick victory over France, with the reinforcement of the East by troops no longer needed on the Western front. The precise tactic was to ensnare French forces in a huge enveloping movement with the right of the German armies hooking around Belgium to come behind the French and the left approaching Paris, having defeated an anticipated French assault through the Lorraine gap.[54]

As history records, the plan failed. Some historians have blamed the failure on the younger von Moltke, who replaced Schlieffen as Chief of Staff in 1906, and made some modifications to the plan. Others, such as Liddell-Hart, see the pernicious hand of Clausewitz in Schlieffen's original plans for a 'decisive battle'. However, another interpretation, which defends Clausewitz, is that Schlieffen and von Moltke ignored two of Clausewitz's holy trinity: politics and friction. The Schlieffen Plan assumed that every last detail had been worked through, and that every contingency had been anticipated. The question of friction was overlooked. Politics was simply ignored altogether. Based on a plan that was refined for over two decades, the German General Staff placed their hopes in a rationalist calculus of war that left nothing to chance. If they were Clausewitzians, they had not read or understood the following passage:

Everything in war is simple, but the simplest thing is difficult. The difficulties accumulate and end up by producing a kind of friction that is inconceivable unless one has experienced war. Countless unforeseen incidents ... combine to lower the general level of performance, so that one always falls short of the intended goal. Friction is the only concept that more or less corresponds to the factors that distinguish real war from war on paper ... This tremendous friction ... brings about effects that cannot be measured, just because they are largely due to chance.[55]

This, in fact, could function as the ideal explanatory epitaph for what happened to the Schlieffen Plan in the first weeks of the First World War. A series of errors by German commanders, the capacity of the French to reorganize, and the fact that they did not panic meant that the assault failed. Indeed, in what has become known as the 'miracle of the Marne', German forces were repelled and forced to retreat to the Aisne river. As the various battles unfolded, the Germans were locked into predetermined plans which allowed for no reorganization. To repeat an argument made in Chapter 1, this mentality owed more to the influence of Jomini than to Clausewitz. It is important to realize that the German plans had ossified after constant rehearsals through the medium of a series of war

games – *Kriegspiel* – pioneered by the Prussian military academy.
Arguably this locked the Schlieffen Plan into a mechanistic formula. As
de Landa observes:

> the Prussian high command reverted to a Jominian view of strategy,
> destroying the informal links that had been forged between strategic
> planning and political leadership. When Schlieffen became chief of staff
> in 1891, the main source of friction in combat, the independent will of
> one's opponent, began to disappear from operational planning, paving
> the way for the eventual ascendancy of the war-game mentality in
> strategic matters.[56]

After the failure of the Schlieffen Plan the Western front became two
static lines of firepower dug into fortifications stretching from the Flanders
coast to Switzerland. The opening battles, The Battle of the Frontiers and
that of the Marne, had cost an enormous number of casualties, half a
million on each side, but they had been characterized by mobility and the
chance of victory. By contrast, 1915–17 saw battles of attrition where
massive artillery bombardments were used to soften up the opposing
defences prior to an infantry assault. But initially successful attacks were
often repulsed, leaving the attackers in a killing ground hundreds of yards
wide. As Bloch had predicted, the slaughter was unparalleled. Breech-
loading rapid fire artillery and the machine-gun exerted a terrible toll. Now
the material military artefacts of modernity had been unleashed on the
peoples of Western Europe. Strategy and tactics failed to catch up with the
technological revolution as generals, schooled in the cult of the offensive,
sought to deny the reality of the new weapons. In Germany and France
great hopes had been placed on the vigour and idealism of youth. The
Germans believed that students would fight more daringly than working-
class recruits or canny old hands who were keen to survive. Keegan
records how the university authorities in Bavaria exhorted their young
men to fight:

> Students! The muses are silent. The issue is battle, the battle forced on
> us for German culture, which is threatened by the barbarians from the
> East, and our German values, which the enemy in the West envies us.
> And so the *furor Teutonicus* bursts into flame once again. The enthu-
> siasm of the wars of liberation flares, and the holy war begins again.[57]

The untrained German students were formed into the XXII and XXIII
Corps, and met the British in battle at Ypres in October and November

1914. The result was a predictable slaughter, known in Germany as the 'Kindermord bei Ypern'; 36,000 of them were killed and buried in a common grave at Langemarck. But this was hardly unique. All over the Western front the flower of Europe's youth was falling in a war of mechanized slaughter. In the end, the casualties of the First World War were truly mind-boggling. In one of the bleakest days for Britain in 1916, 57,000 casualties, with 21,000 dead, were suffered at the opening of the Somme offensive. In all, the Somme saw 415,000 British casualties from July to November 1916. At Passchendaele in 1917 another quarter of a million perished, while nearly 150,000 were lost at Arras in 1917.[58] At Verdun in 1916 the German attackers lost 336,000, to the French's 362,000. All told, during the whole war the French lost 1,700,000 men from a population of 40,000,000, while Germany lost 2,000,000, and the British Empire forces suffered losses of 1,000,000.[59] Never before in world history had such slaughter been conceivable. But now the logic of war and the pathology of the nation were bound together. The huge number of deaths meant that few, if any, families remained untouched by tragedy. The telegram conveying the news of the death of a loved one was ubiquitous.

But the nation and war were bound together in other ways as well. The scale of the conflict and the use of the mass instruments of factory production saw the industrial worker as a key asset in the state's death struggle with its rivals. The logic of this was inescapable: the citizens of the opponent and his cities and industry would have to be included in strategic assessments, assessments that would lead to the targeting of civilians.

The scale of the carnage in the First World War revealed something utterly new in the construction of state and society in the West. The inclusiveness that Hegel saw as the essence of the state had brought the masses into mainstream political life as both warriors and citizens. If they were not warriors directly, they were assets in the industrial logistics of total war. Thus, as Western societies approached the status of genuine democracies, the *quid pro quo* for the new citizens was to surrender their lives in the service of the state at war. Societies could bear these huge losses because of a culture which emphasized the wholistic claims of nationalism. Thus it can be argued that as modernity perfected its configuration through the genesis of the modern nation-state, the rationalization of industrial production, and the homogenization of political identity in nationalism, it revealed its character as one of war. In this view, total war and modernity walk hand in hand: 'The brutality of the twentieth century, which has taken many forms ... is easier to understand if we see the totalitarian features of warfare as a reflection of modernity itself.'[60]

The revolutions which had moulded populations into the malleable aggregates which could be used in mass warfare were clearly sensed by Charles de Gaulle:

> the culmination of long years of change, suddenly brought together by the cataclysm. For generations universal suffrage, compulsory education … industrialization and city life … the press, … political parties, trade unions, and sport had all fostered the collective spririt … The mass movements and mechanization to which men and women were subjected by modern life had preconditioned them for mass mobilization and for the brutal, sudden shocks which characterized the war of peoples.[61]

Of course, cataclysm had struck European peoples before in the shape of famine, war and pestilence, but the general conditions of life before the modern period militated against high expectations concerning material and social conditions. It was the modern period which had promised ever-increasing betterment in the material conditions of men and women and proferred doctrines of uninterrupted progress.

The ease of identification of the causes of the willingness to engage in slaughter between 1914 and 1918 has been possible only in retrospect; at the time the carnage was a massive body blow to the edifice of self-confidence evident in nineteenth-century culture. In fact, some European intellectuals had succumbed to a mood of pessimism well before 1914, as many of the symptoms of mass society seemed to mock the European Enlightenment's celebration of individual reflection and judgement. Also Nietzsche's proclamations about the meaninglessness of modern life and his emphasis on the nihilism of science and rationalization haunted many thinkers at the dawn of the twentieth century. But the war itself made concrete the fears that many critics and philosophers had articulated before 1914. The ideology of progress was dead. As Coker argues, 'The Great War was the first historical event of significance to confront modern man with a question whose implications were particularly grave: was it any longer possible to see progress in terms of a long historical trajectory, and could progress itself any longer be considered necessarily redeeming?'[62]

THE FUTILITY OF WAR

Ropp notes how the American Civil War was the first in which large numbers of literate soldiers were able to give their account of the fighting.[63] This process was even more pronounced in the First World

War, when many literate middle-class men shared for a time the life of the ordinary soldier. They were nearly all deeply scarred by the experience; but the process was a catalyst to creativity. Ropp comments: 'The shock – to men whom society had taught that war would be short and glorious – produced the greatest of all war literature.'[64] An important point about this literature is that it allowed an interpretation of the war outside the normal discipline of military science or the reflections of members of the political elite. Ordinary men were simply expressing the sentiments and emotions that arose in the trenches. This, of course, does not make it the definitive account of the Great War; it is one textual presentation amongst many, but a key one because it meshes with changing assumptions about modernity and the post-war social order. In the writings of the war poets the central message which comes through is that of the futility of war. The mass deaths, the mechanized slaughter, the random selection of victims, all seemed meaningless to men who sought a more personal rationale for the forces they found themselves enveloped by. Between 1915 and 1917 the static war of attrition also enhanced the sense of battle being pointless. At Ypres in 1917 the British ultimately captured 45 square miles of territory at a cost of 370,000 men. As a result of the massive 19-day bombardment by artillery, which used a year's production of shells by 55,000 munitions workers, what the British captured was essentially a swamp. It had cost them 8,222 men per square mile.[65] Small wonder, then, that many participants articulated a sense of futility and despair.

For British readers the writings of the most important war poet, Wilfred Owen, were brought together by Edmund Blunden. Indeed, it is Blunden who is responsible for providing us with the account of Owen and the other poets as men, an account which has become nearly as important as the poems themselves. Another poet known to Blunden was Henry Williamson, who wrote the following as a 19-year-old at the Somme:

the wide and shattered country of the Somme ... among the broad, struggling belts of rusty wire smashed and twisted in the chalky loam, while the ruddy clouds of brick-dust hang over the shelled villages by day, and at night the eastern horizon roars and bubbles with light.

And everywhere in these desolate places I see the faces and figures of enslaved men, the marching columns pearl-hued with chalky dust on the sweat of their heavy drab clothes; the files of carrying parties laden and staggering in the flickering moonlight of gunfire; the 'waves' of assaulting troops lying silent and pale on the tapelines of the jumping off places.

I crouch with them while the steel glacier rushing by just overhead scrapes away every syllable, every fragment of a message bawled in my ear ... I go forward with them ... up and down across ground like a huge ruined honeycomb, and my wave melts away, and the second wave comes up, and also melts away, and then the third wave merges into the ruins of the first and second, and after a while the fourth blunders into the remnants of the others ...

We come to wire that is uncut, and beyond we see the grey coal-scuttle helmets bobbing about, ... and the loud cracking of machine gun fire changes to screeching as of steam being blown off by a hundred engines, and soon no one is left standing.[66]

These images reveal not just a critique of war, but a loathing for industrialized war and the machine. The 'drab heavy clothes' speaks of the visual poverty of the industrial landscape and the anonymity of mass labour. The 'steel glacier' is a mechanical force, the noise of which prevents human communication, as did the machines in many factories where workers sometimes learned sign language in order to communicate. In Williamson's account, the soldiers die not as individuals, but in 'waves', mowed down by machines. There is no heroism or valour here. The same sentiments were continually expressed by Wilfred Owen and by Blunden himself. Coker believes that poets such as Owen were predisposed not against war as such, but against mechanized, industrialized war: 'Was not Owen's main complaint less the reality of death in battle than the experience of industrialised warfare?'[67] But this doesn't seem a very powerful point to me, as the First World War was precisely an industrialized war. Coker goes on to attack the image of the war presented by men such as Owen, the 'unhappy warrior', who he accuses of robbing the war and death of meaning. The point of this critique is to give a broader account of the reception of the war in Britain than is evident in the work of the poets. But surely this misses the point. As Coker acknowledges, the texts of the war poets are one representation among many. The poetry must be decoded with the context and the social background of the poets in mind. Thus, to some extent an attempt at a factual rebuttal of the observations of men like Owen seems pointless. The war poetry serves as a testament to the distress felt by men whose preconception of war gave them an utterly false image of what was awaiting them in the trenches. Against the pre-war hyperbole of heroism and glory, they offered a poignant rebuttal based on the idea that the offensives which resulted in such mass death were futile. Of course, as Coker argues, if every ordinary soldier had felt as Owen did, then the British army would have been unable to sustain the remarkable degree of morale that it managed right until the end of the war. But a variety of factors sustain men in adverse and horrific conditions, including fatalism and the bond of comradeship. Many ordinary soldiers felt the horror described by a Williamson or an Owen, but would not articulate it in the same way or submit to the idea that it was all they had experienced.

An important point made by Coker concerns the social conditions of ordinary soldiers in domestic society. Before 1914 there was no cornucopia for ordinary working-class people. Standards of diet and housing had improved, but were still poor. Conditions of work in many industries were appalling. The Boer War had occasioned much surprise about the state of physical health of the nation's working classes. But the problems were not all resolved by 1914. Coker notes how 1,000,000 volunteers were rejected by the War Board as medically unfit. Montagu described the rejects as 'gargoyles out of the tragical-comical-historical pastoral edifice of rural life'.[68] The point here is that the conditions of life for many who joined up were a great improvement: a decent diet, exercise and a clean place to sleep were often new experiences for the lads from the factories. Also war has a habit of juggling with the dynamics of social order and raising expectations. Thus, as Coker argues, there were other perpectives to those of the war poets, perspectives of men who may have believed that their lot was improving. But the conditions for the ordinary soldier were still not good, and many died horrible deaths in Flanders – men such as Bill Hubbard of the City of London Regiment, Royal Fusiliers, who was found dying in no-man's-land by his comrade Alf Razzell. In a moving testament recorded by Roger Waters, Razzell recounts how he tried to carry Hubbard back to the British trenches across the wilderness of bomb craters, but failed because his comrade could not bear the pain of being moved. Hubbard was left to die without medical attention, a fact which haunted Razzell for the rest of his life.

Even if the account of the war poets can be challenged, it is still clear that the Great War was a transformative experience which left a cultural legacy of pessimism. Those who were marked by it found it impossible to communicate its reality to those they returned home to. Coker notes how the poets never recorded their own heroic deeds. But as any close relative of a war veteran knows, most men are reluctant to recall the details of the worst fighting. Real heroes are much more reticent than Hollywood might suggest. In history and culture the Great War was a wall which marked a fundamental boundary, a clear delineation of past and present. Millions of men and some women had experiences they found impossible to describe or relate to what had gone before. Pick argues that this image of transformation may be misleading. Paul Fussell has given the clearest account of the war as rubicon, an indelible boundary. But Pick believes that *The Great War and Modern Memory* is too much premissed on an illusion of a pre-war world of stasis and fixed assumptions.[69] This is probably right; but it still doesn't mean that the war was not a fundamental right of passage from one world to a new one. It is true that before the Great War writers invoked images of machines out of control, of mechanistic forms of slaughter and of human alienation. But 1914–18 actually turned Europe into a real charnel-house: 'The carnage was absolute, the madness total.'[70] At Verdun a French officer couldn't tell the earth from rotting corpses: 'one could not distinguish if the flesh were mud, or the mud were flesh'.[71]

WAR AND AESTHETICS

A critique of anything presupposes standards of judgement and criteria of assessment. The 'moral' critique of the Great War was founded on standards believed to characterize pre-1914 Europe. More particularly, norms and values emphasizing the growth of civilization and the linear development of human progress were corroded by 1914–18. The slaughter seemed to contradict any Christian tenet about the value of human life, and its evil was therefore self-evident. Worse, the Great War showed how soldiers might depart from a moral and legal conception of war. Conduct in the war, such as the bombing of Rheims Cathedral, revealed how the boundary between the sacred and the profane might be crossed; war opened up the prospect of mass criminal action. Thus, for a variety of reasons, the war challenged many of the imagined values of the modern era and also specific military notions of chivalry and heroism.

But it was possible to judge the war experience from other perspectives. An aesthetic rather than a moral view could distance the appraiser from any emotional engagement with the events and their victims. This is not to say that the slaughter was enjoyed, for this would be more a sign of derangement. But once a critical distance was attained, it was possible to see the war in terms different from those of moral outrage or the betrayal of history. Moreover, it should be pointed out that some found their life experience enhanced by war. The war turned ordinary life upside down; but what of those who found normal life unsatisfying? Before the war many critics had sensed the need for the values of martial pursuits. William James believed that if war were abolished, a moral equivalent for it would have to be found. After all, where was the glory and honour in a bourgeois life, the pursuit of wealth and a selfish orientation towards family? Many may have come to distrust the political buzz-words of the time: patriotism, nationalism and fatherland; but many also found joy in comradeship, in playing a role in something greater than the network of competing egos. Further, self-sacrifice in service of an ideal seemed a moral good. Durkheim had long argued that the utilitarian conception of society as competing egos, where self-interest equalled the general interest, was false. He believed that when society attempted to institute such a vision in real forms of organization, it would lead to anomie and moral confusion.[72]

An individual who found the Great War invigorating was Adolph Hitler. Hitler was at Langemarck, where the student volunteers of XXII and XXIII Corps were cut to pieces by the British. Hitler found the war experience the most fulfilling of his life. What the case of Hitler shows is how an individual lost in anonymity in society can be literally reconstituted by historical events such as war. Hitler revelled in the comradeship, the pursuit of the national cause, and the exhilaration of the danger. Germany's defeat gave him his historical mission and the conditions to fulfil it. Hitler sought to avenge the death of heroes betrayed by the 'stab in the back'.

Another participant at Langemarck was the writer and critic Ernst Jünger. As Coker notes, Jünger drew drastically different conclusions from his experience to Hitler. Jünger believed that war was the crucible where in man's essence was defined. In the trenches men had found themselves, and had refashioned German identity:

> In the depth of its craters, this war had a meaning which no amount of arithmetic could possibly quantify. One could already hear in the cheering of the army volunteers who sounded the voice of the formidable German daemon, a voice which combined wearines with old values with longing for a new life. Who could have thought that the sons of the materialist generation could have greeted death so ardently? ... Just as the real fulfilment of an honestly lived life is the gain of one's own deep character, so the result of this war cannot be anything but the recovery of a deeper Germany ... Deep under the areas where the dialectics of war aims are meaningful, the German met with a superior force: he encountered himself.[73]

In Jünger's view, defeat didn't matter; the real function of the conflict had been to knit the German nation together and to reconstitute idealism. In this sense, war made possible a form of transcendence, something lacking in the lexicon of bourgeois liberalism. Here it is ordinary life which in a way is terrifying, a routine with no drama or pathos. More generally, I would argue that Jünger's ideas show how modernity denied man emotional consolation, and in Peter Berger's memorable phrase created the 'homeless mind'.[74] I am not seeking here to restate the thesis of Adorno and Horkheimer in *Dialectic of Enlightenment*, but it seems that modernity's compulsion to saturate cognition with technical, utilitarian and scientific norms creates an enormous burden, manifested as a search for meaning. The cognitive technical machinery of economic advance and the apparatus of domination of nature require forms of enchantment. In war this is reflected in attempts to find meaning where mass death and mechanical slaughter would seem to make meaning elusive.

CONCLUSION

The aesthetic appreciation of war after 1918 was more pronounced in continental Europe than in the USA or Britain. The creed of liberalism, with its emphasis on individual rights, was less easily moulded to an appreciation that something good may have emerged from the trenches than were collectivist philosophies searching for new rationales for organic social identity. In the Anglo-Saxon world it was generally held that the costs of the Great War had been too great. In military science there began a search for a new way to conduct war that would short-circuit the costly war of attrition. Over time, this refashioning of strategy latched on to air power as the solution. The potential of air war had been vividly imagined before and during the First World War, but its overall impact was not great. But the war gave a huge catalyst to the development of aircraft. As daring young flyers did battle over northern France, something else was also apparent. If heroism and chivalry were dead in battles on the ground, the gladiatorial combatants in the air seemed to have reinvented it. Rickenbacker and von Richthofen were the stuff of heroic stories and legends. Modern war had lost its enchantment in the trenches. But a central thesis of this book is that modern war reinvented itself in the air. In the next chapter I will show how a new culture of war grew up in the mystique of air war. This culture was developed in the democracies which manufactured the new instruments of strategic air war and brought to the world the possibility of total global annihilation.

3 The Enchantment of War in the Air

INTRODUCTION

The First World War triggered a number of profound changes in the Western cultural and philosophical attitude to human experience. One of the most fundamental was in the understanding of what war signified. The idea of war as a rational instrument of state policy or as an uplifting experience for man was largely discredited. Especially in countries where liberalism was the dominant social philosophy, many sought not to think about war at all. But the West did not give up on war completely. A new technology and a new theory of war were developed against the backdrop of the 1914–18 experience. This was the birth of an air strategic conception of war.

What I seek to show in this chapter is how the pursuit of an alternative to the war of mass attrition led to the creation of a modernist philosophy of air war which re-established a positive cultural gloss for war. For Western countries air warfare has helped to rescue the state from the consequences of the mass loss of life associated with huge land operations. While totalitarian states were still prepared to fight such land wars, the liberal democracies were not. Air war has had other advantages as well. The role of the flyer helped to re-establish a notion of heroism and chivalry in war. Further, the technology of air warfare has itself become something of a cultural icon. Moreover, the way in which aerial weapons deliver death and mayhem to the enemy has helped to distance citizens in the West from the moral consequences of war. Here the specific grammar and language of modern strategy have been pivotal. As the destructive power of airborne munitions has grown, ultimately to the point where global destruction has become feasible, the language of strategy has become ever more devoid of accurate referents. The likely real consequences of war for people have been hidden behind a cloak of clinical terminology straight from the lexicon of utilitarian, instrumental rationalism. As I show in Chapter 4, this was essential for the elites managing the machinery of nuclear deterrence. In principle, nuclear weapons could undermine a modernist theory of war. Modernity seeks to colonize the future; its watchword is control. But Soviet hydrogen bombs threatened to cancel the future. They also meant that Western destiny was no longer entirely in Western hands. As a consequence, I interpret nuclear strategy largely as a discourse designed to bring these wild cards under control. First, though, let us see how the nuclear dilemma grew out of the creation of the machinery of conventional strategic air power in the United States and Britain.

THE END OF HEROIC WARFARE?

In the eighteenth century a powerful tradition had been born which stressed the rational and individual character of human action. In the post-Enlightenment nineteenth century this optimism congealed into various narratives of progress linked to conceptions of scientific and technological development and human betterment. But not everyone was happy with a secular philosophy of progress rooted in materialism. As the years passed to 1900, a growing constituency sought to invoke a more romanticized and martial conception of society. As we saw in Chapter 2, this was based around the doctrines of social Darwinism, nationalism and organicist romanticism. In many respects bourgeois philosophical conceptions of modernity were pushed to one side; but nevertheless, the material instruments of bourgeois industrialization grew ever more powerful. In the nineteenth century scientific and technical innovation developed its own dynamic. As Whitehead noted, this was more important than any specific invention: 'The greatest invention of the nineteenth century was the invention of the method of invention ... the process of disciplined attack upon one difficulty after another.'[1]

Nowhere was this process more in evidence than in industrial-military research. In the nineteenth century one innovation after another served to massively increase the potency of battlefield firepower; breech-loading rifles, smokeless gunpowder, the machine-gun and breech-loading artillery transformed the battlefield that men were to encounter in 1914. Now infantry men could fire 15 rounds a minute; machine-guns could disgorge 600 bullets every 60 seconds; and heavy artillery, 20 shrapnel shells filled with steel ball.[2] As Bloch had predicted, the battlefield became a hellish place. Yet the mentality of those who went to war in 1914 was not tuned to the new material realities of battle. The culture of war and its material under-side were out of joint. The philosophy of war was configured precisely around the frustration with bourgeois values mentioned above. Even the stoical Sigmund Freud welcomed the outbreak of war in 1914 and its awakening of national sentiment.

The Great War began between nations saturated with propaganda built on notions of heroism, chivalry and the *telos* of historical mission. But all this died in the mud of Flanders. While the men there saw countless examples of individual heroism, this was not the image conveyed to those outside the field of battle. The dominant cultural images were of collective, mass slaughter, of death at the hands of the factory instruments of the machine age, of filth and drabness, of incompetent commanders blind to the suffering caused by their folly, of bodies enmeshed in barbed wired, and of a landscape pulverized beyond recognition.

In the wake of 1914–18 serious military analysts sought to refashion military thinking in order to find a means of resolving the dilemmas of the static war of attrition. Here air power would be central. In the work of Basil Liddell-Hart, J. F. C. Fuller, Guilio Douhet, William Mitchell and Hugh Trenchard, the theory of strategic air war began to take shape.[3] But this theory was not sketched on an empty canvas. Speculation about the war-plane had existed for decades before air war was feasible. This speculation was very much wrapped up in the science fiction of the time, and reflects general attitudes to progress and scientific development at the end of the nineteenth century. In order to grasp the reasons for the particular reception of the theory of strategic air war, it is necessary to examine the culture into which serious accounts of aerial warfare were absorbed.

THE AGE OF FANTASY

The era of manned flight began in November 1793, when two aeronauts ascended to a height of 3000 feet above Paris. Many in the watching crowds became hysterical as they witnessed the doctor and the army officer break free from man's terrestial home. Flight was the medium of travel which broke the chains binding man to the earth, and as such was dramatic and revolutionary. Men had tunnelled below ground, they had conquered the oceans; but now, after thousands of years of speculation, they were floating above ground. Legends, such as that of Icarus, had cautioned against such a bold challenge to the gods, and the hysteria in Paris bore testament to this combination of wonder and awe. Flight was exciting, but it was frightening too, as it challenged many deep assumptions about man's place in the world. In his masterly study of the rise of American air power Michael Sherry even suggests a religious aspect in man's attitiude to flight: 'Flight also resonated with the deepest impulses and symbols of religious and particularly Christian mythology – nothing less than ·Christ's ascension.'[4] But flight also had a more utilitarian component. Flight allowed a new perspective on territorial space; it allowed man to see the topography of the Earth more precisely. Flight thus complemented and enhanced a modernist impulse to assess, to map, and to control. It was also a form and a symbol of power that would carry the possibility of terrorizing men and women below. From the beginning, its military potential was uppermost in the minds of those in the forefront of its development.

The first treatises on the military uses of aviation were written by Major-General John Money and the Prussian officer J. C. G. Hayne at the end of the eighteenth century.[5] Both could see the potential of balloons for observation; but even as early as the civil war in France there were plans to drop bombs on Toulon. By 1812 the Russian Czar, Alexander I, was so impressed by the potential of flight that he accepted the plans of the Prussian inventor Franz Lepping to provide an armada of balloons. In one of the more bizarre turns in aviation history a thousand Moscow prostitutes were rounded up to sew taffeta into sections for the new aerial craft.[6] But nothing came of the Czar's initiative, and the extended period of peace in Europe after 1815 slowed down the more frenzied search for military aviation. The first real air raid took place in 1849, when Austrian balloonists dropped a handful of bombs on Venice, although plans for bombing had been hatched earlier by the American John Wise during the Mexican War of 1846–8.[7]

In the American Civil War and in the Franco-Prussian War, balloons showed their worth in reconnaissance and artillery target spotting. However, the most detailed speculation about future air war in the late nineteenth century came in science fiction. As Kennett notes, 'Popularizers of science saw them in the future and described them to their readers.'[8] Two important contributions here were Alfred Robida's *War in the Twentieth Century* (1883) and Jules Verne's *Clippers of the Clouds* (1887). As Franklin and Weart have noted, this literature was part of a wider cultural movement which saw science as the medium of human salvation.[9] It was also linked to race *angst*. In much of the science fiction which anticipated the use of air power, the possessors of the new technology were white, while its victims were black or Asian. In Robida's book, war is imagined between Australia and Mozambique; but the most repeated instances of this genre involved America defeating racial inferiors with its slick advanced technology.[10] Two themes emerged in this literature which warrant comment. One is the notion described above of a technical fix to the problems posed by threatening aliens and hordes; the other is a more general belief that new weapons will actually benefit mankind, because as war becomes more terrible, it will become unthinkable.[11] Co-inventor of the plane, Orville Wright, exposed a complacency which was commonplace: 'The aeroplane has made war so terrible that I do not believe any country will again care to start a war.'[12]

Of course, it is not easy to specify any exact links between a wider cultural concern with aircraft and more precise strategic formulations. What we are reviewing here is a context in which thinking about the military uses of flight began. But what must be emphasized is that at the turn of the century books and articles were the essential ingredients of popular culture. Many war and science fiction articles were serialized in magazines, and became a staple diet in the wider culture. The cultural context was thus significant. Kennett notes its importance:

> The popular literature of the late nineteenth century, because of its scientific and futuristic elements, had more than a casual relationship to the dawn of airpower and more particularly to perceptions of that power. This sort of literature not only bred in its readers a faith in science and the inevitability of 'progress', but it also created a kind of anticipation.[13]

It is important to realize, though, that there were differences between Europe and the USA. The plane as an ingredient in a culture of techno-philia was more pronounced in the USA. According to Franklin, this was exemplified in the work of Thomas Edison. He describes Edison's book *The Conquest of Mars* as a 'mindless glorification of the cults of progress, empire, individualism and technology'.[14] Edison himself could see no incipient militarism in his and other inventors' restless search for advanced weapons: 'There is practically no military sentiment in the United States, nor ever has been, but we have proved ourselves to be amongst the world's most powerful fighters whenever we have had to fight.'[15] This quotation illustrates neatly a tendency in US thinking to see American war-making as an act of self-defence, always undertaken reluctantly. As we shall see below, it contributed enormously to the understanding of aviation in the USA as essentially a benign phenomenon.

In Europe the arrival of the plane was always accompanied by more apprehension. At the beginning of the twentieth century, a series of conferences in The Hague sought to control the uses of the coming aerial weapon. But the operation of the apparatus of the war machine was not to be restricted. In Germany in 1886 Count von Zeppelin began sketches for the design of a dirigible, which the Germans adopted in 1908. By 1914 the Germans were using Zeppelins to bomb Liège, and by 1915 they were attacking Great Britain. The potential of the war-plane had been clear in 1909, when Bleriot flew across the Channel. What was obvious now was that the territorial boundaries of a state could be breached with impunity. In Britain this rocked the age-old confidence that her best defence lay in her physical isolation from Europe. Britain responded with a Navigation Act in 1911 claiming exclusive control of her air space.[16] Thus, having defined itself previously in terms of terrestrial boundaries, the state was now claiming jurisdiction over the skies as well. But it was all to no avail. After the outbreak of war, experience showed that, incrementally, air warfare would penetrate ever more deeply into the state's domestic terrain.

The first raids using actual aircraft took place in 1911, when the Italians, at war with Turkey, attacked Tripoli in Libya. The Italians dropped Cipelli bombs weighing a mere 2 kilograms. These were no more than converted hand grenades, and gave only a foretaste of what was to come. In 1912 the French used incendiaries in raids against tribesmen in Morocco. Both raids broke the Haig Convention of 1907.[17] The logic of air war was unfolding. In 1910 the combined air fleets of the great powers stood at a mere 50; by 1914 they had 700 planes. Despite attempts at legal control, it was clear that the war-plane would play a role in the coming war.

AIR POWER IN THE GREAT WAR

In 1913 the Assistant Secretary of War in Britain saw the war-plane as providing 'merely an added means of communication, observation, and reconnaissance'. This described the role of the plane in the early stages of the conflict very accurately; the major use given to the war-plane at the beginning of the First World War was geared to events on the battlefield. Tactical roles for aircraft included reconnaissance, observation and straffing. But as the war developed, a strategic conception of air power grew in plausibility and attraction. The fundamental principle of strategic air warfare was to use the plane to attack the enemy's society: to damage or destroy assets that were deemed vital to the war effort. With industrial warfare, this meant the opponent's factories and industrial infrastructure. But tacitly some strategists realized that the will of the enemy could be targeted as well. Strategic air warfare always had a terroristic dimension. Particularly with social Darwinism still prominent in the ideologies of ruling elites, it was believed that inferior races or classes might soon capitulate in the face of mass bombing raids. In addition, the borrowing of other categories from biology by theorists of war led to the idea of society as a complex and interdependent organism with 'vital organs' and 'nerve centres' that could make it vulnerable to collapse. For a variety of reasons, there was a broad consensus that aerial bombardment would have profound effects, and that industrial societies were especially vulnerable to strategic air war. But behind the technical rhetoric were other more conventional motivations for air war; it fitted perfectly with a mentality of revenge which could be enacted even if one's ground forces were coming off second best.

In the 1914–18 war strategic bombing emerged haphazardly, according to no overall plan. At the time, there were many who doubted its moral justification; but as the war went on, those inclined to restraint were increasingly silent or ignored. In 1914 the Germans bombed Liège and Paris, with the British launching raids on Köln and Düsseldorf. But in 1915 the Germans upped the stakes with raids on London which killed civilians. The scale of German raids increased in 1917, with raids by the new, advanced Gotha planes, which had a profound symbolic effect on British leaders, who sensed the end of British immunity from attack. The aim of the German raids was to try and divert British resources away from the front. Ironically, as Sherry points out,[18] the Germans were not too impressed with their handiwork. But it made a big impact on British thinking, where a notion of strategic bombardment was soon advanced by the independent air force created in 1918 with Hugh Trenchard as commander-in-chief.

In Britain assumptions about the moral weakness and volatility of the lower classes led to a tendency to see the urban masses as easy targets for a campaign of terror bombing. The historian and critic J. F. C. Fuller was particularly prone to wild thinking on these matters.[19] With hindsight it seems to me that these ideas were deeply insulting to the men who had fought so bravely on the Western front and to their families at home. After all, they had come from the factories and the farms. But these ideas were not prone to a factual rebuttal; they were deeply held prejudices. The bombing did indeed cause some panic in London, perhaps because of its novelty. No less a person than David Lloyd-George left the capital in search of a safe haven. But there was no evidence of the mass hysteria which Fuller associated with bombing raids. Nevertheless, as I have indicated, the bombing had a great impact on the British authorities, who proceeded to plan for air war on a much greater scale.

As bombing escalated between Germany and Britain, so too it spread to other fronts. While the Italians remained somewhat cautious, as they had their own people living in the Austro-Hungarian Empire, the Austrians, using their advanced Taube aircraft, launched a great many raids over their southern border after 1915. During the war Venice was hit 42 times. In March 1917 Benito Mussolini was in a military hospital hit by an Austrian raid. In September of the same year another raid on Venice hit a hospital, where 42 people were killed. What was becoming clear was that gradually the inhibitions about killing civilians were being eroded. As Kennett notes, 'Early in the war bombing began to reach beyond the actual battlefields of the contending armies, and the distinction between combatant and noncombatant began to blur.'[20] As one raid increased the terror element, so another would be launched in reprisal. Sherry captures it nicely: 'Bombing escalated through a series of challenges and responses, raids and reprisals, all initiated as much to satisfy popular demands for revenge and punishment ... as to achieve any tangible gain.'[21]

At the start of the war, bombing was tactical; but as we have seen, it progressed gradually to a strategic role. In the war itself this lacked a theoretical rationale, as strategic thinking often lagged behind the popular imagination. But despite this, an assumption took hold in Britain that larger and more destructive raids were justified and effective. Hugh Trenchard had not been enthusiastic about bombing at first; but by 1918 it was clear that civilian support for bombing had overcome military reticence. Lord Weir, Trenchard's superior, gave the following instruction in 1918: 'I would very much like if you could start up a big fire in one of the German towns ... I would not be too exacting as regards accuracy ... The German is susceptible to blood-iness, and I would not mind a few accidents due to inaccuracy.'[22] Trenchard was able to reassure Weir thus: 'All the pilots drop their eggs well into the centre of the town generally.'[23]

Strategic bombing, including raids on civilians, grew in attraction, because it fitted an image of punishing an aggressor who deserved harsh treatment. It was easy psychologically, because it distanced the civil authorities and the wider population from a direct confrontation with the consequences of their actions. British bombing of Germany began very much as an act of revenge, as Lloyd-George said: 'We will give it all back to them and we will give it soon. We shall bomb Germany with compound interest.' In the war, as Germany's campaign of bombing faltered, Britain sought bigger and more powerful aircraft that could take air war into the heart of the enemy. By 1918, by using planes such as the Handley-Page V / 1500,[24] it was planned to mount massive attacks with incen-diaries on commercial and industrial targets in Germany. These raids were never undertaken, but it is worth noting that while Germany dropped some 330 tons of ordnance on Britain, approxi-mately twice that tonnage was returned. By 1918 Britain had the largest aircraft industry in the world,[25] and had laid the ground-work for a commitment to strategic bombing which was enacted during the Second World War.

THEORIES OF AIR WAR

During the 1914–18 war the great American proselytizer of air war, William Mitchell, came to Europe as an observer. Mitchell, a veteran of the wars against Spain and the Philippines, was quick to see what he regarded as the decisive nature of air warfare. In the war the USA had lost 48,000 dead in battle and another 56,000 from disease;[26] despite these numbers of dead being small by European standards, Americans were quick to see the ground campaigns as costly and futile. Support for the war had been engineered through a massive propaganda campaign aimed particularly at Irish-American and Scandinavian-American communities, but the results of the work of the Committee of Public Information soon dissipated after 1918, when the authorities turned their attention to the problem of Communist infiltration.[27] For Mitchell and his supporters, creating a rationale for the development of air power was thus going to be more difficult than it would be in Europe, where the problem was considered more urgent. In the USA isolationism went hand in hand with an anti-militarist sentiment which dominated in the 1920s. Also, Mitchell tried to convert the military establishment by the risky strategy of ramming air power down its throat. But although he fell foul of the authorities, particularly the entrenched interests of the navy, he managed to establish popular support for aviation by decoupling it from militarism. Mitchell's efforts showed very clearly how aviation could be used to restore mystique and optimism to a modernist vision of progress.

After the war, as we have seen, little survived of a heroic notion of combat. But the flyers, despite the truth of strategic bombing, emerged as the most likely inheritors of a noble conception of war. The flyers were individuals; they engaged in gladiatorial combat with their opponents: 'to others and often to themselves, aviators were knights of the air locked in individual combat, proof that the mechanical age possessed gallantry'.[28] As Sherry argues, within American culture they were able to unite two central ingredients in mainstream US values: individualism and technological superiority. 'Air power derived its appeal by promising to place the glitter of modern technology in the service of traditional values.'[29].

In the USA air power also appealed to a vision of war rooted in race *angst*. While no real antagonism persisted towards Germany after the war, there was a feeling of hostility to Japan. In Mitchell's work, such as his articles for the *Saturday Evening Post* in 1924 and *Winged Defense* (1925), the threat of war against Japan was always implicit. It was argued that Japan's 'paper cities' would make an ideal target for the bomber. More generally, Mitchell and his publicists attempted to show how air war would be cheaper and more humane than previous forms of armed conflict. In *Winged Defense* he argued that air power 'is a distinct move for the betterment of civilisation, because wars will be decided quickly and will not drag on for years'.[30] According to Mitchell, air forces would attack 'centres of production and not so much the people themselves', but Japan would be 'an ideal target'.[31]

Because of America's strategic position, Mitchell could present air bombardment as a defensive strategy. There was no risk of the USA being bombed, therefore the role ascribed for the war-plane was to locate and destroy ships approaching the US coast. In 1921 Mitchell had shown that this was possible in war games using captured German battleships. But generally there was scepticism that warships approaching the USA would be easily detected. Against this scepticism, Mitchell launched bitter attacks, labelling naval commanders as 'fossilized Admirals'. Ultimately, though, the champion of air power went too far. In 1925, after his personal attack on the Secretary of War, John Weeks, the President, Calvin Coolidge, ordered his court-martial. However, this defeat by the authorities did not mean that the case was lost with the wider public. In the USA Mitchell became something of a legend: the press repeatedly presented an image of him as a brave, lone hero standing up to the entrenched interests of the militarists. But the legend obscures a paradox which we have noted before. The reluctance in the USA to support large formal military institutions has usually been taken in orthodox scholarship as a sign of a lack of bellicosity. However, I see the strategic culture of the USA as distinct from that of Europe, but as no less potent. In America, air power appealed to a sentiment that sought to make war less burdensome and less costly than in Europe, by exploiting the benefits of science and technology. Ideally, war was to be fought 'over there', thousands of miles from American shores. Losses to one's own side were to be minimized, and the maximum firepower utilized against the enemy. As Coker points out, America was a new society with a new creed; it was appropriate that it should adopt a novel approach to war.[32] Freedman associates notions of punishment, rapid victory and efficiency with the American military credo.[33] To be sure, the USA did not have a distinct grand strategy in the 1920s and 1930s, but it didn't need one. Building on the links established by the Navy Consulting Board, what the USA possessed was the capacity to rapidly generate the institutional basis for massive levels of military production, by forging organizations of state, economy and military together. It certainly did not lack a culture able to transmit enmity to other races and nations. With air power the USA saw the promise of a means to defeat enemies without them having to be laboriously overcome. In addition, the idealism which attached to heroes such as Rickenbacker and Lindenbergh allowed the harsher aspects of military aviation to be pushed to one side. Temporarily, air power threatened the interests of the entrenched institutions of the army and the navy, but ultimately it gave the USA a new creed of war and a tool for managing global order.

Like Mitchell, the Italian theorist Guilio Douhet (1869–1930) faced a military court because of his criticism of his superiors. Douhet had witnessed bombing raids during the Great War, and had read newspaper accounts of panic in London during German raids.

His *Command of the Air* (1921) brought together ideas he had sketched over a number of years, and marked the first ever attempt at a general theory of strategic air war. Douhet believed that air power could greatly increase the destruction that war could wreak. More importantly, he thought that the war-plane could unleash destruction far faster than battle on the ground. Armies on the ground were locked into static lines of combat, but air power could bring havoc to a much wider radius of action. Douhet enthusiastically endorsed an escalation of the scale of destruction, because, like Mitchell, he believed this would end wars more quickly. He anticipated that cities would become 'unapproachable flaming braziers'[34] which would quickly compel surrender. Influenced by theories of mass psychology and the elitist pessimism promulgated by thinkers such as Mosca and Pareto, Douhet saw the masses as the Achilles' heel of the modern nation. The key would be to undermine civilian morale:

> It seems paradoxical to some people that the final decision in future wars may be brought about by blows to the morale of the civilian population. But that it was the last war proved, and it will be verified in future wars with even more evidence. The outcome of the last war was only apparently brought about by military operations. In actual fact, it was decided by the breakdown of morale among the defeated peoples – a moral collapse caused by the long attrition of the people involved in the struggle. The air arm makes it possible to reach the civilian population behind the line of battle, and thus to attack their moral resistance directly.[35]

Douhet argued that no restraint would be shown in war: 'The purpose of war is to harm the enemy as much as possible; and all means which contribute to this end will be employed, no matter what they are.'[36] Here, though, was the moral justification for strategic bombing; the more terrible war became, the quicker it would end. But what if morale was stiffer than theorists such as Douhet believed? Contrary to his assertion in the passage above, the Great War showed that people were capable of soaking up terrible punishment without capitulating. Within the amoral framework proposed here, at what point would destruction cease? In fact, what we have here is a naive technological determinism which assumes that the strategic dilemmas posed in the First World War, themselves the result of technological innovation, will be resolved by another innovation, the strategic bomber. In one sense Douhet has a point. In the First World War the tactical difficulty was the new power of the defensive position; in contradistinction, it is true that no really effective defence has been forthcoming against the bomber. However, with ground warfare, the criteria of victory and defeat were fairly clear. But this is not the case with the aerial offensive. If the morale of the enemy does not collapse, as was the case in Vietnam, at what point should strategic bombing be terminated? In my view this futurist and modernist refashioning of war has only one logic: that of nihilism. Douhet's unbridled optimism about technology thus feeds directly into the theoretical rationale for strategic operations with atomic weapons. His own expectations about bombing turned out to be wildly optimistic; but after Hiroshima and Nagasaki it was no longer fanciful to speculate on the consequences of the prompt destruction of whole cities. From the 1950s this escalated to the point where strategic operations had as their objective the destruction of whole societies with estimates of casualties in the hundreds of millions[37]. Total war thus became total destruction.

Another contribution to the development of the theory of the aerial offensive came in Basil Liddell-Hart's *Paris, or the Future of War* (1925). Liddell-Hart (1895–1970) was seriously wounded in the First World War, and, like Douhet, he sought a means of rescue from the destructive war of attrition of the trenches. But, unlike Douhet, Liddell-Hart was to emerge as a distinguished scholar of military affairs, who later rejected his earlier formulations on air power. Nevertheless, the 1925 publication is important, as it resonates with the assumptions and cultural attitudes of the time. Thus it is legitimate to see it as a significant contribution to the development of new notions of war in the 1920s and 1930s.

Like Douhet, Liddell-Hart saw the essential advantage of the bomber as its capacity to bypass the armed forces of the enemy and strike directly at the opponent's society: 'Aircraft enables us to jump over the army which shields the enemy government, industry and people, and so strike directly and immediately at the seat of the opposing will and policy.'[38] Also Liddell-Hart followed Douhet in his belief that 'the worse the better'. The more terrible the destruction, the more rapid war's termination. Alive to the potential of new technologies, he also had no qualms about the use of gas as an air weapon.[39] Although not as pessimistic about the lower classes as Fuller, who envisaged attacks, mass panic and capitulation in a matter of hours, Liddell-Hart also believed the masses to be the soft under-belly of the modern nation. As noted above, this view seems gratuitous, given how the ordinary soldier had performed in the Great War. In Chapter 2 we saw how Coker believes that the war poets, in their critique of the futility of war, robbed the dead of meaning; but equally significant is how the upper classes could maintain contempt for the lower orders after 1918. Perhaps all this shows is how engrained class prejudices were, and how little they accommodated historical experience. For whatever the reason, Liddell-Hart, Fuller and Douhet believed a terroristic bombing campaign would soon engender bedlam and mayhem.[40]

One of the many merits of Michael Sherry's masterly study *The Rise of American Air Power* (1987) is its use of sources from outside the orbit of orthodox military science. In his analysis of the complex doctrine of strategic air war he notes the ideas of the inventor and critic H. G. Wells. While many thinkers sought solace in the technical fix provided by air power, Wells was extremely prescient in his vision of the future. Although scientists remained sceptical about the prospect of atomic weapons, Wells's *The War in the Air* (1908) revealed an uncannily accurate account of future events. The book describes a German attack on US cities which quickly prompts the authorities to surrender; but the mass of citizens demand revenge, and as the state loses control, the world slips into a prolonged war. The major insight which enabled Wells to rise above the level of analysis of many of his contemporaries was that air war would not be decisive and lead to the rapid termination of hostilities. In his phrase it would be 'at once enormously destructive and entirely indecisive'. It is this, of course, and not his account of a German attack on New York, which foretold the future. But what was also a real insight into the future was the image of cities at the mercy of aerial attack out of the blue, of death unleashed by opponents thousands of miles away. More specifically, the bombing raids of the Second World War bore out his vision of protracted air war. In Germany allied bombing was to reduce town after town to rubble and cause nearly 700,000 civilian fatalities without crushing the population's morale. Also, although heavy damage was done to key industries such as petrochemicals, German war production actually peaked at the time of the heaviest allied raids. In Japan the damage was even greater, with the 20th Army Airforce under Curtis Lemay able to turn cities into the mass infernos envisaged by Fuller. But, again, morale did not crack as city after city was set ablaze.

Wells's vision of air war attracted much attention, but made not a jot of difference to the development of the technology and the planning for war. He believed that his image of a hellish war in the future might lead to the banning of the war-plane, but here he only indicated his own naivety. After the war, and particularly in America, the plane was absorbed into an optimistic vision of the role of technology in man's future. The aeroplane came to symbolize not the pessimism of those such as Wells, but the optimism associated with a new beginning. As Sherry contends, 'Prophecy, political debate, and cultural imagination shaped a benign image of aviation.'[41] In films such as *Wings* (1927) and *Hell's Angels* (1930) a tendency began which became more marked in the nuclear era: that of dissociating the war-plane from its effects. Cultural appreciation emphasized the technology and the flyers, but ignored the consequences of aerial firepower. This process arguably reached its apotheosis in the Gulf War of 1991, where TV coverage stimulated a techno-philiac appreciation of the air war against Iraq. In the USA, aviation industry trade publications, such as *Aviation Week* and *Space Technology*, presented the conflict as a clear victory for US technology, as if the agents in the war were machines. Little interest was ever shown in the scale of human suffering which the machines caused.

REFINING THE ART

In the 1930s the Italians used strategic bombardment against Abyssinia, and the *Luftwaffe* was brought into play against the Republicans in the Spanish Civil War. For the democracies this made possible the convenient assumption that the totalitarian states were those who would breach the rules of civilized warfare. But, in fact, the democracies themselves were practising aspects of air war against recalcitrants in their colonies. As Grey points out, the French even had a bomber called the 'Type Coloniale'.[42] The Royal Air Force under Hugh 'Boom' Trenchard developed a policy designed to control colonies without having to occupy them. In the 1920s 19 of Trenchard's 25 operational squadrons were stationed overseas.[43] Trenchard believed they could play a key role in pacifying troublesome tribes in the Middle East, a policy endorsed by the charming and erudite marshall of the RAF, Sir John Slessor.[44] The aim of this policy of Control without Occupation, was to pacify tribes humanely; as Asprey observes, it was a form of 'gunboat diplomacy from the air'.[45]

He continues: 'Lawless tribes would be warned, and if failing to come to heel, would be punished – their villages bombed and herds dispersed.'[46] But as Asprey points out, the weakness of the policy lay in what would happen if and when a tribe ignored a warning. An RAF report of the time showed what occurred on one occasion when a commander lost his patience with some rebellious herdsmen:

> The eight machines … broke formation and attacked at different points of the encampment simultaneously, causing a stampede among the animals. The tribesmen and their families were put to confusion, many of whom ran into the lake, making good targets for the machine guns.[47]

Notwithstanding the slippage that can take place between policy formation and execution, this action in the Middle East shows how the allegedly humane, selective character of air power has always been a myth. When aerial intimidation failed, the response was always one of escalation. In the case of British policy in the Middle East in the 1920s and 1930s, the euphemism of air control as a humane method simply masked the truth; when intimidation failed, innocent men, women and children were targeted. In essence, it was colonialism on the cheap, and a means of refining aspects of air policy.

As well as in the Middle East, the British used air power in India and Pakistan to buttress colonial rule, with the Pathan tribesmen in India coming in for particularly brutal treatment. But they were not the only ones. The French used the war-plane in their colonies in North Africa, and the Americans used it in Central America, particularly in Nicaragua. In an extraordinary incident in the USA, the plane was used to restore order in Tulsa, Oklahoma, in May 1921. Having been attacked by thousands of whites, who rampaged through their area of the city, black residents of Tulsa retaliated. In turn, they were bombed by whites, who dropped dynamite from eight planes which circled over the black communities, killing 150 to 200 people.[48] Racist forms of containment did not occur just on foreign soil.

The use of air power as an instrument of colonial rule was a fairly low-key work-out in the 1920s and early 1930s. But in general the 1920s was not a good decade for the aviation industry in Western countries. The war had finished, with massive overproduction, and political support for aircraft development became patchy and unenthusiastic as the prospect of war dimmed.[49] But as the 1930s developed, the whiff of war was again in the air, and states turned their attention to the threat posed by Hitler.

In the USA a gradual shift in the perception of air power occurred as the storm-clouds gathered over Europe. But, even before, many had seen the possibilities of conflict in Asia. The expressed isolationism of the period has always been exaggerated in my opinion, as US leaders never took their eye off the ball in the Asia–Pacific region. As we have seen, thinking about air power in America was always tinged with a casual racism which perceived the war-plane as an ideal weapon to use against Japan. As Mitchell had noted of Tokyo, 'Incendiary projectiles would burn the city to the ground in short order.'[50] More detailed attitudes to the Japanese were revealed in a Command and General Staff School study of 1935 called *The Psychology of the Japanese Soldier.* Here we learn that Japanese 'Samurai swords will be found rusty and their rice mustardised'.[51] But although the image of the enemy was clear, the tactics and strategy were not. In the 1930s the Air Corps developed the doctrine of Precision Daylight Bombing, but it was still not clear what the targets would be and how war would be terminated. Was it the will, or the material assets, of the enemy that would be sought out? In contradistinction to the offensively minded 'militarists' in the navy, Air Corps advocates had stressed coastal defence as the role for the bomber. But coastal defence was hardly going to justify the prestige and resources that air power enthusiasts sought. Thus the doctrine of precision bombing made it clear that air power would strike deep into the enemy's society, but at the same time the notion of precision kept alive a moral justification, in that attacks would be surgical and humane.[52]

In the early 1930s the means to achieve this form of strategy were designed and created in the form of the B10 and B17 (Flying Fortress) bombers. The contract for the latter, which had a much larger radius of action than previous planes, was awarded to Boeing in 1933, but B17s did not go into mass production until 1938. In Britain the industry had been in the doldrums in the 1920s, but it did survive the Depression because of government support. In 1934, Prime Minister Baldwin's announcement that the RAF would have parity with the *Luftwaffe* marked the effective beginning of rearmament in Britain, which would capitalize on the skills of companies such as Bristol Engines, Rolls-Royce, Avro and De Havilland to catch up with and surpass the German effort. The results of Baldwin's policy shift were dramatic. In 1936, an industry which

had had a mere 21,000 employees in 1930, was close to having a
work-force of 80,000. Companies such as Bristol Engines doubled
their work-force size in a single year.[53] The race was on to achieve
dominance in military aviation in the next war. In Britain it
inspired new levels of co-operation between private industry and
the state, which helped to create the planes, such as the Spitfire,
Hurricane and Lancaster, which took such a heavy toll on Germany
during the Second World War.

British thinking on air power was, as I have suggested, very much
based on the experience of being under bombardment during
1914–18. In the 1930s it was further refined by fear of Goering's
Luftwaffe. In fact, the German air force was not the Leviathan that
Goering's propaganda suggested. In the 1930s it was useful as an
instrument of diplomatic coercion; but as events revealed, it turned
out to have little strategic capability and has subsequently been
referred to as a 'shop window' air force. To reiterate, it was the USA
and Britian which theorized and instituted strategic air warfare.
As Sherry emphasizes, 'in the 1930s, only England and America
seriously developed the concept and the instruments of strategic air
war'.[54] After Guernica, many were intimidated by German air power,
but Goering lacked heavy bombers like the B17 and the Lancaster.
The Germans were reliant on versatile planes like the Junkers 88,
which could perform many roles, but none to the highest standard.
The blitz against England and Wales was terrifying, but it was not
of the same order as the British and Anglo-American offensive
against Germany. Germany simply lacked the means: 'The Germans
never made a concerted effort to wage strategic air war, although
occasionally they shifted tactical aircraft to strategic missions when
opportunity, miscalculation, or fits of desperation came into play.'[55]

With regard to the German war effort, it is worth making a point
which some historians get wrong. A typical example here is
Keegan's *A History of Warfare*, which, as I showed in Chapter 1,
makes some dubious observations on Clausewitz. Keegan also
repeats an oft-made, false cliché about Hitler. According to Keegan,
Hitler had an obsessional interest in 'revolutionary weapons'.[56]
As Albert Speer's memoirs make clear, nothing could be further
from the truth. According to Speer, Hitler 'was filled with a fundamental distrust of all innovations which, as in the case of jet aircraft
or atomic bombs, went beyond the technical experience of the First
World War generation'.[57] The best study of Hitler, that of Joachim
Fest, shows how Hitler, in fact, had no interest in revolutionary

weapons at all; rather, his interest was in the detail and quantification of existing weapons and logistics.[58] The issue I want to raise here is who was best geared to waging modern war? Although Guderian's new tactics for mechanized warfare were novel, they were hardly revolutionary. Much of German war culture was traditional and subjectivist. For Hitler the key asset of the *Wehrmacht* was its racial composition and its will to victory. The reactionary modernism of the Nazis actually recalled much myth and superstition of the folk past. In terms of instrumental effectiveness, the result of the cult of the irrational was often entirely negative. The assault on 'Jewish science' cost the Germans dear in terms of the effectiveness of their war machine, as did the exclusion of Jews and other groups from the armed forces. Modernist, rational war was actually waged by the Western allies. In Roosevelt and Churchill the allies had leaders who understood the logic of the industrial war machine. The aerial destruction of Germany and Japan was a central ingredient in the calculated, instrumental culture of modernist war.

FROM THEORY TO PRACTICE

In the United States the perception of events in Europe in the late 1930s had a profound impact on the emerging consensus for a large, strategically capable air force. As France and Britain were cowed by Hitler's increasing chauvinism, the view taken in Washington was that Germany's air power was a critical ingredient in the Nazis' ability to intimidate their European neighbours. While Neville Chamberlain was negotiating the Munich Agreement in September 1938, which subsequently became regarded as an infamous act of appeasement, the US ambassador to Germany, William Bullitt, remarked to Roosevelt, 'If you have enough airplanes, you won't have to go to Berchtesgarden.'[59] Earlier the same year, after the Italians had bombed Barcelona, an article in the *New York Times* suggested that 'bombers could destroy centuries of civilization in a few minutes'.[60] FDR and his advisers knew this was an exaggeration, but at the same time the US administration believed that air power would play a key role in the coming conflict. Ostensibly to arm France, Roosevelt now decided that US production must be massively increased. According to Roosevelt, Britain had 'cringed like a coward' at Munich, but this was not going to happen to America.

In the wake of Munich, US strategists began to see a key deterrent role for the war-plane. Roosevelt was clearly thinking in terms of deterrence, and his views were shared by key thinkers in the Air Corps, such as Lieutenant-Colonel Carl Spaatz and Lieutenant-Colonel Donald Wilson. As the latter noted, 'What could be better than a force so strong that actual conflict is thereby avoided.'[61] Spaatz's thinking was rooted in the general speculation of the 1930s about war with Japan. He wondered whether the 'mere existence' of a bomber force on Luzon might 'restrain Japan from open and active opposition to our national policies'.[62] If it did not, then probably, 'sustained air attack alone would be sufficient to force Japanese acquiescence to our national policies'.[63]

These ruminations came a step closer to reality in May 1940 when Roosevelt, addressing a joint session of Congress, announced that the USA would aim for a manufacturing capacity of 50,000 planes a year. In 1939 it had been agreed that the army and navy air forces would have an inventory of 5,500. But now the aim was for much larger numbers. Also in 1939 it was decided to go ahead with the B29, despite the fact that the navy had opposed a bomber larger than the B17. Thus the technology for the coming massive air assault on Japan was being prepared.

Just as at the beginning of the 1914–18 war, 1939 saw leading politicians suggesting that the bombing of civilians would be immoral and perhaps counterproductive. In the late 1930s this had been Churchill's position, and it was also endorsed by Roosevelt, who spoke of this 'inhuman form of barbarism'. Earlier Churchill had severely reprimanded Trenchard for the RAF's attacks on tribesmen and their families in the Middle East.[64] In America the actual strategy that was to guide bombing was still ill-defined, but in general the real significance of the new bomber force was disguised behind the assumption that its role would be defensive. In Britain matters were more urgent, and the moral reticence quickly evaporated. On 8 July 1940 Churchill said he wanted 'an absolutely devastating, exterminating attack' on Germany, and on 25 August sanction was given for a raid on Berlin.[65] German night raids on British cities began in September 1940, but severe raids had already been launched on cities such as Warsaw and Rotterdam.

Partly with revenge in mind, the British replied to German raids with an air onslaught that was to last for five years. From May, British Bomber Command had agreed to raids away from the combat zone, and the bombing of civilians had tacitly been endorsed, despite

Roosevelt's pleas. This tacit focus on civilian morale became explicit with the arrival of Air Marshall Arthur Harris as Chief of Bomber Command in February 1942. Harris made it clear that a policy of bombing 'area targets' had been adopted. In February 1942 a British Air Staff directive stipulated that operations 'should now be focused on the morale of the enemy civilian population and in particular of industrial workers'.[66]

From 1942 massive raids were launched against German cities. However, it must not be thought that previously civilians were spared. The truth was that the inaccuracy of bombing was such that precision attacks on military targets were illusory. In addition, daylight raids had been so costly that the RAF concentrated exclusively on night raids. The problem of inaccuracy had been dramatically illustrated at the beginning of the air war when German planes had accidently attacked Freiburg in May 1940. In another incident the British, who were aiming at submarine pens, managed to obliterate the towns of St Nazaire and Lorient. But military targets were also often close to civilian areas, making the claim about avoiding civilians otiose. Thus in many ways Harris was simply being more open about something which was already happening. But he did have larger forces at his disposal. In March 1942 new fire-bombing techniques were used against Rostok and Lübeck. In May the first 1,000-plane raid devastated Cologne. In July 800 bombers struck Hamburg.[67] In the Hamburg raids 80 per cent of the city's buildings were destroyed, and between 30,000 and 48,000 people killed.[68] After the raid 40 million tons of rubble choked the streets. In many respects the lurid expectations of some of the science fiction writers who had predicted air war were coming true. But they were wrong, as was Douhet, about the consequences of such destruction. War was not promptly terminated; the destruction and death of innocent civilians could go on for years. By November 1943, 19 German towns had been reduced to rubble by the Combined Bombing Offensive.[69] In a move that indicated how far moral restraint had been relaxed, 1944 saw plans for a project to tow unmanned bombers crammed with explosives over Germany and release them to crash-land at random. This 'War Weary Bomber' project was never enacted, but, as in the plans to drop the anthrax virus on Germany, it reveals how moral taboos were being abandoned. In 1945 Operation Clarion was designed to bring air attacks against small towns and villages in Germany, as morale became even more explicitly the target. But this plan also resulted from the fact that 50 of the largest towns and cities had already been laid to waste.[70]

Most controversial of all was Dresden, which was attacked on 13 February 1945. Dresden was an important cultural centre, and had little military utility as a target. In February 1945 it was swollen with refugees fleeing from the advancing Red Army. On the night of the 13th British bombers filled the town with incendiaries; the next morning it was attacked again by American heavy bombers; then, finally, US fighters straffed those still alive and visible in the inferno below. The damage done was colossal. For many years after the war it was believed that perhaps a hundred thousand people perished in Dresden. In the last decade or so this figure has been revised downwards to something in the region of 35,000, but it was still an enormous loss of life.[71]

The Dresden raid gained a notoriety after the war that put it at the centre of arguments about the moral behaviour of the Allies *vis-à-vis* the Axis powers. It was immortalized in Kurt Vonnegut's novel *Slaughterhouse Five* (1969). Vonnegut was a prisoner of war in Dresden during the raid, and survived with others who hid in a massive meat safe. When they emerged into the daylight, Vonnegut and his colleagues could not believe the sight they beheld. There were charred and melted corpses everywhere; bodies were piled together in a way that made them indistinguishable from each other. Death and destruction were everywhere; hell had materialized on Earth.

After the war Vonnegut found that he could not come to terms with his experiences in Dresden, which he decided to write about. His surreal novel, published 24 years later, reflects the fact that ultimately he came to see Dresden as too bizarre and terrible to be treated in an orthodox narrative style. If life was literally mad, then a literary form appropriate to madness was called for. As in Kubrick's film *Doctor Strangelove* (1964) this off-beat approach works well. The killing of thousands of innocent civilians is depicted as the result of a society that manipulates individuals and destroys the vestiges of conscience and judgement. The main protagonist, Billy Pilgrim, is the hapless victim of forces he can't understand or even detect. But although Vonnegut's horror is entirely understandable, the truth is that Dresden was not quite the unique event that some critics believed it to be. He described it as 'the greatest massacre in European history'.[72] But a few months before, in September 1944, Darmstadt had been destroyed merely because it was there and the available technology made it possible. Another raid by US forces in early February 1945 left 25,000 dead in Berlin, but led to no great outcry. As the campaign mounted, the destruction of cities became routine. Leaders such as Churchill who had taken a moral stance before the war had a hand in the decision to 'increase the terror'. Dresden attracted attention because of an Associated Press story which miraculously got past the censor, and some US leaders feared a public reaction. In Army Air Force circles there was some soul-searching over the strategy, but the pretence was still maintained that the policy was one of precision bombing of military targets.[73]

The fear of a public reaction to Dresden was naive for a number of reasons. Despite the official credo of liberal democracy, Western states had a long track record of committing brutal acts against other peoples. Further, the propaganda during the war was designed precisely to dehumanize and depersonalize the enemy. In the case of the Nazis and the Japanese, this was not difficult. After the destruction of Berlin, an editorial in the *New Yorker* revealed the dominant attitude: 'it serves the bastards right ... it was a necessary action, efficiently and economically carried out'. To really consider that normal, decent people were being killed in the bombing raids would have demanded a degree of reflection that was unlikely in the heat of war. Cinematic and print images of the bombing were effective in showing how the British had suffered in the Blitz; but they did not invite sympathy for the enemy. As Franklin remarks, 'Missing from the verbal and cinematic pictures of Anglo-American bombers was the world of the bombed, which appeared in stories about our side, especially Britain, under Axis attack.'[74]

Again, one is prompted to some reflection on the nature of modernity. The Second World War, a total war, was a conflict between whole societies, with their material and cultural domains fully geared to protracted struggle. The organizational capacity of the modern state extended beyond mere administration to the manipulation of culture. For the Western allies a degree of consensus was created which belied the supposed individualism of liberal discourse. Arguably Hitler was more afraid of the consequences of total mobilization than either Roosevelt or Churchill. The Western countries also ruthlessly applied the technologies that gave them a quantitative and qualitative edge. Here air power was pivotal. As I have repeatedly argued, the use of air power allowed a psychological and cognitive distance to be maintained between perpetrator and victim. In the post-war reflection on war crimes, the killing of hundreds of thousands of civilians, through the means of strategic bombing, barely entered into the condemnations, which centred mainly on Japanese and German barbarity. In Britain there was a tendency in some quarters to dishonour the Head of Bomber Command, Arthur Harris, but this served to imply that the fault lay in the morality of a few individuals. Further, it disguised the role of the politicians who actually directed policy. In general terms, victorious nations did not want the humbug of reflecting on their less noble acts. The real truth of the bombing campaign against Germany simply did not fit the dominant self-image of the West. But bombing was also a remote enough act for it to remain outside the mainstream memory of the war.

As I have indicated, some critics have raised the issue of Dresden and other raids on Germany. Others who have not chosen to deal with the moral issues have assessed the technical effectiveness and performance of strategic bombing against the expectations raised by theorists such as Douhet. A study which deals with these latter issues is Robert Higham's *Air Power: A Concise History*. His conclusion about the British raids is scathing: 'If the object had been to encourage the Germans to fight, no better technique than the clumsy [British] air offensive of 1940–1943 could have been devised.'[75]

The USA's bombardment of Japanese cities was even more terrible, and even more misjudged than the combined air offensives against Germany. The racial inferiority of the Japanese was believed to make them more susceptible to panic in the face of bombardment: 'Americans assumed that Asians would panic or collapse in the face of bombing which Englishmen or Germans could endure.'[76] Here the racist predictions of what incendiary bombs might do to paper cities came true, but not the naive expectations about the collapse of morale. In November 1941 George Marshall told press bureau chiefs, 'we'll fight mercilessly. Flying Fortresses will be dispatched immediately to set the paper cities of Japan on fire.'[77] This was no idle threat. In due course in 1944 and 1945 the B29s of the XXth and XXIth AAF burned city after city to the ground while operating from Guam, Saipan and the Timan Islands.[78] Again, within AAF circles concern was raised about the policy, and courageous men such as Haywood S. Hansell spoke out about the ineffectiveness and the immorality of the bombing of civilian targets. But Hansell was replaced by Curtis Lemay, who had no such qualms.

American raids against Asian cities began with those under Japanese occupation such as Hankow and Bangkok. However, in 1944, as more B29s came into service and as bases were found closer to Japan's shores, a full-scale onslaught against Japanese cities began. No cities were spared, except for four on the special target list for the planned atomic attack. The worst destruction befell Tokyo. In the winter of 1944–5 US scientists were working on plans to optimize the burning of Japanese cities. New munitions were developed, such as the M47 napalm bomb and the 500 pound M69, which contained a large number of small magnesium incendiaries. Also new experimental raids were carried out. These were perfected in the early months of 1945, and reached their peak in a raid on Tokyo on 10 March 1945. Vonnegut had called Dresden 'mass murder'. However, the XXIth Army Air Force raid on Tokyo in March 1945 was certainly the most violent and destructive act in human history. The attack on Tokyo was aimed at ten square miles of the eastern sector of the city, where 1.5 million people lived. The aim of the attack was to ignite targets in an X-configuration, which would make fire sweep outwards so that the whole rectangle within which the X was located would become a giant inferno. The plan worked perfectly. The bombing created a tidal wave of fire which melted metal and tarmac. It left no hiding-place as it leapt over canals and roads. At the end of the three-hour raid 16 square miles were burned out, 267,000 buildings were destroyed, 1 million people were homeless, and between 84,000 and 120,000 people were dead.[79]

In many respects the scale of this carnage speaks for itself. Any rhetorical outrage expressed here would make not a jot of difference to the way the incident is remembered or interpreted. What is more useful is to try and assess what an act such as this meant, and why it was possible. The possibility was essentially technical; the means existed to launch such an attack, and the development of ever more effective military means has been at the heart of the Western way of making war. But the raids on Japan indicate a cultural model of war and conflict which is not reducible to any material calculus.

The Japanese warrior culture was one of the strongest and oldest in the world. Before the effects of Western culture were experienced in the nineteenth century, the warrior ethos was at the centre of the Japanese status and class hierarchy, with the right to carry a sword the symbol of honour of the samurai.[80] Courage and physical bravery were central to the masculine code of ethics. Coupled to the powerful instinct for tradition and consensus, this made the Japanese soldier a formidable enemy, as the campaigns of the Pacific War revealed. This was a radically different culture from the one existing in the United States, with its emphasis on individualism, scientific progress and material comfort. But, at the political level, the USA also had a highly moralistic creed associated with the fusion of notions of rights with religious conceptions of exclusivity. From this perspective, the unique and exceptional continent that white Europeans had settled was a vast and beautiful wilderness, theologically configured for a chosen people to engineer a new destiny for man. With this kind of understanding, it is hardly surprising that the original inhabitants of the continent were simply swept away and excluded from the script.[81] Further, little attention was paid to the abused, downtrodden African-Americans, who were also excluded from the official version of American destiny. In the war with Japan, Americans were thus able to draw on a long tradition of assumed cultural pre-eminence, which invariably had a racist tinge. As I have shown above, thinking about air war against Japan had long had strong racial overtones. In *A History of Warfare* Keegan maintains that Japanese conduct during the war exhausted any sympathy that Americans might have had for the victims of Hiroshima and Nagasaki.[82] This is undoubtedly true, but a fuller picture emerges when the real attitude of the USA to Japan before 1941 is assessed. As we have seen, the predisposition to respond with wrath and indignation and to seek bloody revenge against Japan was well entrenched within American culture before hostilities began. On 8 December 1941, after the attack on Pearl Harbour, Roosevelt addressed a joint session of Congress; he assured his audience that Americans, 'in their righteous might, will win through to absolute victory' and to 'inevitable triumph'.[83] The final crushing of Japan with atomic weapons was a fitting conclusion to this teleological assessment. The most powerful industrial economy in the world had developed a technology that allowed American forces to enact a terrible revenge against an enemy that had long been seen as outside the sphere of human authenticity.

CONCLUSION

Building on the doctrinal innovations of the 1920s and the technical developments of the 1930s the Western allies unleashed strategic air war in the Second World War. But during that war the promise of the immediate results predicted by Douhet and others materialized only with the advent of the atomic bomb, which generated a radically new set of problems. In the post-1945 era many of the most gifted thinkers in the USA wrestled with the dilemmas thrown up by the advent of nuclear weapons. Within the extended debate that took place, a clear schism existed between those inclined to see the atomic weapon as revolutionary and those determined to interpret the bomb in a more traditional framework. In the next chapter I shall argue that nuclear weapons did create a revolutionary situation, but not in the form that orthodox scholarship has indicated. The actual use of the bomb in 1945 grew out of the already established practice of using strategic bombing to raize cities to the ground. In the United States the discussions of the 'Interim Committee', which had the task of deciding nuclear policy, chiefly concerned which cities would be attacked, not whether the attack should take place. The moral inhibitions about this form of warfare had long since been abandoned by 1945, a situation eased by the remoteness and abstraction of this form of strategic violence. In my view, this is the quintessential form of modern war, the process whereby Western countries have asserted global dominance through their use of superior military firepower. It derives from the essential mission of modernity; as Campbell asserts, modernity represents 'European dominion over other peoples and lands, the place of science in the construction and ordering of the polity, and the rise of technocratic and instrumentalist rationalism'.[84] These were the forces that enabled the Axis powers to be defeated. In the case of Japan it can be seen in the clash of two opposed cultures of war; as Keegan notes, the practical consequences of this opposition was that 'The United States ... deployed a plethora of advanced technical means against Japan in the effort to beat down courage with firepower'.[85] The West thus regained its supremacy because of its superior technical means. But despite this, the post-1945 world could never be the same as before. In the justifiable outrage that has been expressed about Japanese conduct in the Second World War, an important point is often overlooked. In the Second World War Japan effectively ended the West's complacent assumption of racial superiority. As the Japanese pushed the white man out of South-east Asia, an important fact of global proportions was learned. As Asprey observes, 'Japanese conquest and occupation of Southeast Asia had shattered the myth of white supremacy.'[86] But another and more profound problem grew out of 1945. The atomic bomb crushed Japan, but it brought to the world a means whereby the most powerful Western country was vulnerable to total obliteration. Engelhardt argues that this simple fact shot a hole through the major American narrative of triumphalism.[87] As he puts it, 'The atomic bomb that levelled Hiroshima also blasted openings into a netherworld of consciousness where victory and defeat, enemy and self, threatened to merge.'[88] After 1945 the certainty of the forward march of modernity was thrown into doubt. For a time the bomb seemed to offer the opposite vista. Douhet's naive ideas about the impact of strategic bombing seemed finally to have come true with the atomic bomb. But this only worked if the USA had a monopoly. From 1949, after the detonation of 'Joe 1', American culture had to come to terms with the prospect of total destruction. For the planners of the security state, the problem was that any military interventions could escalate into nuclear conflagration, or worse, that the USA might be subjected to a sneak attack which would leave it only the choice of suicide or surrender. From this point onwards strategic articulations were confounded by fundamental dilemmas of contingency and uncertainty. Cultural representations of war also had to deal with the problem of a possible terminal and meaningless ending to the project of modernity. Writing in the early 1980s John Schaar gave his account of where this process had reached:

> We have finally made the engine that can smash all engines, the power that can destroy all power. Security today, bought at the cost of billions, means that we shall have fifteen minutes' warning that they intend to annihilate us, during which time we can also annihilate them. The most powerful state today cannot provide security but only revenge ... The dream of total security through total power has ended in the reality of total vulnerability.[89]

In the next chapter we shall see how intellectuals attempted to resolve these issues in the discourse of nuclear strategy.

4 Intellectuals and Strategic Discourse

INTRODUCTION

In 1945 the United States emerged as the undisputed, one great power of the post-Second World War era. With the end of the world dominance of the European powers, this meant that the USA attained hegemony through the assumption of a global role. It also meant that the USA was in a position to spread its own version of political ideology to the states which needed its civil and military aid. In effect, this amounted to nothing less than proselytizing for a new enlightenment. This cultural/ideological offensive was underpinned by an enormous index of material power that was manifest in numerous resources at America's disposal: the 20 billion dollar gold reserves, the 12 million men/women in uniform, the fact that the USA produced 50 per cent of the world's manufactured goods and owned half the world's shipping.[1] Included in this inventory of global might there was a technology which made previous military instruments seem insignificant. Through the efforts of scientists and administrators, working on the largest engineering project in history, the USA possessed the atomic bomb. Initially justified as a counter to a possible Nazi weapon, the bomb seemingly brought the war to a dramatic end in August 1945. Its awesome power was revealed in the attack on Hiroshima, where, in a matter of minutes, 68,000 individuals perished, while another 76,000 were seriously injured.[2] The casualty statistics, though, were not really the point. The issue was that one weapon could destroy a whole city. Immediately, then, it was necessary to speculate on the possible effects of the use of fifty or perhaps a hundred such devices as the prospect of war with the USSR loomed after 1947. In the West, but more specifically in the United States, a debate began among military planners concerning the impact that atomic weapons would and should exert on military doctrine and real defence policy. While the technology itself was unique, so too was the USA's geostrategic position. America needed to be able to project its power thousands of miles from its own shores, in order to protect allies in

Europe and Asia. In effect, it needed to develop a grand strategy, virtually from scratch. In the following decades this was achieved with remarkable speed. What was extraordinary about the process was the degree of involvement of intellectuals in it. Thus a distinctive feature of American thinking on defence in the post-1945 period was the power and influence it accorded to intellectuals. As William Kincade notes, 'What stands out, however, in contrast to the strategy-making of other powers and times, is the role of the civilian or "scientific" American strategists and the influence of their theories.'[3] My aim in this chapter is to reflect on the causes and consequences of this process, and to chart and illustrate some aspects of its evolution.

KNOWLEDGE AND POWER

Today it is not usually supposed that intellectuals possess significant political or social power. However, special circumstances concerning the atomic bomb and the American state have given specific academics and intellectuals more power than is usually recognized. In the first place the bomb was an intellectual project; its development represented half a century's speculation by the world's top physicists. Its very feasibility was suggested to Roosevelt by Einstein as a counter to a possible Nazi bomb. Subsequently, a scientist became head of the Manhattan Project, and Oppenheimer and others then attained enormous power through the aegis of the Atomic Energy Commission. But what is even more unusual is that social scientists accrued significant power within the US state. Political scientists and economists shaped and defined the new culture of war. According to Rothstein, intellectuals of a realist orientation filled a gap within the American state which resulted from the USA not having a long-standing foreign policy-making elite. Many of these were European émigrés whose experience of totalitarian regimes in Europe gave them strong reasons to support the ideological slant of US-style liberalism.[4] In addition, the new global responsibilities of the US and the security dilemmas created by the bomb resulted in a quantum leap in the amount of intellectual work needed in the area of policy advice and guidance. Intellectuals were needed in the construction of cultural hegemony.

In military circles the use of intellectual expertise was already established by the practice of recruiting special services operatives from universities. The whole image and career of the academic/intellectual in the USA in the post-war period has been different from that in Europe. In Germany the role of universities in supporting the Nazis in the 1920s and 1930s undercut their potential as agents of the post-war state. In other European states the strength of communism after the war in academia led to similar problems of trust. But the American experience was that there was a significant residue of loyalty that could be tapped, particularly because most American institutions had been purged of Communist influence in the 1930s. In international relations the trust was enhanced because scholars were committed to the very tenets of Cold War practice which embodied their theoretical horizons. As Michael Banks notes, 'So confident were many of the authors of their understanding of the basic political structures of the world and the forces that moved them, that they permitted the discipline to become the handmaiden of superpower rivalry.'[5]

Another important reason why certain academics and intellectuals attained power is that decision making in the sphere of nuclear weapons planning was highly secretive. Potential controversy over collaboration was forestalled because much of it was covert. The general population had some vague idea of what nuclear policy entailed, but the detail was utterly secret. Many of the key publications of the period were written by elite members, to be read only by other members of the policy-making clique. As Engelhardt puts it, 'American policy makers soon found themselves writing obsessively, not for public consumption, but for each other, about a possible war of global annihilation.'[6]

Secrecy also entailed a degree of conspiracy between certain agencies and individuals, as in some cases it presupposed deception. A BBC *Panorama*, broadcast on 9 March 1994 revealed a series of covert nuclear experiments in the USA in which citizens were exposed to radiation without their knowledge or consent. Some of these were even undertaken under the pretext of medical treatment for pregnant women. It was done with the connivance of a handful of scientists and doctors, and it was successfully kept dark. Its revelation by US Energy Secretary Hazel O'Leary has caused much shock and dismay, but from the 1940s to the 1970s, during the apocalyptic confrontation with the USSR, it was believed in some quarters that such steps were justified. Secrecy has always been at the heart of the nuclear project. In January 1950, when the decision was made to build the H-bomb, no more than a hundred individuals knew of this epochal move.[7] Throughout the

1950s, the establishment remained suspicious of any processes that would widen the base of informed opinion. In the early 1950s, attempts by *Scientific American* to publish critical articles were prevented by the AEC, which had thousands of copies burned.[8]

In academic debate on strategy the key institution was the RAND Corporation. Here scientists and social scientists pondered the question of nuclear war. But there was no sense of needing to contribute to public opinion. RAND, originally part of Douglas Aircraft, was working for the air force. As Fred Kaplan explains, 'there was the elitist assumption, pervasive at Rand, that influencing military officers and Pentagon officials was what really counted, that airing views to the general public served no purpose and might, in fact, be seen as displaying disloyalty to Rand's sponsor the US Air Force.'[9] In this climate there was little concern for any ethical problems that might be created by secrecy. Through think-tanks such as RAND, individual academics could be recruited when it was clear that they were completely loyal. Other colleagues would often not know what work was being undertaken. Thus the whole process was under very strict control, a situation which persisted until the mid-1960s, when Vietnam split the US academic community, and ended bipartisanship on issues of foreign policy.

STRATEGY AND LEGITIMACY

The ideological significance of the work of the strategic planners in the 1950s was that it created a taxonomy, a framework through which nuclear defence issues came to be grasped by the political-intellectual elite. The concepts developed disclosed the world of nuclear planning in a language which was acceptable to the political elite and also useful in the sphere of political justifications. As I shall argue, this was the critical contribution that intellectuals could make. The potential for concern and agitation over nuclear issues was immense. In elite circles there was often anxiety, as when Eisenhower screened the top-secret film *Operation Ivy* (1953) in the White House. In the film an entire atoll disappears in the wake of an H-bomb test; according to Spencer Weart, Eisenhower and others present were visibly shaken by the scale of the destruction.[10] Hence, I shall contend, there was a need for a mode of discourse which would remove the neurosis and anxiety from nuclear speculation. As I have argued elsewhere, a key reason why this was possible is that nuclear strategic theory lacks empirical data. There has been no concrete realm of lived experience to contradict the extrapolations of the theorists of Armageddon. Also the theorists were spreading a message that was attractive. If there was to be nuclear war, then we would hope that it could be controlled, that we could recover, that civilian targets could be avoided, and that perhaps, in some bizarre sense, the West could win. The last point was very significant in military circles, as motivating the armed forces to merely enact suicide, when the loss of their own society was certain, would not be easy. It is not surprising, then, that USAF and SAC found the doctrine of Mutual Assured Destruction distasteful. Nor is it surprising that in the late 1970s and the 1980s intellectuals were recruited to help find a route away from strategic stalemate.

The growth of state power in the sphere of defence had the potential to raise enormous problems. In the USA traditional values tended against big government and permanent and large military institutions. Moreover, with nuclear weapons the problems were amplified in a number of respects. Atomic weapons raised the spectre of global destruction, and were likely to frighten the domestic population. Thus, as Michael Howard pointed out some years ago, reassurance was a vital component of nuclear deterrence. In addition, nuclear weapons necessitated secrecy and heightened internal security to prevent theft, sabotage and contamination. Their presence in society was and is, in itself, a cause of tension and anxiety. Because of this the nuclear state has had to appear to be 'in control' of its nuclear operations. Policies which included the possibility of nuclear confrontation and perhaps nuclear accidents needed to be seen as rational and credible.

Anxieties about nuclear security were not just a question for the general population; as indicated above, they pervaded political elites as well. After the epochal document NSC 68 was drafted for the State Department's Policy Planning Staff by Paul Nitze in 1950, it was widely recorded that some of Truman's officials were deeply disturbed by reading it. Ever since America has had nuclear weapons, some political leaders, scientists and strategists have contested their legitimacy and morality, while others have simply felt naked fear. Scientists, in particular, have been ambivalent about their own creations. In order to fashion hegemony, the state has thus faced

conflicts, division and naked anxiety. However, the nuclear state in
the United States did secure a consensus on nuclear security. The
means and style of achieving this have varied, with overt coercion an
ingredient in the 1950s. However, a key element in the articulation
of nuclear security has been the discourse of the civilian intellectuals
who fashioned a cohesive ideology of nuclear rationality. Michael
MccGwire sees it thus: 'in America, a significant proportion of
government officials and consultants in the fields of defense and
foreign policy have been drawn from those who have taught or
studied these theories at university. It was these theories that defined
the agenda and provided the strategic discourse throughout
NATO.'[11] Particularly in the 1950s and 1960s, a modernist-liberal
and technocratic colonization of the public space of defence was
achieved in the United States. From the mid-1960s the academic
community was split, but not those advising on the issues of nuclear
weapons. As Colin Gray has recently affirmed in *Political Studies* the
community of advisers remained committed to a consensus even in
the turbulent 1980s.[12]

The significance of the earlier nuclear discourse arises from the
particular problematic of nuclear security. With conventional war it
is necessary in domestic society to present the 'face of the enemy'.
Propaganda discourse justifies the fate of the adversary through the
articulation of powerful negative images. In the recent Gulf War
the US public was subjected to prolonged propaganda about the
Iraqis and, in particular, Saddam Hussein. Above all else, this
propaganda inserted a genuine sense of threat and hostility in the
public space where the war was debated and justified. But the Gulf
War was always going to be won; there was no risk of nuclear escalation, and the USSR was sidelined. By way of contrast, this approach
could never work with nuclear conflict. A nuclear show-down
always needed to be a step away from reality. It was necessary to
dramatize a threat; but this was geo-strategic, not personal. Nuclear
diplomacy was not typically an exchange of insults and overt
threats. My thesis is that the strongest hegemony over nuclear
issues was attained by a liberal technocratica, a fusion of 'reason-
ableness' with scientism and instrumental rationality – in other
words, a clear attempt to fashion a modernist interpretation of
nuclear policy. In the USA ready- made discourses existed concerning a modernist understanding of American destiny and the role of
science in that destiny. Thus the discourse of nuclear control sat
comfortably on prepared ground.

TRADITIONAL CONCERNS

From a traditional liberal viewpoint the role of intellectuals in defence planning raises difficult questions about the relationship between the state and universities, and also the moral responsibilities of intellectuals. In Hitler's Germany two contradictory trends in this area had both appeared equally disastrous. On the one hand, scholarship for its own sake and ascetic aloofness insulated academics from the effects of state brutalism; on the other, obedience to the legitimate authorities and the belief in the state as the ultimate arbiter of ends incorporated German universities into the Nazis' grotesque plans for extermination, slavery and eugenics. As the intellectual exile Franz Neumann revealed, his career at Breslau, Leipzig, Rostock and Frankfurt was blighted by anti-Semitism and other manifestations of restoration and nationalist ideologies. Neumann explains how the arrival of the totalitarian state made impossible a situation that was already difficult for intellectuals because of nationalism. In the nation-state we see 'the bureaucratization of modern society and, with it, the trend to transform the intellectual into a functionary of society'.[13] But in totalitarian systems there exists a need to 'completely control man's thoughts, and ... thus transform culture into propaganda'.[14]

In certain respects Neumann's comments go to the heart of the major dilemma I wish to highlight in this chapter. Post-war reflection on the issue of the role of intellectuals has tended to see any problem as existing in the totalitarian context. But in principle the Nuremberg trials highlighted legal criteria which transcended the jurisdiction of the nation-state. However, intellectuals in the US mainstream, who offered their services to the containment, warfare state, seemed oblivious to reflection on some of the inherent problems this posed. One reason for this is an inherent narcissism, which seems implicit in Enlightenment narratives concerning the West. But the Enlightenment model of the university and of the intellectual was already outmoded in 1945. The dominant understanding of what the purpose of universities was in the twentieth century had changed dramatically. A century or more earlier, American universities had often celebrated an Enlightenment yearning for critical self-reflection and open debate, which corresponds to the classical liberal view of intellectual life. In his plans for the University of Virginia, Jefferson believed the academy should 'unmask their usurpation, and monopolies of honours, wealth and power'.[15] But in the 1900s the twin aims of higher education had become scholarship and service. As regards the latter, Socrates had posed the dilemma as one between the inclination to combat and that to cater. By 1945 it was clear which of these was the guiding light in the USA. As Roszak remarked, 'service came to mean the indiscriminate adaptation of the university to every demand that monied interests and the general public could make'.[16] According to him, this culminated in a situation where, 'the ideal of service has matured into a collaboration between the universities, the corporate world and the government'.[17]

During the Second World War the links between the state, science and academia were both necessary and uncontroversial. However, for some, disquieting signs were apparent before 1945. In 1944, as US troops occupied Stuttgart, the failure of the Germans to get close to production of atomic weaponry became clear to members of the Alsos mission, whose goal was to investigate the German research. In consequence, scientists on the Manhattan Project began to argue that the bomb need not be used in anger. The scientists, though, were quickly rebutted by the overall head of the project, General Leslie Groves, and in some cases doubts about state policy began to emerge. What should have been clear was that traditional understandings of the role of science in society no longer applied. In the inter-war years the greatest natural scientists had worked together with little regard for national interests and state power. The scientists comprised a community committed only to truth. But the rise of the Nazis and the persecution of Jewish and other scientists brought state power brutally into the world of intellectual inquiry. At the beginning of the Second World War American and British atomic scientists could no longer risk open discussion of their work. Particularly with the military promise of nuclear fission, the state moved to colonize the terrain of intellectual endeavour.

In the Second World War the justification for this was an obvious expediency. But the temporary measures meant to harness intellectual power to the dynamics of state policy became a way of life. The institutionalization of a security threat in the form of the Cold War created an enduring legitimacy for 'patriotic' scientific endeavour and policy advocacy by social scientists. Clearly, I regard this as controversial; but let us look at another point of view. In his book *Strategic Studies* (1982) Colin Gray takes up the precise issue that we are dealing with here. Gray declares immediately and honestly that the strategic analyst seeks political influence: 'In addition, he has always sought to balance scholarly professional work with public policy advocacy.'[18] The brief of the analyst is to 'discover ways in which the US can preserve vital interests and function in the international order as a global superpower'.[19] Gray also concedes the epistemic weakness of strategy: 'Unlike many other fields of inquiry, strategy does not entail a quest after truth.'[20] Following Bernard Brodie, Gray takes the line that the issue in strategy is practical: simply, will the idea work?

Some of these ideas were reiterated in a recent review article by Gray in *Political Studies.* In my view he rightly chastised some of the more bizarre and idealistic claims that have been recently made about international peace and order.[21] However, the problems evident in his earlier work remain. Realists such as Gray are, in my belief, too closely tied up with the practices of the state. What I fail to see is how the analytical procedures of intellectual investigation lead to the normative commitment: in this case, to support the US state in its practices of securing particular advantages for one polity. As Charles Reynolds has argued, this is litle more than special pleading.[22] Why is the policy expert loyal to the US state? This question never arises, and reveals a residue of unconsciousness concerning normative aspects of the project. The ideological decision to be loyal is simply incorporated into the technical endeavours of the policy expert. It may be that the US state is actually pursuing policies which are disastrous for the rest of the world. I am not suggesting this for one minute; the point is that Gray is tying his endeavours as a scholar to a specific, particular interest. In Gray's work this arises because certain central features of political life are immutable. The key concept is force; the central datum is conflict; and in the international arena rivalry and nuclear weapons are facts of life. According to Gray, critics are wrong to see defence analysts as warmongers, because they do not invent the reality they describe or theorize. There is an immutable datum that defines international relations: 'Deplorable though it may be, the fact remains that the world of international politics is a jungle wherein the strong and ruthless devour the weak.'[23]

But these are not 'facts'; this view characterizes one paradigm in international relations which Gray is assuming is the only tenable position by according it ontological primacy. By downplaying theory in this way, he can also present his discourse as the 'world'. However, the field of international politics does not generate obvious data that can be read off mechanically. It is a terrain of interpretation.

Whether Nicaragua was a threat to the USA in the 1980s is not a factual question, but rather an issue laced with interpretive and ideological elements. Similarly, there can be no obvious rendering of an issue such as the US embargo against Cuba or US behaviour towards Vietnam after the end of the Vietnam War. More generally the question is of the central balance; the conflict with the former USSR was also never a datum. A passage in the earlier book shows how the contentious can be reduced to the obvious: 'The general military fact underlying this book is the appreciation that the United States must endure, through much of the 1980s, a condition of multi-level weakness *vis-à-vis* the USSR.'[24] An alternative view is that because of the views of analysts such as Gray the USA spent around one thousand million dollars in the 1980s contending with an adversary that was imploding. The technical advice, the policy advocacy, was not some value-free expertise which came from a substantive body of theory and data characterized by epistemic rigour. This advice – advice actually given to the Reagan administration – represented the opinion of strategists such as Gray that the USA had been too soft with the USSR and that a tougher line was indicated. It is essential to realize that the policy advocacy of the nuclear strategists was deeply embedded within ideology. Certain intellectuals were providing rationalizations for what were often highly contentious policies. Looking back, Gray believes that the policies that were advocated were an outstanding success: 'As statecraft, the U.S. defence programmes of the 1980s were politically successful beyond the wildest dreams of their most enthusiastic supporters.'[25]

I would suggest that the jury is still out on this issue. With the criminalization of Russian society, the outbreak of numerous civil wars, and the prospect of widespread disintegration in the former USSR, not to mention doubt concerning the post-Yeltsin era, there is still much to play for. Also it is far from clear that the social costs imposed on the USA in order to pay for the Reagan strategic vision will not have harmful and lasting consequences. Nor should we forget that some realists in the USA, notably John Mearsheimer, see the end of the Cold War as a trigger to political disharmony amongst the Western alliance. The point is that this is really all just opinion. But in all this conjecture, what has happened to truth? For Gray, scholarly truth and the truths of statecraft are not synonymous: 'scholarly truth can differ from truth in the realm of statecraft'.[26] The truth of state policy lies in its effects, but these cannot be read off as though they are obvious. The consequences of the end of the

Cold War are a matter of contestability; they demand interpretation, and they reside within the framework of theoretical investigation.

As the treatment given by Gray indicates, few policy advisers seemed to grasp that ethical and epistemological issues were raised by advocacy. Thus the incorporation of the endeavours of social scientists into the domain of military policy planning seems to have emerged in a fairly unconscious fashion. The crisis of the Second World War was permanently replicated in the Cold War and reinforced by the McCarthyite 1950s. As Irene Gendzier has shown, collaboration also extended to the creation of a paradigm of political development wherein US foreign policy goals and the interests of developing countries were seen as identical. As she demonstrates, this collusion was exposed by Vietnam: 'The alleged neutrality of social science research was exploded before the evidence of complicity between well-known scholars of development and political change, and the policy planners in charge of military operations in Southeast Asia.'[27]

In the humanities and the social sciences the forging of links between academia and defence and intelligence agencies developed during the Second World War through the activities of the Office of Strategic Services. This organization scoured universities in order to locate experts in special areas, and in particular highlighted the skills of political scientists and international relations scholars. In 1965 John Gange, then President of the International Studies Association, remembered that 'The Office of Strategic Services was like a big university faculty in many respects – sometimes staff meetings were just like faculty meetings.'[28] The relationship also worked in the opposite direction as well. One-time director of the CIA, William Raborn, revealed that, 'in actual numbers we could easily staff the faculty of a university with our experts. In a way, we do. Many of those who leave us join the faculties of universities and colleges.'[29]

THE RAND CORPORATION

Given these linkages, it is entirely unsurprising that in the post-1945 period academics were drawn into the world of nuclear target planning and more general speculation about nuclear war. The key institution in this respect was the RAND corporation, which, as noted above, emerged during the Second World War from the connection between Douglas Aircraft and the United States Air Force.

The historical significance for nuclear strategy of RAND was explored in the 1980s in two seminal studies by Fred Kaplan and Gregg Herken.[30] More recently the significance and the defects in RAND thinking have been explored by Manuel de Landa.[31] He reveals how RAND's original mathematical orientation determined the social-science perspective which was later developed. According to de Landa, RAND thinking reduced the question of the Soviet threat to a mathematical simulation based on a zero-sum game. To begin with, this was an intellectual exercise, but, as I argue below, the Kennedy administration institutionalized RAND theorizing. As de Landa notes, 'Although born at RAND during the 1950s, Systems Analysis did not become an institution until Robert McNamara became Secretary of Defense for the Kennedy Administration. He brought with him an army of "whiz kids" from RAND, and used them to limit the power of military decision-makers.'[32]

In the 1950s RAND gradually became a centre of fusion between the world of academia and formal government service. Although RAND had a permanent staff, it was typical for the corporation to recruit from universities. A famous example was Bernard Brodie, who came to RAND via the Centre for International Studies at Yale and the Air Targets division of the Air Force. In 1945 Brodie and other colleagues at Yale sketched an intelligent and perceptive theory of deterrence in a study called the *Absolute Weapon*.[33] However, this study did not become relevant to US nuclear doctrine until the declaratory policy of assured destruction was enunciated in the 1960s. In the early days at RAND, work on nuclear planning was concerned with speculation about nuclear war and the air force's confusion over a new strategy. Key questions concerned the potency of the bomb, the likely casualties if the weapon were used, and the number of bombs needed.[34] This was novel and worrying for some social scientists, and Brodie's colleague Jim Lipp dropped out because of moral anxieties. As Fred Kaplan observed, 'Nobody had ever killed 35 million people on a piece of paper before.'[35]

As this process unfolded, it became increasingly unclear where the boundary between the state and universities could be drawn. The traditional liberal arts view of intellectual work no longer explained the role of intellectuals in society, but no alternative notion was forthcoming. As I have suggested, in the context of the Cold War a residue of unconsciousness clouded the issue. The state had articulated a new code for scientists and intellectuals which had barely been noticed, because the ends to which the endeavour was geared seemed legitimate. In the 1960s and 1970s the issue exploded on US campuses because of Vietnam, but by then the incorporation of the university was irreversible. In general, after 1945 Western liberal states continually expanded the role of state organs without any explicit forms of justification for increased public power. In the USA a critical ingredient in this process was the creation of an intellectual, military and industrial triangle motivated and sustained by the Cold War. As Campbell has argued, the articulation of the modalities of the Cold War has been central to the project of securing America's identity in the contested terrain of domestic society.[36] In particular, the invocation of danger has functioned as a highly consensual force. At the beginning of the Cold War a sustained effort was needed to convey the message of peril, threat and danger. But at the same time the dangers of nuclear armaments needed to be displaced and neutralized. Events in Europe in 1948 gave Americans a clearer image of an enemy, and also gave Truman much needed leverage in his battle with Congress for larger appropriations. Behind closed doors there were fundamental anxieties about the atomic strategy, but the deteriorating international situation militated against open discussion. In January 1950 Truman gave the go-ahead for construction of a hydrogen bomb, and America's commitment to an atomic strategy of actual or threatened mass destruction was sealed. Fundamental questions, though, remained to be answered. Should the USA strike first or second? Was the bomb a means of deterring or winning wars? Were US strategic bases vulnerable to surprise attack? How could atomic bombs best be delivered to their targets?

These questions and many others were posed and answered by scientists and social scientists working at RAND and American universities in the 1950s. Their efforts were central in the sphere of policy discourse. As Herken reveals, 'Since 1945, American policy on nuclear weapons has been sometimes determined – and always influenced – by a small "nucleus" of civilian experts whose profession it has been to consider the fearful prospect of nuclear war.'[37] Their efforts led to a debate which framed a limited public airing of questions, which has since been dubbed a 'golden age' of strategic thinking. From 1960 the defence intellectuals were actually brought into government. Thus what began as indirect policy prescription became real guiding principles of US strategic policy.

The process which galvanized intellectual interest in defence policy in the 1950s was the Eisenhower administration's 'New Look'.

At the heart of the new policy was an increased reliance on nuclear weapons, created by fiscal restraint and the new specific notion of extended deterrence, called by Secretary of State, Dulles, 'massive retaliation'. The policy, while popular with the Strategic Air Command, aroused bitter controversy elsewhere, and sparked a contest in which the administration was pitted against all other participants. The policy was regarded by many RAND strategists as crude and inflexible and likely to lack credibility. Also leading defence writers in universities turned their critical talents against the new doctrine.

At RAND Bernard Brodie highlighted the lack of refinement in nuclear planning. In the Strategic Air Command the aim was to maximize damage to Soviet urban industrial targets. As one writer put it, the plan was to leave Russia 'a smoking, radiating ruin at the end of two hours'.[38] Brodie, by contrast, was postulating the use of smaller, tactical nuclear weapons against Soviet ground forces. However, a grim prospect now haunted these speculations. The USA's original plans for atomic weapons had reactivated the doctrines of strategic bombing. However, these ideas presupposed an American nuclear monopoly, which had ended in 1949. Even worse, from a US perspective, the USSR had developed the hydrogen bomb in 1953, and would soon possess the means to deliver it to the continental United States.

This new reality lay at the back of a whole tradition in strategic theory which had to grapple with novel circumstances. The threat of nuclear apocalypse had to be incorporated in a discourse of scientific control and rationality. What mattered here was not that the theories were coherent, factually corroborated or credible. The point was to have an edifice of scientific rationality, to sustain the myth that apocalyptic military power was under control. The myths were important for the public because of the issue of political order and anxiety; the potential risks of a doomsday military policy for domestic society were enormous. However, the rigour of nuclear discourse was also necessary for planners and political elites. The implementers had to believe in their own project. Critically, from the horizons of American culture, the enterprise had to be under control and the military artefacts compatible with a vision of scientific process.

This project was centred on the RAND corporation, where experts in maths, physics, games theory and econometrics developed a technocratic categorial framework of nuclear war. This framework disguised the fact that the dialectical relationship of destruction between the superpowers was not amenable to an overarching system of management. The USA could influence the process only indirectly. The concepts developed by defence intellectuals in response to this issue were counter-force theory, graduated deterrence, limited war, intra-war deterrence, escalation dominance, crisis management and game theory. Klein argues that the effect of this work was to colonize dissent and legitimize nuclear planning: 'the effect of their work is to co-opt critique by enframing strategy within a technologic of deterrence.'[39] As I have indicated, underlying this is a powerful ideology which is pivotal in the US self-image. The ideology is best understood as a technocratic representation of liberal progressivism. It focuses on ideas of abstract reasoning as a problem-solving tool, where thought is a form of engineering device. In the American context it has led to the idea that science and technology can overcome any problems posed for humans, and that the scope of modernism is unbounded.

In the case of weapons technology, the application of this ideology is obvious. However, it is essential to realize that the social sciences have been viewed in this light as well. With the Soviets able to attack the USA with atomic weaponry, a whole new field of inquiry was disclosed. What were Soviet intentions? How did the leadership perceive the USA? Which threats would frighten the USSR most? How would the public respond to defence policy which had created a doomsday machine? How could the USA best signal its intentions? When crises developed, how could they be controlled? In classical realism the 'ifs' and 'buts' of war and diplomacy had never been ironed out by any faith in scientific management. However, in the nuclear age the contingencies, the unforeseen, the accidental and the interpretive were unacceptable to US defence intellectuals. Thus at RAND the systems analysts, mathematicians, economists and political scientists were seeking to bring defence issues under scientific control. According to Spencer Weart, the search for coherence and order was illusory. He writes of the enterprise in these terms: 'From the 1950s on, the sharpest analysts left ambiguities, internal contradictions, and blind leaps of logic in their writings. Most changed their position from one year to the next and sometimes, it seemed, from one page to the next.'[40] In the mid-1950s a work which crystallized the intellectual crusade for nuclear rationality was William Kaufman's edited collection called *The Requirements of Deterrence*.[41] Kaufman, a political scientist at the Princeton Centre for

International Studies, was specifically responsible for the concepts of graduated deterrence, limited war and mutual restraint. In response to the policy of massive retaliation, his overall critique emphasized the lack of credibility and flexibility of Dulles's plan. The major policy goal which Kaufman sought to put in place was a US capacity to deter Communist aggression at every conceivable level, including a substantial conventional deterrent. Kaufman was one of the first strategists to seek to put the nuclear genie back in the bottle. The particular emphasis Kaufman put on conventional forces appealed to the army, and his work was widely read by army generals. However, this policy preference was never enacted; rather, Kaufman's ideas were applied to a nuclear format, where graduated deterrence was viewed as a scale of incremental uses of tactical nuclear weapons. The ideological significance of his views lay in their presumption that it would be possible to control warfare in a discriminate and subtle fashion. Hence Kaufman was a pathfinder for the NATO dogma of the 1960s and 1970s known as 'flexible response'. The important political myth which was created was the idea that a nuclear war could be a finely tuned process which was always under political control. This was crucial in public debate about defence issues, so that the generalized anxiety of the layman could be offset by the cool and sober expertise of the defence specialist. Kaufman's policy relevance was rewarded in 1956 by a move to the RAND corporation, and later by posts in the Kennedy administration. At RAND Kaufman found that many of his ideas were gaining credibility, and that a consensus about counter-force was already in place.

Another RAND theorist who advocated counter-force was the redoubtable Herman Kahn. Kahn, a physicist, had originally worked on mathematical models of bomb design, but during the 1950s he addressed himself increasingly to issues of strategy. Always likely to shock his audience, he once told air force generals, 'Gentlemen, you don't have a war plan, you have a war orgasm.' Kahn's mission, as he saw it, was to bring precision and rationality to war doctrine, and his ideas were widely aired. Prior to the publication of his *magnum opus On Thermonuclear War* in 1960, he did hundreds of talks and briefings, and was heard by thousands of people.[42] Kahn's undoubted influence was enhanced by the fact that he was a noted futurologist, and, thanks to Kubrick's *Dr Strangelove* (1964), in which the central character was loosely based on Kahn, a national figure.

It should be noted that Kahn's ideas were at the more bizarre end of the continuum of strategic thinking. He often sparked controversy when he depicted nuclear war as something that might not be as terrible as many people imagined. In *On Thermonuclear War* he cited indices of the survivability of nuclear war by comparison with existing medical pathologies. As Coker shows, the way in which Kahn spoke of atomic war indicated his distance from the phenomenon: 'His unconscious detachment made possible the equanimity with which he contemplated the prospect of nuclear war.'[43] I contend that this indicates not just a personal trait, but the wider intellectual culture within which nuclear issues were considered. Emotion and fear were expunged from the discourse. Despite Kahn's seeming eccentricity, it would be naive to assume that his theories lacked policy relevance. Kahn proposed deterrence based on a doomsday machine which was very controversial, but, as Kaplan notes, 'the Doomsday Machine was only a slightly absurd extension of existing American and Nato policy'.[44] In order for the USA to obtain political utility from its nuclear arsenal, Kahn believed that it must have the capability and the will to initiate nuclear war or to threaten to do so. In light of this, he was an enthusiast for extensive civil defence programmes, and he had a clear commitment to the idea that the USA could recover after a nuclear war. Although some of his ideas were freakish, such as the need to have radiation meters in shelters in order to distinguish the ill from those who were faking, other ideas percolated into the strategic grammar of the early 1980s. Escalation dominance, intra-war deterrence and fighting a protracted nuclear war were cornerstones of recent Pentagon policy, and were all evident in his 1960 publication. At the time fellow scientists were divided about Kahn's ideas, but the power of those ideas came from the appearance of scientific rigour which characterized the work. Stuart Hughes described *On Thermonuclear War* as 'one of the great works of our time'.[45] A different view was taken by Noam Chomsky: 'Kahn proposes no theories, no explanations, no factual assumptions that can be tested against their consequences, as do the sciences he is attempting to mimic. He simply suggests a terminology and provides a façade of rationality.'[46]

In contrast to Kahn, some of whose eccentric and apocalyptic theories were regarded as provocative, Kaufman exerted a real influence on defence planning and the emerging strategic grammar of the late 1950s. Indeed, Kaufman's career reveals the fusion of the university and the national security apparatus rather neatly. In the late

1950s Kaufman did a series of briefings for air force generals which sought to sell the strengths of counter-force, limited war and mutual restraint. In the air force, counter-force was already in vogue, as the Strategic Air Command was the vehicle which would strike at 'time urgent' targets in the USSR. However, the 1950s plans amounted to the unrestricted obliteration of Russia and, as later in the British case, a fixation about destroying Moscow. In consequence, air force generals were unhappy about the intellectual niceties of Kaufman's theories. At an infamous briefing at SAC headquarters in December 1960, the new CIC Thomas Power made the following point to the political scientist: 'Why do we want to restrain ourselves ... Restraint! Why are you so concerned with saving their lives. The whole idea is to kill the bastards.'[47] Nevertheless, the air force was, in fact, in accord with Kaufman's views. The reason was that counter-force was a mechanism for articulating a vision of strategy which undercut the appropriations of the other services. Also, while purple language could be used in the privacy of briefings, this was not the lingua franca of political legitimacy. The RAND taxonomy helped to neutralize anxiety about the Strategic Air Command, a process endorsed by a significant and loyal Hollywood output in the 1950s around the theme of the bomber. As Franklin notes, 'By the mid-1950s the strategic bomber had become a major icon of American culture.'[48]

Although William Kaufman's ideas appealed specifically to SAC, the truth was that ideas coming from RAND, Princeton, MIT and Harvard offered new justifications for increased numbers of weapons across the board. Eisenhower set up the Science Advisory Committee in 1957, and again academics from MIT and Harvard figured prominently, especially Kissinger, Schelling and Halperin. At RAND Albert Wohlstetter's concern over vulnerability, expressed in the R290 study on SAC basing, fed directly into the Gaither Panel report, *Deterrence and Survival in the Nuclear Age.* This report, handed to Eisenhower in November 1957, was highly pessimistic, and recommended the spending of an extra 44 billion dollars on defence over the next five years. Another significant contribution was Kissinger's *Nuclear Weapons and Foreign Policy*,[49] which was commissioned by the Council on Foreign Relations while the author was a junior academic at Harvard. The book, which was widely read, was especially popular in army circles, as it supported their drive for increased deployment of tactical nuclear weapons as a counter to Soviet power. The essential message of the work was that US military technology would only have utility if politicians were prepared to use it.[50]

The climate in which these ideas were expressed was one of acute anxiety on defence matters. The defence intellectuals, writing in universities and think-tanks, reflected this anxiety, and concentrated their attack on the seeming complacency of the Eisenhower adminis- tration. On specific matters of policy some intellectuals were close to real centres of power, especially if their departments were doing work directly for the CIA, as the Centre of International Studies at MIT was.[51] However, as regards the central questions of defence policy, the contribution of academics as they shuttled between uni- versity and think-tank was, as I suggested above, to create a taxon- omy, a grammar and semantics of strategic analysis. The concepts they developed disclosed the reality of weapons and defence plan- ning, and set the terms of debate for the next three decades. This was not, then, a disinterested account of a pre-existing state of affairs. The facts of strategic planning were enclosed in concepts of deterrence, counter-force, limited war, first and second strikes, and escalation dominance. This, in itself, is a major contribution to the politics of defence. In particular, these ideas set the boundaries for legitimate and illegitimate criticism; they distinguished between friend and foe. But after 1960 defence intellectuals actually saw real war plans, and in the case of Vietnam provided both operational concepts and policy initiatives.

FROM RHETORIC TO POLICY

The arrival of the Kennedy administration in Washington in 1960 brought academia into the White House, the State Department and the Pentagon. Indeed, the number of Cambridge men and Rhodes scholars in the government was a constant source of pride to the President and his close advisers. At the Pentagon, the new Secretary of Defence, Robert McNamara, had been president of Ford America. However, this background in business did not dispose him against intellectuals. On the contrary, McNamara brought in a large number of analysts from RAND who had previously worked at MIT, Princeton and Harvard. McNamara's goal was to bring defence under rational and scientific control, to organize the budget more effectively, and, in particular, to maintain political control over nuclear weapons. In order to achieve this, he believed the skills of mathematicians, political scientists, economists and systems analysts would be crucial, and such specialists were duly put into key roles in the national security machine. Above all, in the early days, the new secretary sought to rationalize nuclear strategy. To this end, the new administration put into effect the Single Integrated Operational Plan, which Secretary Gates had initiated at the end of the Eisenhower period. The aim of this was to integrate the separate war plans of the three services into an overall framework programmed into the computers of the National Military Command Centre in the Pentagon.

The first SIOP was finished in December 1960, and was dominated by SAC. The plan envisaged an attack with immediately available munitions, which would mean the detonation of 1459 warheads with an explosive power equivalent to 2,164 megatons, against 654 targets in Russia, Eastern Europe and China. In this 'optimum mix' strategy, estimated fatalities were 175 million.[52] If the entire force available were to be used, then 3,423 weapons would be delivered with a yield of 7,847 megatons. Here fatalities would be 285 million, with a further 40 million injured.[53] Air Force Chief of Staff Tommy White thought the plan excellent. But SAC commander Thomas Power was concerned about a point of detail: he asked White what would happen if China was not involved? White replied, 'I hope nobody thinks of it because it would really screw up the plan.'[54]

The atavism and crudity of the view cited above could have no place in the discourse of a modernist, rational strategic policy. McNamara was briefed on the SIOP in February 1961, and immediately decided that it must be reworked. The intellectual put in charge of reworking the SIOP was Daniel Ellsberg, who had come into the government via RAND and Harvard. Ellsberg was in a unique position to tackle the problem, because he had actually seen the real war plans. Quite by accident, Ellsberg had stumbled across a document called JSCAP Annex C, which had never been viewed by any civilian, including the President. While the document was shocking in itself, as it called for the obliteration of the USSR, what particularly disturbed Ellsberg was the realization that planning and discussions at RAND had borne little relation to operational realities. The air force and SAC had been happy to bounce ideas around in RAND briefings, but the analysts had not been given access to real plans. RAND theorizing in the 1950s can thus be seen as a vivid form of textuality. The intellectual agenda, the strategic grammar and the tactical niceties of deterrence created a lucid framework of legitimacy for policies which actually connoted nihilism: SAC simply intended to bomb the USSR into non-existence.

RAND thinking had been premissed on growing US vulnerability and on the need to find a rationale for SAC. Concern about vulnerability had always been a major issue at RAND; it was clear in the early 1950s in Wohlstetter's R290 basing study. In the mid-1950s it coalesced into the infamous bomber and missile gap scares. These show clearly how issues of calculation and rational assessment were really subordinate to cultural perceptions of vulnerability. CIA and air force intelligence estimates constantly exaggerated the level of threat; but, nevertheless, politicians on the right, such as Senator Stuart Symington, still believed the official estimates to be conservative. Thus the intelligence estimates made available to RAND personnel were false. In fact, there was no bomber gap and no missile gap, and SAC had a rationale which was massive superiority.

The myth of US vulnerability had been at the centre of the Kennedy critique of the Eisenhower defence policy. Within days of coming to office, Kennedy was briefed on the nature of the myth by his scientific adviser Jerome Wiesner who had come into the government from MIT. In the meantime Ellsberg had gone back to RAND to deliver a sensational briefing on the missile gap. He told an astonished audience that there was a gap, and that the ratio was 10:1; then he added that it was in the US's favour.[55]

The revision of the SIOP undertaken by Ellsberg was known as Project One. Project One again reveals the overwhelming presence of the ideology of control and instrumental rationality which pervaded the RAND corporation. The likely brute facts of confrontation, which only films and novels have attempted to depict honestly, disappeared beneath a veneer of precision, calculation and cold analysis. RAND thus established a counter-factual rhetoric which articulated a value-neutral framework for nuclear war. Thomas Power was once asked what happens when nuclear war begins. He replied, 'My mind just stops there.'[56] The RAND revision of the SIOP reveals how and why this is possible. The language of strategic discourse leaves no room for real death and destruction. Hence its practitioners can enter a conceptual world where the horrors of nuclear war have been eliminated. Project One left 'invulnerable forces in reserve'; it effected 'targeting discrimination'; it tightened 'command and control'; it regretted 'collateral damage'; and it culminated in the policy of 'second-strike counter-force'. The SIOP revision concluded a period when there had been intense intellectual interest in nuclear strategy. But after Cuba, concern moved elsewhere. In intellectual circles interest in strategy now shifted to another domain. To put it simply, the concepts of limited war, intra-war deterrence and escalation dominance were now applied to the escalating conflict in Vietnam.

INTELLECTUALS AND COUNTER-INSURGENCY

The historical and intellectual roots of US involvement in Vietnam lay in Truman's containment doctrine and in the domino theory. Truman's aim had been to contain Communist expansion on a world-wide level, and he was willing to commit conventional forces in order to achieve this goal. By comparison, the Eisenhower years saw a reliance on nuclear weapons and a geo-strategic focus on Europe. As a presidential candidate, Kennedy had attacked this policy, and upon entering office, he was committed to responding to Communist aggression everywhere and at every level. Moreover, after Cuba, Kennedy and his advisers perceived the main threat to be insurgency in the Third World and, particularly, Chinese support for wars of national liberation. As Ambrose notes:

> There was also universal agreement on the need to prove to the Chinese that wars of national liberation did not work and to show the Third World that America stood by her commitments. These views were held most strongly by JFK's personal advisers, led by Walt Rostow and McGeorge Bundy.[57]

An important reason why intellectuals were so significant in the Kennedy years was the President's habit of setting up *ad hoc* commit-tees which often bypassed the usual agencies. As Ambrose indicates, two of the key intellectual advisers in the Kennedy administration were McGeorge Bundy and Walt Whitman Rostow.[58] According to Halberstam, the former, who sat on the committee which managed the Cuban missile crisis, was arguably the brightest star in the Kennedy constellation, a man of high intellectual attainment and impeccable upper-class credentials. Bundy, the son of Harvey Bundy, who had been a friend of and aid to Henry Stimson, had been edu-cated at Groton and Yale, and had gone from Yale to teach political science at Harvard. Kennedy appointed him as Special Assistant for National Security Affairs, which gave him a leading role in Vietnam. Bundy's deputy, Walt Rostow, who acted as Chief of the State Department's Policy Planning Staff, was also a leading intellectual, but he was from a radically different background. He was born in New York in 1916, the son of a Russian-Jewish immigrant.[59] He graduated from Yale, was a young Rhodes scholar, and while in his twenties was recruited for the Office of Strategic Services. In 1950, at the age of 34, Rostow founded the MIT Centre for International Studies with money provided by the CIA.[60] In 1953 he and colleagues produced a CIA-funded book, *The Dynamics of Soviet Society*, which was available to the public only in an abridged version. However, the loss of academic freedom did not bother Rostow. For him the highest goal of academic work was to serve the nation-state.

Rostow's impact on policy can be seen in the report he submitted to Kennedy after a fact-finding mission to Vietnam undertaken with General Maxwell Taylor in October 1961. Following an earlier expedition headed by Lyndon Johnson, Rostow and Taylor endorsed the advice which the Vice-president had brought back. They recommended an increased military presence. He further advised Kennedy that North Vietnam should be bombed in a graduated escalation which should match Hanoi's support for the Viet Cong. Kennedy accepted the recommendations, apart from the one to bomb the North.[61] At the time of the Rostow mission there were 1,364 US advisers in Vietnam; by November 1963 there were 15,000.[62] In 1961 another critical academic input came from economist Eugene Staley of Stanford – home of the army's think-tank. In the summer Staley visited Saigon, and made a series of suggestions to the Diem government. Of these the Strategic Hamlets programme was the most significant. The original idea was to bring peasants into protected havens to isolate them from the VC, prevent recruitment, and to stop VC hiding in villages.[63] The reality was rather different. The villagers were coerced off their land at gun point in order to create free-fire zones for the ARVN and later American forces. The programme was instituted in 1962–63 and involved the movement of 8,700,000 into hamlets. Bernard Fall described it as 'the most mammoth example of "social engineering" in the non-communist world'.[64] As to methods, it was described by Marine Colonel William Corson as 'forced resettlement, physical oppression, coercion and political "persuasion" by the club'.[65]

In the Kennedy years Bundy's role was essentially to be the intellectual arbiter. He would weigh the advice the President was receiving, and then point up the pros and cons of particular paths. At this time, and throughout, the major advocates of using increased force were Taylor and Rostow. However, by 1965 the situation had

changed. As the Pentagon Papers illustrate, a major concern of the
Johnson administration was the question of American credibility.
Despite intelligence reports, which were sometimes plain lies, the
truth was known; the war was going badly. The ARVN were perform-
ing poorly; morale was low; and there were massive defections to the
Communists. For Bundy, who was not especially interested in Asia,
this was an important issue, as it was for Johnson. Credibility
involved demonstrating to allies that US security guarantees meant
something. For the administration it meant not retreating in
ignominious defeat. After a year's very uneasy relationship with
Johnson, Bundy and the President began to see eye to eye on the
issue of credibility.[66] In January 1965 Bundy suggested to Johnson
that he make a trip to Saigon to check, first hand, the situation on
the ground. By early February he was in Vietnam. On the 7th the VC
launched a mortar attack on the US base at Pleiku, killing eight
American soldiers. Bundy visited the injured and was outraged; the
cool intellectual exterior cracked. The result was a memo to Johnson
urging instant retaliation and a graduated series of bombing raids
against the North.[67]

Back in Washington, the Bundy memo was significant in pushing
Johnson towards the decision for wholesale bombing, known as
operation 'Rolling Thunder'. From this time on, the USA incrementally increased the firepower unleashed on Vietnam and the number
of combat troops, ultimately to 500,000. In intellectual terms this was
limited war, graduated deterrence and escalation dominance. In
human terms it was something else. The destruction of Vietnam was
unprecedented. By 1970 more bombs had been dropped than in the
whole of human history. By 1973 the tonnage of explosives used was
8 million, and there were 21 million bomb craters in South Vietnam.
As well as bombs, the air force also used Agent Orange to defoliate
the countryside. At the end of the war, half of Vietnam's coastal
mangroves had been destroyed, and a third of its hardwood forests
and 6 million acres of farmland has been poisoned by chemicals.
As to casualties, there are no definite figures, but one estimate is
2.6 million dead.[68]

This carnage was enacted by a government racked by doubts, but
convinced of the truth of certain intellectual ideas about power and
the use of military force. The role of intellectuals, though, was not
just a case of Harvard and Yale men giving advice inside the government. During the Vietnam years connections between academia and
the Pentagon extended to the national level, and many universities

were embroiled in scandals as the scale of research for security agencies became apparent. But let me be clear: the cosy relationship between academia and the state had changed. Academics were still serving the security state, but there was now concerted opposition in universities.

The interface between the state and academia widened in the 1960s because of the government's need of experts in development and modernization. As the USA surveyed its relations with the Third World, it became critical to plot a trajectory for the relationship. In other words, rather than fight governments which had instituted Communism, it would be easier to 'manage' Third World developments towards liberalism and capitalism. Just as intellectual capital had brought nuclear strategy under control, so it could engineer social development.

This new tactic, though, was much more difficult. Nuclear strategy was written in documents and programmed into computers. There were no real-world counter-factuals to contend with. Moreover, the small number of academics who really counted in the nuclear field could be given exhaustive security checks. However, by moving into the intellectual terrain of development and modernization, the state was engaging universities in areas where there was widespread controversy and debate. Departments of sociology and social anthropology proved less tractable than those of economics and political science, and the state patronage sparked by Vietnam produced a reaction against development. Gendzier notes:

> If Political Development Studies were sparked by postwar U.S. foreign policy and the need for a cadre of domestic experts, the war in Vietnam generated the conditions that opened the door to widespread support for counter-development studies.[69]

The most notorious case was the army's project Camelot, conceived in 1963 by the Army Office of Research and Development. The plan was to spend between four and six million dollars channelled through the American Universities Special Operations Research Office. The project was headed by the sociologist Rex Hopper, who by 1965 had acquired the services of 33 leading US behavioural scientists. The research aimed to isolate the causes of social and political breakdown in Latin America, Africa, Asia and the Middle East, and to recommend strategies to forestall such breakdown. The orthodox view of this was that it was part of a development strategy, to ensure that Third World countries trod the path of economic liberalization. However, it must be observed that the project was launched during a period of revolutionary change in the Third World. Thus, it is possible to view Camelot as an anthropological strategy for counter-insurgency.

Project Camelot was aborted in 1965 by McNamara, but as Robert Nisbet has shown, this was not because of the domestic dispute in American academia; it was the result of an international scandal.[70] In 1963 a professor of anthropology travelled to Chile to make contact with Chilean social scientists. He sounded out his contacts to see if they would collaborate in a US army project to study political unrest. The Chilean academics failed to see the attractions of working as agents for the US army in their own country, and shortly afterwards a diplomatic storm broke out between the two countries.[71]

Camelot was a well-known example, but it was the tip of an iceberg. Building on contacts established by OSS, the CIA and the State Department after 1945, there was an extensive network of university–intelligence contacts by the 1960s. Academics at Michigan State University were working on a project for the CIA to train South Vietnamese policemen.[72] In 1967 it was discovered that the Executive Director and the Treasurer of APSA were, respectively, the President and Vice-president of Policy Research Incorporated, which was a CIA front.[73] This led to some scandal in US political science circles, but the international relations establishment was not unduly abashed, probably because American international relations departments were receiving substantial funding from defence and foreign policy agencies. In 1966, William Crockett of the State Department commented:

> The colleges and universities provide us with a rich body of information about many subjects, countries and people through special research studies prepared for many clients and purposes. For example, the United States Government is spending $30m this year on foreign affairs studies in American universities.[74]

REASONS AND MOTIVES

I could list links between universities and security organizations *ad infinitum*, but let us turn now to their causes and consequences. In an important article entitled 'Lying in Politics', Hannah Arendt gives illuminating insights into the *Pentagon Papers* (McNamara's 47-volume history of US policy in Vietnam).[75] Throughout the documents Arendt observes the impetus to retain credibility, to save face and to maintain certain images for domestic consumption. As the prosecution of the war became simultaneously more destructive and less effective, the need to cover up the truth and to ignore dissenting voices – such as George Ball's – increased. In this respect the behaviour of the defence intellectuals became more and more an act of bad faith. By late 1966 many in the administration such as McNamara, Ellsberg, and McNaughton (a former Havard law professor) had lost faith in the policy. However, the ubiquity of deception continued. While Rostow still believed that victory was imminent and that the bombing was working, those around him were playing damage limitation. In Arendt's view the Pentagon Papers reveal that image making, rather than containment, was the ultimate policy, and as she comments, the intellectuals 'played the game of deception and falsehoods'.[76] Collectively, the self-deception which abounded concerned the myths that furnished the policy from the beginning: that communism was a monolith, that there were two states, that the North had attacked the South, and that the war was against the North. As individuals, the civilian advisers had doubts about these particular assumptions; but as a collective intelligence unit, the doubts were submerged under the ideological front of the policy and the image making. As to the reasons for failure, Arendt regards them as remarkably simple: 'the wilful, deliberate disregard of all facts, historical, political, geographical for more than 25 years'.[77]

The acquiescence of the intellectuals in deception points to a fusion of personal motives and general ideological factors. In a commentary on Project Camelot, Irving Louis Horowitz listed some of the motives that drove the 'consultants'. There was first the excitement of a big project, of transcending what C. Wright-Mills had demeaned as 'abstract empiricism'. There was the exhilaration of power, of rising above the humdrum ordinariness of the campus and the classroom. There was the Platonic arrogance inherent in advising and educating an elite. There was an enlightenment zeal about using social science as a vehicle for humanization, and finally a sense of dizzy excitement, of becoming a doer, rather than a thinker.[78]

Part and parcel of the process was thus the basic desire for social advancement. The top advisers were clearly members of an elite;

their establishment credentials were unambiguous. Moreover, their careers indicated that there were glittering prizes. After government service it was quite typical for these men to go on to be presidents of the largest foundations or universities. Thus, in the lower echelons of academia, there was a clear perception of a career ladder that culminated in endorsement by the state.

In the whole of this process there was a fundamental unconsciousness about the politics of these developments. After 1945 there was virtually no oppositional intellectual culture in the USA. In the 1950s McCarthyism moved academic debate to the right, while the syndrome which Daniel Bell called the 'end of ideology' robbed intellectual life of fundamental political reflection. The mainstream of American politics, understood as pluralism, was seen as a neutral political ground devoid of the patent absurdities of the left and the right. Under the sway of behaviouralist commitment to ethical neutrality, US political science should have realized that all purposes were contestable, subjective and lacking foundations. However, this reflection was never applied to core US values. The two-party system, capitalism, materialism and the belief in science were simply unquestioned as the foundation for all academic purposes. In consequence, to serve the state, to bring their values to a world-wide stage was completely non-controversial. In Rostow's modernization theory, all nations were heading towards a rational, productive and affluent future. In assisting the American state, social science was just promoting – at a faster rate – a historical process which was inevitable.

These aspects of American intellectual life explain, I believe, why intellectuals were prepared to be closely associated with policies which caused untold misery and suffering. The core values, the theory and the instrumental rationality preordained the idealism of the American way. Thus Kennedy's idealism, which was wrapped up in the semantics of universalism, was really the universalization of particular American beliefs. On the day that Che Guevara was killed, Rostow called a staff meeting. He announced: 'The Bolivians have executed Che ... They finally got the son of a bitch. The last of the romantic guerrillas.'[79] For Rostow, men like Che were deluded opponents of progress; to liquidate them was an act of liberation. The theory, then, could legitimize any cruelty because it was correct. Numerous examples can be found of this form of logic, but the following is an archetypal case. In testimony to the House Committee on Foreign Affairs, Professor David Rowe, Director of

Graduate Studies in International Relations at Yale, proposed a policy of mass starvation against China. He said:

> Mind you, I am not talking about this as a weapon against the Chinese people. It will be. But that is only incidental. The weapon will be against the government because the internal stability of that country cannot be sustained by an unfriendly government in the face of general starvation.[80]

CONCLUSIONS

The role of intellectuals in supporting, designing and implementing state security policy in the 1950s and 1960s was both significant and controversial. Robert Engler expressed some of the contradictions that were apparent in the Vietnam years:

> Working directly for the military is commonplace, and classified social science projects are widespread. It is reported that MIT has awarded a number of higher degrees for classified theses. One loses the capacity to distinguish between satire and reality when an applicant for a university position in political science, currently employed by the Rand Corporation, explains modestly on his vita, under the heading of publications, that many of his writings are classified and hence not available for listing or inspection.[81]

In the United States the prerequisites for an intellectual branch of the security state were, first, a general atrophy of the idea of the critical and independent university, and second, the concrete institutional links forged in the Second World War by the OSS. In the Cold War the independence of security-relevant knowledge was no longer tolerated, and natural science succumbed to the state's embrace. But at the same time the politically dangerous business of nuclear strategy required a legitimizing discourse, a mode of persuasion which would secure consent. My view is that traditional forms of military-cultural discourse could not engineer legitimacy in the nuclear sphere, because America was vulnerable to obliteration. The inevitable defeat of the adversary because of Yankee ingenuity was no longer assured. Security had become dialectical and symmetrical. Accordingly, the world of nuclear confrontation became disclosed as an area of calculation, management, prediction and rationality.

The elites managing the nuclear apparatus could thus believe that they were involved in a credible and rational process. Even after a nuclear war images conveyed the notion of a still functioning state apparatus, albeit in a wasteland.

The impetus to co-operation with the state was enhanced by the McCarthy years, when neutrality was suspect. Moreover, predominant theories in American political science, such as value-neutrality, the end of ideology, and modernization, insinuated a sense of unconsciousness about collaborations. The security state was a force for the very values which underwrote academic endeavour.

In the late 1960s the problems of collusion were exposed by Vietnam, and a left-liberal reaction set in. However, the fragile liberal consensus of the 1970s was undercut by economic failure and the ferocious assault of the new right. But a new nuclear consensus was not created. The rhetoric and policy of the Reagan administration created an inevitable fissure in the strategic community, which remained until the end of the Cold War. However, the lure of state patronage has not dried up. As Edward Said notes, 'So pervasive has the professionalisation of intellectual life become that the sense of vocation ... has been almost swallowed up. Policy-oriented intellectuals have internalised the norms of the state.'[82]

5 The Rise and Fall of Nuclear Culture

INTRODUCTION

The previous chapter assessed the role that intellectuals played in constructing a discourse of strategic rationality in the United States after 1945. The significance of this was that it generated a framework for the analysis and refinement of theories of nuclear war which preserved a modernist veneer of control and rationality. Here the language and grammar of strategic discourse were pivotal. The prospect of global destruction and the consequences of the generation of forces capable of species annihilation were hidden deep within a technical vocabulary taken from hybrid disciplines, such as operational research and systems analysis. In my view this was chiefly a manoeuvre to enable elite members and policy advisers to communicate without having to confront the full reality of a possible nuclear war.

In the wider society little was known about the technical detail of nuclear war plans. The public heard only elements of what Paul Nitze referred to as 'declaratory policy', which was rather different from what Nitze termed 'action policy'. The master precept of declaratory policy was deterrence, which grounded nuclear strategy firmly in the ideological foundation of defence. Few writers outside RAND or SAC wanted to explore the consequences of actual nuclear attack on the USSR. Deterrence allowed nuclear policy to be seen as responsive; nuclear weapons were the means to hold back the tide of Soviet military power, which it was believed would be used to overrun Western Europe. By the early 1950s it was held as axiomatic that America's nuclear weapons were protecting the West from an otherwise inevitable Soviet attack. Churchill put the dominant assumption well: 'It is certain that Europe would have been communized and London under bombardment some time ago but for the deterrent of the atomic bomb in the hands of the United States.'[1]

Despite the legitimacy accorded to nuclear policy, there were of course many reasons for anxiety. In 1949 the USSR had its own nuclear device, and world events indicated that war could well be on the agenda. But in the USA the 1950s was a decade of unparalleled consensus, which allowed the anxiety to be managed. Western Europe had a powerful and intellectually independent left, whose credibility had been enhanced by its role in the war. But this was not the case in the USA. As the Cold War intensified, the possibility of any generalized dissent in America became remote as repressive devices, such as the House Un-American Activities Committee, bore down on those considered disloyal. Ironically, the group exposed to the most scrutiny were the very scientists who had given the USA its technological supremacy. In the 1950s physicists and mathematicians comprised more than 50 per cent of the individuals identified as Communists in Congressional hearings.[2] Yet no American atomic scientist was ever shown to have turned traitor.[3]

The reasons for the coercive control of the scientific community were complex. But one key factor was that these were the people who could undermine the consensus about state security policy and the role of nuclear weapons in defence. As I revealed in Chapter 4, some scientists had expressed misgivings about the ultimate purpose of the Manhattan Project, once it was clear that the German atomic research had failed. These grumblings continued after 1945, and reached a peak when the USA decided to develop the hydrogen bomb in 1950. In an article in *Scientific American* Hans Bethe made the following points:

> We believe in peace based on mutual trust. Shall we achieve it by using hydrogen bombs? Shall we convince the Russians of the value of the individual by killing millions of them? If we fight a war and win it with H-bombs, what history will remember is *not* the ideals we were fighting for but the methods we used to achieve them.[4]

But these were not arguments that the American state wished to see debated in the wider society. Bethe's ideas were considered heretical, and the AEC effectively censored the issue of *Scientific American* carrying the article. Thus, in order to create the consensus for nuclear weapons policy, the state needed to make clear who was in charge and to isolate any critical voices. In Coker's *War and the Twentieth Century* the atomic scientists come in for heavy criticism.[5] He argues that the pursuit of scientific truth has been just as remorseless as the warrior's pursuit of the enemy. But I believe that the scientists' main weakness was in failing to understand the form of state that emerged after 1945. Many of the greatest scientists were individuals who had fled totalitarian regimes in Europe in the 1930s, or gone to the USA after the war's end. But after 1945 science in the West was just as much under the state's jurisdiction as it had been in the totalitarian states of Europe in the 1930s. The only difference was that after the Manhattan Project science now had even greater technical potential and greater resources. As Bertrand Russell put it, the issue was whether the century could survive science.

In the USA in the 1950s the scientific community faced one simple and stark choice: either it supported the new regime of nuclear security, or it could take actions that would be deemed to be treasonous. The institution which managed this coercive form of discipline was the AEC, which had 150,000 of its employees investigated by security agencies in the 1950s.[6] The potential problem with science was that it had a methodology and normative framework which could lead to the questioning of policy. While this methodology was focused on a specialized research project, it carried no danger; but the greatest scientists had an interest in questions of philosophy, politics, art and aesthetics, which could lead them to ask awkward questions about the assumptions behind policy. In order to erect a discourse of nuclear rationality, it was essential that any such questioning was either suppressed or done esoterically behind closed doors. In the 1950s science had to fall in behind the normative framework designed by the state. Science was one of the interest groups in the pluralist democracy; but these groups were integrated into a corporatist consensus based on the master principle of Cold War politics. This chapter assesses the rise and fall of this consensus in the wider society and the cultural assumptions upon which military policy rested.

COLD WAR NUCLEAR CULTURE

The consensus behind Cold War military policy was achieved in a decade when political legitimacy was high and economic performance unparalleled. Government agencies were powerful, partly because they were trusted. If this is in doubt, then a moment's reflection on the current situation in the United States and Europe shows how distant the world of the 1950s seems. Today consensus has been largely undermined, and the degree of public cynicism about politics is profound. In particular, the fragmented and ravaged society of urban America is conceptually a million miles away from the USA of 40 years ago.

In the 1950s the dominant narrative of American culture and society was one of economic progress, expanding scientific prowess, pluralist democracy and effective social order. As the decade wore on, mainstream political scientists characterized American political culture as representing 'the end of ideology'. According to luminaries such as Seymour Lipset, the USA had effected a historic compromise among the forces thrown up by the Industrial Revolution: 'This change in western political life reflects the fact that the fundamental problems of the industrial revolution have been solved.'[7] Central to this was the growing affluence of the average American citizen, who now resided in a new landscape. Assisted by the US state, which provided the infrastructure, many of the white working class and middle class moved out from crowded, unattractive town centres to colonize the suburbs. The new neat homes in the suburbs were also gradually filled with the expanding range of consumer goods made by companies such as Westinghouse, Hoover and General Electric. In order to reach the suburbs and the new out-of-town shopping areas built to service them, the new suburban Americans also needed more automobiles, usually provided by Ford and General Motors. But as certain critics have noted, many of the corporations providing luxuries for the home were the same ones providing weaponry for the Pentagon. What has subsequently been termed 'Military Keynesianism' was creating a group of corporations that depended on their government contracts for weapons, while also providing consumer goods in the home. Domestic luxury and national defence were co-terminous. Other synergies were also evident. As Charles Wright-Mills revealed in his highly controversial *Power Elite*, political consensus meant that the personnel in these corporations shared the same values as those in government and the military.[8] In consequence, it was easy for them to move between the world of business, government and military service. It was not an accident that in the 1950s the president of General Motors, Charles Wilson, became Secretary of Defence; neither was it a matter of contingency in the 1960s when Robert McNamara made the same move from Ford. As Engelhardt points out, in 1957 1,500 retired or on-leave officers of the rank of colonel or above were working for civilian agencies.[9]

The apex of the corporatist structure which was the framework for American politics in the 1950s was the military. The historian Ernest May describes how Washington in the 1950s was essentially a 'military headquarters'.[10] The Pentagon was 'the dominant consumer of the federal government's discretionary funds ... defense and defense-related agencies accounted steadily for 60 to 70 per cent of all federal personnel ... [T]he main business of the U.S. government had become the development, maintenance, positioning, exploitation and regulation of military forces.'[11]

The state's construction of a network of military institutions emerged in parallel with a period of unprecedented economic growth. The Cold War and affluence went hand in hand. Affluence also cemented the legitimacy of the overall package of corporatist capitalism. There were many who might dissent, but their voices were not heard. Consensus ruled the politics of identity, and the political elite shaped the ideological contours of US self-understanding. Paradoxically, in a decade characterized by a shift to the right, the protest potential that was expressed came from the ultra-conservatives. The new configuration of corporate Cold War liberalism was in fact more complex than many commentators have realized. Its subtleties were certainly too much for Senator Joseph McCarthy, who sought a more fundamentalist form of anti-communism. Useful to a degree, McCarthy ultimately crossed bounds – including attacking the military – which made him a threat to the establishment itself. By stepping off the plateau of consensus, McCarthy fell outside the bounds of legitimate politics.

Cold War consensus was mirrored in a popular culture which increasingly reached its audience in the 1950s through the medium of television. After 1945 a series of semi-documentary programmes reached a mass audience, and recreated the achievements of US forces during the Second World War. Programmes like *Victory at Sea*, screened in 1952 and 1953, were a national institution, and cemented the establishment's view of the military in the wider society. Others included *Crusade in the Pacific, Crusade in Europe, Air Power* and the *Silent Service*.[12] The making of these series was possible because of a large degree of co-operation between the various services and the media: 'To such shows, the services extended offers of help of every imaginable sort – from the loan of a military campus or base as a set to specially shot footage of subs diving or missiles being launched.[13] As I show in Chapter 6, the links that made this possible had been established during the Second World War, when Hollywood had come under the control of the Office of War Information. Here the purpose was the entirely predictable one of producing propaganda. But after 1945 the populace had to be convinced of the need for continually expanded military expenditures during an era of peace, albeit with the interregnum of the

Korean War. In fact, from 1948 to 1953 the DoD budget jumped from 10.9 billion dollars to 49.6 billion. Before Korea, Truman had struggled to convince Congress of the need to fund his policy of global containment. But Korea gave the final stimulus needed to fund and erect the new security state.

The TV shows cited above were a means of securing an identity in America which continued the narrative project of American triumphalism. However, as the previous chapter revealed, representational popular culture was not the only means whereby this identity was constituted as politically binding. At an elite level academic scholarship reinforced the new consensus. In the dominant realist paradigm of international relations scholarship, epitomized in the work of Hans Morgenthau,[14] the nature of global politics was revealed as a force complex where power was the critical ingredient. To succeed in this environment, a state needed statesmen able to make cold and sober decisions concerning the national interest and the effective use of key power resources. Here global politics was *real-politik* writ large. But this perspective should have engendered a critical distance and value-neutrality, where states were defined as essentially homogeneous players in the game of global power politics. However, as Campbell shows, the policy formulations and statements of the Cold War, which were allegedly scripted according to the dictates of realism, were embedded within a discourse replete with moralistic and even religious elements.[15]

What I am trying to pin-point here is the fact that the official narrative of the USA's post-war role in the Cold War has not been captured in the realist account of this process. At some point realist scholarship was actually absorbed into the narrative process it purported to describe. The output of popular culture and that of intellectuals were united in privileging one version of the Cold War process.

CO-OPTING EUROPE

Because of the creation of NATO and the USA's adoption of a policy of extended deterrence, the discursive, legitimating grounds of the new militarism also needed to penetrate the political culture of the European allies. The ideological grounding of Cold War militarism needed to be Atlanticized as the palpable signs of US military power became permanent features of the European landscape. In one of the less researched aspects of CIA policy, a decision was taken in the late 1940s to launch a cultural offensive in Western Europe to challenge the cultural legitimacy of communism and to provide an aesthetic dimension to the edifice of containment.[16] Spearheading this *kulturkampf* were intellectuals, artists, writers and musicians who sought to join the mobilization against Soviet communism, although the real targets of the campaign were European intellectuals rather than Soviet ones. The policy arose because in the late 1940s the State Department began to worry that Western European countries might succumb to communism because of internal subversion – although it should be noted that communism in Italy and France was actually doing rather well at the ballot-box.[17] The ostensible, overt move to ward off these developments was of course the Marshall Plan, which after much wrangling was passed as the European Co-operation Act in April 1948.[18] But a covert face of the strategy involved using Marshall Plan funds (known as counterpart funds) for the cultural war against Communists and fellow-travellers.

The CIA operative in charge of this action was Thomas Braden, who has quite openly admitted the existence of the policy in the press and on television.[19] What was not known until quite recently was that it included trying to engineer a positive reception in Europe for a particular school of American painting, known as abstract expressionism. Unknown to themselves, artists such as Jackson Pollock, had their work exhibited by organizations which were CIA fronts. The rather quaint idea behind this extraordinary manoeuvre was that abstract expressionism revealed a deeply held Western aesthetic of freedom, as compared to the crude social realism of Soviet painting, which expressed mechanical collectivism.

The manipulation of fine art was no more than a Cold War curiosity. But other tactics employed in the *kulturkampf* were of greater note. Using the Congress of Cultural Freedom as an umbrella organiza-tion, the CIA began a covert war of ideas in Europe in order to bind the opinion leaders of Western European countries to the Cold War consensus created in the USA. A major prerequisite for this was to isolate and marginalize the Communist left in Europe: in other words, a strategy of exclusion. Conversely, a strategy of inclusion was launched to bring trade unions and the non-Communist left into the consensus. The Congress of Cultural Freedom was used to fund cultural events which showed the USA in a favourable light, and to make European intellectuals familiar with US cultural attitudes. In a sense, as Longstaff has argued, art ruled over politics.

Leading intellectuals in the CCF included Sidney Hook, Melvin Laskey, Arthur Koestler, Bertram Wolfe and James Burnham. Because the CIA was using the American Federation of Labour as a conduit for funds to Europe, the AFL leader Irving Brown was also recruited.[20] In June 1950 the Congress organized its first major event in Berlin. The convention was to sound a clarion call to Europeans, reminding them of the sins of communism and chastising those inclined to neutralism. Many of the CCF's leading lights were former Trotskyites who believed they had a special insight into the working of the Communist mind. In particular, Laskey and Burnham believed that the European 'soft left' did not understand the aims and means of Stalin and his henchmen.

The Berlin Congress was able to build on the solidarity created by the airlift of 1948–9, when the USA and Britain saved Berlin from the Soviet blockade. But leading speakers at the Congress went over the top in their deflamatory statements. Burnham was committed to a 'roll-back' strategy for Eastern Europe, and was quite prepared to openly envisage the use of atomic weapons.[21] He acknowledged the problem of the bomb, but he argued that there were 'good' bombs and 'bad' bombs. But, as I argued in Chapter 4, this was not the way to legitimate nuclear policy. In order to give reassurance, atomic weapons policy needed to be stated *sotto voce*, what were not needed were statements openly envisaging the prospect of nuclear war. In Berlin delegates from other countries found the rantings from the platform disturbing and unacceptable, and the proceedings ended on a note of rancour.[22]

In the CIA the inaugural of the CCF in Berlin was regarded as something of a fiasco. The 'wild men' were pushed to one side and replaced by tacticians of greater subtlety, notably Julius Fleischman and Michael Josselson. The latter had been in the Office of Strategic Services during the war, and had then moved into the CIA. With Braden, he became the leading strategist in the CIA's war of aesthetics with the USSR.[23]

In 1952 the new team running the CCF organized a festival in Paris under the direction of composer Nicholas Nabokov. The festival was called, 'Masterpieces of the Twentieth Century'. The aim was to bring the best of American literature, music and art to the French capital. By contrast with Berlin, it had been decided to let the art speak for itself, and not subject audiences to propagandistic diatribe. Nabokov referred to the event as his 'dream festival',[24] and by any standards it was an enormous success. A staggering line-up of performers went to Paris, and many produced new works for the occasion. The goal for Braden and Josselson was to counter claims by European intellectuals that the US had a sterile and philistine culture aimed solely at making money. More broadly, it was to show that the culture and way of life being protected by the new Western alliance was superior to the one behind the Iron Curtain. In that respect Braden believed that performances by the Boston Symphony Orchestra would be more effective than a hundred speeches by diplomats or politicians. Art was spearheading the battle for hearts and minds.

The aim of the CCF was to counter anti-Americanism in Europe amongst the intellectual elite and opinion leaders. But other mechanisms were working at a more mundane level. As early as 1946, when the French sent the socialist minister Léon Blum to Washington to ask for aid, the USA included the export of American films in the deal signed by Blum and Secretary of State James Byrnes.[25] In Germany the USA responded to 'lesehunger' by providing millions of American novels and, in more serious vein, journals such as *Der Monat*, which, in an early edition, included a translation of the whole of Orwell's *Animal Farm*.[26]

It is of course far from clear how effective this cultural strategy actually was. What is clear is that the USA was prepared to pump millions of dollars into it. It is also obvious that it was regarded as controversial, the CIA disguising its involvement by passing funds through dummy organizations such as the Farfield Corporation.[27] In France and Italy the Communist left could never be entirely marginalized, but the cultural onslaught for Cold War politics helped to shield consensus positions from the left's influence. Also after 1947 Communists marginalized themselves by their identification with Moscow and Stalinism. By the early 1950s it was clear that the Marshall Plan had been a great success, as European economies began to grow prodigously. The greatest achievement was in Germany, where between 1947 and 1951 industrial production increased by 312 per cent.[28] Unlike France, the Federal Republic was overtly grateful to the USA, and openly swore allegiance to American-style liberalism. This was essential to Cold War strategy, as West Germany was the centre-piece in America's policy of military containment. Moreover, the espousal of 'Western' ideology helped the Germany's new political elite to distance themselves from the nightmare of the Nazi period. In short, the modalities of the Cold War helped the Bundesrepublik to establish an unequivocally

Western identity. Coupled with the pragmatic achievements of the 'economic miracle', this enabled West Germany to emerge as the USA's most staunch Cold War ally.

NUCLEAR POLICY

The NATO alliance created in 1949 believed itself to be confronted by a vast Soviet army able to overrun Western Europe in short order. With hindsight this was probably a pessimistic assessment, which overstated Red Army force levels and capabilities. It was also the kind of 'worst case' analysis which deduces intentions from alleged capabilities. Nevertheless, it was the predominant view at the time. In 1949 there were only 100,000 US troops in Europe, and, all told, the NATO signatories could muster only 12 divisions to face the Soviet leviathan. The long-term consequence of this was that NATO became locked into an atomic strategy for the defence of Europe. But here an unresolvable problem arose. How could nuclear weapons be used to defend a geographical area as densely populated as Europe? As NATO evolved, its Nuclear Planning Group tried endlessly to resolve this conundrum; but the efforts proved futile. Under the Democrats the USA had sought a global conventional capability in order to deter Communist aggression at every level. NATO endorsed this at a meeting in Portugal in 1952 which set ambitious conventional force levels, known as the 'Lisbon goals'. But these were never achieved, and were downplayed by the new Eisenhower administration, which introduced a changed policy known as the 'New Look', which was based on National Security Council document 162/2. The centrepiece of this was the strategic doctrine of 'massive retaliation', which alerted the Soviet leadership to the clear threat of a huge nuclear counter-attack if Soviet forces moved against Western Europe. In a speech to the Council on Foreign Relations, and in a subsequent article in *Foreign Affairs,* Secretary of State John Foster Dulles defined the essence of the policy as 'a great capacity to retaliate, instantly, and by means and at places of our choosing'.[29]

This policy marked an important shift in US thinking. In the late 1940s some analysts had pondered whether the 50 or so bombs the US possessed were enough to make a plan, such as Operation Halfmoon, built on strategic bombing, credible.[30] Indeed, the Harmon Report of 1949 was overtly sceptical about the nuclear option.[31] However, with the decision to develop the nuclear fusion hydrogen bomb in 1950, and its successful test in 1952, as well as cheaper means to produce fission bombs, there was an abundance of nuclear firepower by 1954. As Bernard Brodie noted, nuclear weapons 'can no longer be regarded as exceedingly scarce or costly'.[32]

The fission device dropped on Hiroshima had an explosive power of less than 20 kilotons. It flattened a defined area of the city, and killed 64,000 people with its immediate effects. War plans based on the use of 40 or 50 such devices might result in several million casualties. But the hydrogen bomb opened up the vista of truly awesome levels of destruction. The device which the USA tested in November 1952 had an explosive power greater than 10 megatons – that is, 500 times the magnitude of the Hiroshima bomb. Clearly it could be used to wipe out whole urban/metropolitan areas. In 1949 members of the General Advisory Committee of the AEC, including Oppenheimer, noted that such weapons made the extermination of civilian populations inevitable; the H-bomb was a weapon of genocide.[33] This was a portent of a policy of complete nihilism, and as we saw in the previous chapter, US war plans at the end of the 1950s envisaged enemy casualties in the range of 200 to 300 million. From the point of view of political legitimacy, massive retaliation meant that those living beneath the nuclear shield needed the reassurance that a policy which could lead to unimaginable levels of destruction was somehow 'rational'. But how could this be done?

Political consensus in the 1950s made the task of legitimating nuclear policy easier, because there was a high degree of trust between leaders and those they led. In West Germany, which was admitted to NATO in 1955, the leadership were determined to be good allies and to emphasize their 'Western' identity. In the wider society energies were consumed in the economic miracle which re-established prosperity. In response to the nightmare of the Nazi period, the German populace turned away from forms of political involvement which highlighted normative questions, and focused their attention on their instrumental attachment to the new economic programme.[34] Instinctively, the fear of authoritarianism provided ready-made support for anti-Soviet ideology. Regarding issues of security, the Germans passively accepted the doctrine prescribed by the USA.

Despite consensus and acquiescence, the 1950s showed how NATO's front-line state could be jolted by the clumsy handling of nuclear issues. In parallel with the massive level of strategic armaments in the hands of the Strategic Air Command, the 1950s saw the arrival in Europe of large numbers of tactical nuclear weapons for battlefield use, with yields in the range of 2 to 20 kilotons. The first weapons deployed included the Long Tom cannon and Honest John missile. In the event of war, these were to be used to counter the conventional numerical superiority of the Red Army. But again the problem arose that Soviet forces might be engaged close to West German population centres. In an infamous war game known as Carte Blanche, played in 1955, a scenario was enacted in which Soviet ground forces were halted by a limited nuclear riposte. In the exercise 355 nuclear devices were detonated in two days. The games assessors calculated that 1.7 million West Germans had died, and another 3.5 million had been wounded.[35] This assessment ignored the effects of radioactive fall-out.[36] Carte Blanche was played out in Holland, Germany and North Africa. Another exercise, Sage Brush, was performed in Louisiana. Here 70 devices were used that were all in the range below 40 kilotons. In the Sage Brush game the umpires ruled that all life had 'ceased to exist'.[37]

The results of these exercises were leaked to the press, and caused considerable anxiety. What they showed was that if attention was really focused on what a nuclear defence policy might mean, then anxiety would be difficult to manage. Emotionally, the best way to deal with this was to emphasize the role of deterrence. Europeans became reluctant to discuss war in anything other than generalities, and continued to enthuse over a nuclear policy which they maintained made war inconceivable.

The rationality of scenarios of tactical nuclear defence was further undermined by the fact that after 1956 Warsaw Pact forces were also equipped with short-range tactical weapons. In response, the community of strategic analysts developed the idea of limited tactical nuclear war, where bargaining and diplomacy would control escalation. But this was not debated in the wider political community. Europe had to adopt the make-believe mentality that nuclear war was unthinkable. Bernard Brodie summed up the position neatly in 1959: 'The typical citizen does not believe that there is any chance of nuclear war occurring. In that respect he is completely wrong.'[38]

Throughout the 1950s nuclear war planners tried to resolve these dilemmas, and in the USA some of the defence analysts working in think-tanks were highly critical of Republican defence policy. But Eisenhower remained largely unperturbed, realizing perhaps that the best way to deal with nuclear weapons policy was to leave it on the back burner. In Europe, though, the twists and turns of the nuclear issue threw up yet another problem. After the late 1950s it became clear that the USA itself was vulnerable to attack from Soviet strategic forces. In reality, the threat was greatly exaggerated, but nevertheless it was clear that the USSR now had two strategic bombers (TU 20 Bear and MYA-4 Bison) that could reach the USA. Further, as Sputnik dramatically indicated, the USSR's missile programme was bearing fruit. American analysts were deeply concerned by these developments. In European diplomatic and military circles an unthinkable question began to be asked: if the USA was now vulnerable to Soviet nuclear forces, why would it risk its own cities to defend Europe? This served to accelerate the drive in Britain and France for an independent deterrent – a 'second centre' as the British called it. But it also led to to another bizarre twist in strategic logic. Limited-war scenarios grew out of the desire to minimize destruction in Europe, should war break out. But because some Europeans now believed that the USA might back away from a strategic confrontation with the USSR, there emerged a drive to deploy and target nuclear forces in such a way as to guarantee escalation to the strategic level. What made sense politically was nonsense militarily; coupling the USA to Europe's defence guaranteed massive escalation. In European eyes deterrence was enhanced when the plans for war were literally insane – an idea lampooned in the film *Dr Strangelove* (1964), in which an accidental strike on the USSR by a SAC B52 leads to the automatic detonation of a Soviet doomsday weapon.

Other potential conflicts in security policy erupted in Europe after 1960, with the arrival of the Kennedy administration in Washington. As I showed in Chapter 4, Kennedy brought into government many of the analysts working on defence planning in universities and think-tanks. But the key institutional link was with RAND. Amongst others, Charles Hitch, Alain Enthoven, Henry Rowen, Andrew Marshall and Daniel Ellsberg made the move to the capital from Santa Monica.[39] William Kaufman and Harvard's Thomas Schelling were also hired as consultants. Under Secretary McNamara's leadership, these analysts created a regime which sought to rationalize nuclear policy. But in reality this only served to let the atomic genie out of the bottle. The revolution which the Pentagon instigated brought the issue of war in Europe back to the centre of political debate. Under the umbrella idea of counter-force McNamara wanted a European policy with more conventional forces, smaller-yield atomic weapons, and increased accuracy of nuclear weapon systems.[40] In 1962 another NATO war game, code-name Fallex 62, was played utilizing some of the new thinking. But again, results were leaked and published, this time in *Der Spiegel*. According to the report, nuclear weapons were used only to attack military targets, yet the umpires calculated 10 to 15 million deaths.[41] As Kruschev remarked, nuclear war was 'stupid, stupid, stupid'.

THE AGE OF ANXIETY

In the 1950s consensus ruled the narrative portrayal of security issues. But anxiety was never far beneath the surface of either popular culture or elite representations of nuclear security. While it may not often have been discussed openly, many analysts and politicians felt an acute sense of fear concerning the USA's vulnerability. After NSC 68, as strategic forces were built up, some strategists continued to stress the risk from a Soviet surprise attack. The novel fact for the USA was that its security was now at the mercy of the Soviet leadership. It might be possible to deter aggression, but no direct physical defence against nuclear attack was available. Gradually, in the wider society, a general consciousness of the possible effects of an atomic war became pervasive. In art, film and literature nuclear war issues began to be explored. Also, as the Federal Government began to promote civil defence measures, every American family began to realize that the inconceivable and unthinkable was just remotely possible.

The advent of a perception of a possible future doomsday dented the ideology of modernist progress. In the mainstream narrative of political culture, American society was benefiting from the innovative technologies created by science; but science had now introduced a wild card into the game. A device invented by the USA now threatened the future of mankind. How, then, could such an unsettling development be controlled?

A variety of responses to the bomb have allowed the creed of state security to be maintained. As we have seen, in the 1950s the US public trusted their government, and tended to believe the reassurances they were given. At the time a child-like innocence helped to pacify the population. In Nevada people would actually go to visit the areas close to the atomic test site in order to watch the explosions. Both they, and those resident in the area, were exposed to more radioactivity than was safe, but an alarming naivety about the effects of radioactivity persisted.[42] What was inconceivable to most people was that the Federal Government and the AEC might be engaged in activities that would endanger ordinary citizens.

In the 1950s the political control of Hollywood helped to reassure a film output which glossed over the realities of war, and tried to reassure the public about the nuclear future. As Franklin asserts, 'Almost without exception, movies that dealt openly with atomic weapons from 1952 through 1958 were Cold War propaganda tracts.'[43] The films he has in mind include *The Atomic City* (1952), *Invasion USA* (1952), *Hell and High Water* (1954), *Strategic Air Command* (1955) and *Bombers-B52* (1957). The trend had started in 1952 with the semi-documentary *Above and Beyond*, in which the commander of the plane that bombed Hiroshima, Colonel Paul Tibbets, is played by Robert Taylor. In the film the tragedy of Hiroshima is portrayed as the pressure put on the Tibbets's marriage by the secret training he is undergoing. The clear subtext of the film is that civilians should not meddle in military affairs, that secrecy is essential, and that the bomb is actually a blessing.[44] In other films displacement is achieved by focusing on the flyers and the planes, and not the possibility of war. The message in *Strategic Air Command* and *Bombers-B52* was that the USA's defence was in safe and capable hands and that the war-plane was a beautiful, highly beneficial technology.

The images and representations in these films were a fantasy. In *Above and Beyond* the syrupy love-story has a happy ending; but in reality, the Tibbets's marriage ended in divorce. In SAC the strain of being the backbone of the US's strategic forces led to psychological and emotional problems. As Weart comments, 'Alcoholism was a widespread problem in SAC for decades. The officers' relations with their wives tended to be unusually formal and unromantic, while extramarital sex relations became common.'[45] In the navy, as well, those charged with the awesome task of nuclear retaliation were not as Hollywood portrayed them:

> The public did not know that Rickover's men, like LeMay's, had morale problems and a high divorce rate. Nobody publicized the fact that in a typical year one out of every twenty-six missile submariners was referred to a psychiatrist and some had to be hospitalized for paranoid schizophrenia and other mental illnesses.[46]

Attempts at reassurance provided by popular films were reinforced by a propaganda campaign by the Federal Government and the AEC. The first Federal Civil Defense Administration booklet, *Survival under a Nuclear Attack,* offered citizens the following comforting observation: 'lingering radioactivity ... is no more to be feared than typhoid fever'.[47] In films for children, a lovable little turtle called Bert prompted kids to shelter under their desks at the cue 'Duck and Cover'.

Meanwhile another campaign by the AEC was launched to convince Americans of the peaceful benefits of the atom. 'Atoms for Peace' was launched in the White House in 1946, and rehashed the pre-war conception of a cheap supply of unrestricted energy. In 1948 the AEC and General Electric produced the comic book *Dagwood Spits the Atom,* which was distributed free to millions of citizens. Here a magic genie has been released which will solve all America's problems.[48] In 1956 this theme was expanded in Disney's extraordinary *Our Friend the Atom,* where again the atom is America's friend. Most extraordinary of all, as Trevor Findlay has shown, was a campaign to convince people of the benefits of peaceful nuclear explosions. Contamination was already occurring because of the atmospheric tests, but now the AEC wanted to use explosions for mining and other projects.[49]

But as the 1950s wore on, the AEC and the pro-nuclear strategists ceased to have it all their own way. Consensus and coercion masked a critical perspective which now began to show itself. In 1955 an Atoms for Peace conference denied a platform to Herman Müller, a former Nobel prize-winner, who had researched the effects of radiation on DNA. Eisenhower supported the AEC line, but some critical stirrings were apparent in the press.[50] In the wake of this, a groundswell of opinion developed in support of a ban on nuclear tests. In the middle classes an awareness dawned that radiation might harm babies through damage to genetic material. Within the emotional argument over nuclear weapons there was now a bifurcation. Consensus was sought for the nuclear policy against the USSR on the emotional grounds of patriotism and anti-communism. There was a dim perception of the risk of nuclear war, but cognitively the possibility was largely denied. However, the effects of nuclear tests on children and the unborn was a problem of the here and now which some scientists claimed was real. The opponents of nuclear weapons and nuclear testing now had an emotional anchor for their critique.

In 1957 the saintly Albert Schweitzer called for a test ban, and the same year the prominent American biochemist Linus Pauling organized a petition signed by 2,000 scientists, who revealed their disgust with the AEC. Subsequently the hearings of the Joint Committee on Atomic Energy revealed the scientific community to be split, with Edward Teller at one end of a continuum and Pauling at the other. The AEC admitted at these hearings that there was some risk, but Teller made ludicrous claims to the effect that some radiation might actually be beneficial.[51] Teller wanted more tests, an ABM programme and a national system of shelters.

Counter-offensives were also launched by groups seeking more bombs and those who emphasized the USSR's growing lead in strategic weapons – a lead that was entirely fictional. In 1957 Eisenhower received the Gaither Panel report on the US's overall strategic position. The report was similar to NSC 68 of 1950, with its emphasis on US weakness and the need for a massive increase in strategic forces. The Gaither report, *Deterrence and Survival in the Nuclear Age*, demanded an extra 44 billion dollars to be spent over the next five years, with new deployments of Thor, Jupiter and Titan missiles.[52]

In the mainstream media, the normative stress always underscored the pro-nuclear position. But the state did not have total control of all discursive forms of representation. As Franklin points out, 1950s hard-core science fiction offered some surprisingly radical views on both issues of war and wider social questions.[53] Failure to control this output probably resulted from underestimating its significance and the nature of its audience. The most avid consumers of science fiction were children, now reading magazines with a content unknown to their parents. In the 1950s comic sci-fi introduced a novel range of grotesque intruders and threats into the narrative portrayal of white, affluent, suburban America.

In film media *The Day the Earth Stood Still* (1951) and *Five* (1951) just preceded HUAC's total control of Hollywood, and both were critical of the nuclear arms race. After 1951 sci-fi films dealt with atomic issues more indirectly, usually by depicting a struggle with monsters and aliens. Nevertheless, films such as *Them* (1954) and *The Beast from 20,000 Fathoms* (1953) showed new threats to man's survival created indirectly by nuclear weapons. The monsters in these films were invariably mutations resulting from atomic tests or strange alien creatures from other planets. Sci-fi was unveiling a new genre of 'others' that threatened modern man. As Susan Sontag has argued, these films reveal an 'imagination of disaster', which shows how the atomic age raised to consciousness the real possibility of the total destruction of civilization.[54]

Implicit here was a new ambivalence towards science. Before the Second World War, popular cultural representations of the scientist often depicted a crank or eccentric. But with the Manhattan Project, science had merged with big government and big money. Scientists were now serious people in smart suits. Also the post-war home was full of useful inventions created by scientists, which improved the quality of life. In the value system of corporatist pluralism, science was now situated at the centre of state and society. But at the same time there was the question of who controlled science, and whether the forces now unleashed by scientific research were actually too powerful. As Biskind argues, 1950s sci-fi revealed a conflict between the men of authority – usually soldiers – and the men of science.[55] At least in some quarters, there was a belief that science was dangerous, as well as beneficial.

As Ira Chernos has argued, nuclear issues have also mingled closely with millennial and eschatological fantasies, where themes of death and rebirth have merged with religious motifs of sin and redemption. Here the bomb is essentially a theological construct, with the awesome power now absent in an anthropomorphic God congealed in a scientific device.[56] In Elias Canetti's memorable statement, 'God has waited patiently and steps forward from the atom.' [57] The bomb is the *Deus ex machina*; it demands reverence and respect.

Again, this raises interesting issues about the atomic bomb and modernity. On many levels the bomb seemed to undermine a modernist image of progress. In the atomic bomb, the urban mass society of consumer affluence and order confronted its possible nemesis. Future-oriented notions of progress now posed the dilemma of termination. As Julian Cracq suggested, history had 'essentially become a warning addressed by the future to the present'.[58] From an Enlightenment point of view, the human race's end in a nuclear holocaust would be utterly farcical, and would undermine central tenets of modernist thought. Coker notes:

> By the 1950s it was no longer possible to see history as Vico had 150 years before as a cycle governed by providence. Nor was it possible to see it as Hegel's progressive force that emerged through the dialectical development of the World Spirit. It was even more difficult to imagine it as a natural process governed by scientific laws which, reversing Hegel on his head, unfolded dialectically.[59]

In the 1950s neither version of the modernist utopia could transcend the bomb. Both the USSR and the USA were vulnerable to annihilation, and their future, unlike mutual destruction, was far from assured.

In representational culture, films with monsters and blobs usually ended with the defeat of the 'other'. Sontag has construed this as the vicarious defeat of nuclear war.[60] But other representations, particularly in the sci-fi genre, depicted the complete or near extermination of the human race. In some cases this served as a warning; but some popular culture in the 1950s seemed tired of the world, and perhaps ready to embrace Armageddon. The religious encoding of the nuclear issue, as we have seen, allowed ideas of rebirth and regeneration to penetrate some accounts of the nuclear dilemma. Here was another potential breach in nuclear rationality. From a millennial perspective, the destruction of a rotten, corrupt world called forth a new beginning, and this would be a desirable end. Moreover, as Weart points out, individuals who felt they had no place or status in this world might actively seek the apocalypse: 'If a person who already felt victimised believed that catastrophe would end in release, perhaps even in a rebirth of all the world, should he not want to drop the bombs?'[61] In the discourse of nuclear strategy there was a perception that there was just the remotest chance that an accident might trigger war. But what if someone unstable had their finger on the nuclear button? The official narrative of the security state presented the nuclear guardians as sober, rational and cautious. However, back in the 1940s, Secretary of Defense James Forrestal had exhibited worrying behaviour, and had committed suicide by jumping out of a window. The real nightmare, though, was that the far right might manage to place a religious zealot in the White House – a situation which seemed far from remote in the 1980s.

Belief in a post-apocalypse world that was better than the one that modern man actually inhabited was not just a fantasy for the religious. In US culture a major response to the bomb has been the construction of a genre of survivalist science fiction in which individuals recapture the original spirit of the pioneer in the wilderness. As Franklin argues, this links with deep-seated strains in US culture concerning individualism and the frontier. Again, the attraction of the bomb is precisely its capacity to destroy the negative features of the modern world: 'The city – envisioned as a hopeless morass of pollution, overcrowding, decadence, and enfeebling interdependence – is obliterated, thus freeing the would-be frontiersman to live out his yearnings for primitive, manly self-reliance in a restored wilderness.'[62]

Millennial and survivalist fantasies were ostensibly not based on the fear of the bomb which we are discussing here. However, they helped to blast a hole in the consensus position on nuclear weapons, because they raised to consciousness the possibility of nuclear destruction. The mainstream position had always been that although we were prepared for nuclear war, it was virtually inconceivable. This understanding has been that of the centre, and it has been best articulated in the dry, technical language of official strategic documents. It has been a welcome message; it speaks to people in the same style as the airline pilot whose calm words before take-off reassure the anxious. Here we do not want excitement or emotion; we require the voice of sober, technical competence.

But with nuclear weapons, even the centre had to remind us what to do if the worst transpired; civil defence measures brought disaster to life. Coupled with the increasing presence of the nuclear issue in popular culture, these served to universalize the reality of the nuclear predicament. Towards the end of the 1950s the containment of atomic anxiety began to fail. While strategists and their masters kept the faith, many in the public and some leading scientists began to speak out against the arms race. In popular culture the flood-gates opened: 'The warnings that had been dammed up in the isolated reservoir of hard-core science fiction now burst forth in a flood of science fiction reaching a far wider audience, including novels read by millions and movies seen by tens of millions around the globe.'[63] Some of the major publications included Neville Shute's *On the Beach* (1957), Helen Clarkson's *The Last Day* (1959), Walter M. Miller's *A Canticle For Liebowitz* (1959), Mordecai Roshwald's *Level Seven* (1957) and *A Small Armageddon* (1962). There were also major films, such as *On the Beach* (1959), *Fail-Safe* (1964) and *Dr Strangelove* (1964). These critical voices did not mean that the whole edifice of state security would immediately be challenged. But some were stirring against the consensus. In Britain on Good Friday 1958, protesters marched to the nuclear facility at Aldermaston. In April 1957 a protest was made by 17 leading German physicists. In the USA Herman Kahn's *On Thermonuclear War* was reviewed in *Scientific American*, where it was described 'as permeated with bloodthirsty irrationality'.[64]

Everywhere, no matter what their political orientation, individuals had an image in their mind's eye of the mushroom cloud which signalled Armageddon. In dreams nuclear war surfaced as the new ultimate nightmare, and those concerned found themselves fearful of the future for their children. Nuclear fear was becoming ubiquitous. Coker notes: 'The fear of nuclear war, unforeseen, sudden and inescapable seemed to be encoded in the consciousness of 20th century man.'[65]

The nightmare dreamscape of nuclear war became a possible reality in 1962 during the Cuban missile crisis. After John F. Kennedy was informed by the CIA that parts for SS4 and SS5 intermediate-range missiles were being unloaded from Soviet ships in Havana, the USA put a naval blockade around Cuba. Kennedy warned Nikita Kruschev that the USSR risked 'dire consequences to the whole world'. Kruschev responded by underlining the fact that the risk was of 'reciprocal extermination'. Meanwhile, in October, Soviet ships sailed towards the American blockade. In Washington shovels and sandbags were sold out, as one in eight Americans took civil defence precautions and one in fifty built or purchased a fall-out shelter.[66] Now citizens were 'thinking the unthinkable'; the bizarre world of Herman Kahn's *On Thermonuclear War* had become reality. In his opus on nuclear war he had argued that in order to effect deterrence, it would be necessary for the USA to credibly threaten to go to the nuclear brink. Now Kennedy had done precisely that, and a mesmerized Kahn carried his radio everywhere during the 13-day crisis to ensure he missed none of the action. Fantasy and reality had merged.

The odd thing about the Cuban missile crisis was that it brought home the potential insanity of the nuclear arms race, but also marked a turning away. After Cuba interest in matters concerning atomic weapons virtually disappeared in popular culture and scholarly journals. The debates continued in the military, government and think-tanks, but outside these circles interest was muted. Critical political interest turned to the Vietnam War. Also détente, established in the late 1960s and cemented in the SALT 1 treaty of 1972, seemed to pacify the wider public. Bertrand Russell lamented the fate of the Campaign for Nuclear Disarmament: 'most people feel utterly paralysed by the vast impersonal machinery of war and state power'.[67] While attention was elsewhere, the strategic liberal establishment declared the arms race a draw, and enthused over a stalemate, which became known as 'mutual assured destruction'. But assured destruction was not the policy of either superpower. Behind the veil of deterrence, both sides continued to seek weapons that could hit their opponent's forces in such a way as to make a first strike plausible. At the same time, counter-force targeting was enhanced by the new technology of MIRV, multiple independently targetable re-entry vehicles. With MIRV a number of warheads could be put on the same 'bus' in the tip of a missile and be targeted independently. One missile could cover a number of separate targets. At the same time the superpowers also sought more accurate systems in order to enhance 'single shot kill probability'. While both sides talked deterrence, actual deployments revealed a search for a strike force which could disarm the opponent. Missile-carrying submarines remained a problem, but in 1957 the US Navy had developed SOSUS – Sound Surveillance System – and in 1962, during the Cuban crisis, every Soviet nuclear submarine in the vicinity of Cuba had been located and trailed. Thus, while the perception may have been that the arms race was more restrained, new, destabilizing technologies came to fruition in the 1960s and 1970s. By the late 1970s both sides were more massively defended, but felt less secure. A new, chronic anxiety was spawned.

DISMANTLING CONSENSUS

The 1970s was a trying time for political elites in the West. The post-war boom was over, and economic difficulties were compounded by problems of political and social disorder. Beginning in 1968, Europe was racked by student unrest and increasing trade union militancy. The Keynesian social compact was failing. In the United States the Civil Rights movement and the anti-Vietnam War protests created a major threat to social order. In the early 1970s the costs of the Vietnam War created an economic crisis, which led to the end of dollar convertibility and other drastic protectionist measures by the Nixon administration. Then in 1973 the office of the Presidency was besmirched by scandal and disgrace. Watergate showed that the very centre of the US state was rotten.

If things were bad at home, they were arguably worse overseas. After the Yom Kippur War of 1973, OPEC used its control over global oil supplies to restrict output and quadruple the price of a barrel of oil from $2.50 to $10. The USA and Holland were singled out for harsh treatment, but throughout the West it was clear that prosperity was dependent on cheap supplies of Middle Eastern oil – a fact that made the West a hostage to political instability in that region. After the crisis Western economies succumbed to stagflation; an unwelcome combination of stagnation and inflation.

OPEC also spearheaded a drive by developing countries to challenge the West in other areas. Largely through the United Nations, the group of 77 non-aligned countries drew the West into a debate about the need for a new international economic order, which would redistribute wealth from the rich North to the poor South. Little came of this other than talk, but it showed the West to be on the defensive.

Worst of all for the governing elites and their advisers in the 1970s, the power of the USSR seemed to have massively increased. Détente was supposed to be linked with good behaviour on the part of the USSR. For the West this meant the Soviets not supporting wars of national liberation in the Third World – in other words, not exporting socialism. But for Soviet leaders détente was about the central balance; it was a way of stabilizing the core military strategic relationship in order to ensure peaceful coexistence. Thus détente did not prevent the USSR advancing its goals in Africa and the Middle East. Angola, Mozambique and the Horn of Africa appeared to be now in the Communist orbit.

In the strategic relationship, SALT 1 was meant to stabilize the arms race by preventing a dash to deploy defensive ABM sytems. In the ABM treaty of May 1972 the superpowers relinquished their right to defend themselves against nuclear attack. The political right in the USA were profoundly unhappy about this. But, worse, SALT 1 set an interim limit on offensive missiles which allowed the USSR a larger number of launchers.[68] The left didn't like it either, because it did nothing to hinder the development of MIRV, which the US had deployed on Minuteman 3 in 1970, with the USSR responding in 1974. At the SALT 1 meetings Henry Kissinger believed he had an assurance that the USSR would not replace their SS9s and SS11s with larger missiles.[69] However, these assurances were false. Throughout the 1970s the USSR tested and deployed larger ICBMs such as the SS17, SS18 and SS19. The SS18 was a gigantic launcher with the capacity to carry 30 mirved warheads. SALT 2 in 1978 limited the number of MIRVs to ten per missile. Nevertheless, the USSR now had a formidable strategic weapon able to deliver more megaton-nage than anything in the US arsenal. Ultimately the USSR deployed 308 SS18s in three modifications: Mod. 2 carried eight 900 kiloton warheads, Mod. 3 one gigantic 20-megaton warhead, and Mod. 4 ten 500 megaton warheads. The SS18 was also more accurate than previous Soviet missiles, with a claimed accuracy of 350 metres (circular error probable). (CEP determines the radius of a circle within which 50 per cent of missiles will fall when aimed at a given target.) With a CEP of 350 metres the SS18 could be used to attack hardened counter-force targets, such as missile silos.

In the USA the Soviet missile buildup galvanized the far right into a sustained attack on the Carter Presidency. From the beginning some politicians had been trenchantly opposed to SALT. In Washington, Senator Henry Jackson had long been a bitter opponent of détente. Now in the mid- and late 1970s he was joined by a growing group of advisers, politicians and activists who openly sought to undermine Carter. A key individual here was Richard Perle, who worked as Jackson's staff assistant in the 1970s. Perle was a right-wing zealot with an obsession about arms control, Soviet ICBMs and the USSR's emigration policies.[70] Able, youthful and energetic, he built a reputation as Carter's fiercest critic. He was a key member of the so-called Madison Group, which in a series of meetings at the Madison Hotel in Washington plotted to block SALT 2.

In the late 1970s the right's anxiety was not new, but it was more intense than before, and it confronted a liberal centre that was already on the defensive. Throughout the decade right-wing journals and authors had been attacking what they construed as a sell-out by the centre. According to the right, liberals had intentionally given the USA's strategic superiority away by their pursuit of the policy of assured destruction. This was the central proposition in Edward Luttwak's *The Grand Strategy of the Soviet Union*, which lambasted the liberal position.[71] But it could also be found in the work of Colin Gray, Robert Rummell, Paul Nitze, Robert Tucker, Richard Pipes and many others.[72]

The work of individuals to undermine the liberal consensus was supplemented by the creation of pressure groups which sought to undermine détente. In the late 1960s the Committee to Maintain a Prudent Defense Policy had sprung up in Congress in opposition to SALT. In 1976 the Committee on the Present Danger, originally created at the time of Korea, reformed under the leadership of Paul Nitze and Eugene Rostow, both veteran right-wingers. Even more strident was the American Security Council, which in 1978 merged with the CPD to form the Coalition for Peace through Strength. These groups had the services of many former strategists, and they were able to focus a powerful critique on the policies of the Carter administration.

The particular issue which the right seized upon had a history going back to the 1950s: the vulnerability of US strategic forces. In the past, analysts such as RAND's Albert Wohlstetter had been concerned when Soviet forces were palpably inferior. Now, confronted with formidable rocket forces, the USA actually had something real to fear. But the scenario which came to dominate strategic thinking in the late 1970s still had a remarkable air of fantasy about it. US analysts were anxious over what they termed the 'suicide or surrender' scenario. The new Soviet ICBMs – the SS17 and SS18 – were believed to be capable of knocking out 90 per cent of the USA's land-based missile force. It was argued that, after a surprise attack by Soviet forces, the US President would have only submarine-based strategic forces with which to retaliate. As these were less accurate than land-based systems, their targets would be industrial/urban areas, rather than military assets, which had to be hit accurately. But a strike by US submarine forces would simply call forth Soviet retaliation; it would be an act of suicide. Therefore the rational act would be to surrender. In effect, the right believed that the USA no longer had a deterrent; it had a window of vulnerability. Director of Defense Research and Engineering Richard Delauer expressed it with blunt simplicity: 'The Soviets don't have to pull the trigger. They have superiority. They've got a deterrent and we don't, and that's the window of vulnerablity.'[73]

The right's concern about nuclear inferiority was not just a question of fearing a Soviet attack. In the mental world inhabited by people such as Delauer and Perle, strategic superiority gave its beneficiary a critical resource in the game of world politics. Thus Soviet geo-political gains in the 1970s could be construed as partly the result of US strategic inferiority. Here in fact is a critical difference in the views of liberals and conservatives on nuclear weapons. Beyond the point at which deterrence has been established, liberals see strategic superiority as politically irrelevant. Conservatives, on the other hand, always see a bargaining edge in strategic advantage. Thus, when Reagan came to power in 1980, the right sought superiority in order to coerce Soviet behaviour.

It is not my intention here to investigate in detail the 'suicide or surrender' scenario or the technical aspects of the conservative interpretation of the strategic balance in the late 1970s. 'Suicide or surrender' grew out of a tradition born at RAND, where analysts played statistical combat: a process of modelling the possible outcomes of different scenarios of nuclear war. This particular scenario was modelled by the Studies Analysis and Gaming Agency (SAGA), which was a Joint Chiefs of Staff organization located in the basement of the Pentagon. SAGA is now the Joint Analysis Directorate, which continues to provide essential inputs into defence plans. Modelling has been essential because, as several commentators have pointed out, there was actually no real data on which to base assumptions about the outcome of nuclear war. Pierre Spey put it bluntly and succinctly when he said: 'Strategic analysis is a dream world. It is the realm of data-free analysis.'[74] What became clear in the late 1970s was that analysts who had spent their professional lives modelling thermonuclear war had lost touch with political reality. In his masterful study of the defence intellectuals, Fred Kaplan formed the following conclusion: 'The insidious aspect of the legacy was that it loomed so constantly throughout their professional lives that it was, by now, difficult to think of them as mere theories. They had taken on all the appearances of a scientific-based reality.'[75]

The sense of strategic inferiority felt by the far right was compounded in the late 1970s by the Soviet invasion of Afghanistan and the Iranian seizure of the US embassy in Tehran. As the President sat in the White House unable to devise a means of freeing the hostages, it seemed that the USA really had succumbed to a fundamental malaise. The Tehran crisis and the abortive rescue attempt in April 1980 ('Operation Rice Bowl') sealed Carter's fate. In 1980 the incumbent of the Oval Office went down to a heavy defeat at the hands of Ronald Reagan. The far right now had their own man in the White House.

EMBRACING ARMAGEDDON

A myriad of policy critiques in the 1970s brought many of the former assumptions about nuclear deterrence into disrepute. But inside government a key one was an intelligence estimate in 1976 by so-called Team B. The Team B reports came about because hardliners had long been dissatisfied with the CIA's national intelligence estimate (NIE). For some time members of the President's Foreign Intelligence Advisory Board (PFIAB) had wanted an alternative, independent assessment. In 1976 the new Director of the CIA, George Bush, yielded to pressure and agreed to set up a 'Team B'. 'Team B', made up of individuals on the right and far right, concluded that the USA had long underestimated Soviet defence expenditure. There was now an 'expenditure gap'. They also believed that Soviet intentions had been misunderstood. The alternative report concluded that the USSR sought 'power on a global scale and strategic forces that would have a first strike war winning capability'.[76]

Upon entering office, Ronald Reagan appointed many advisers who endorsed the 'Team B' approach. In response to the perceived threat to USA strategic forces, the USA now sought to reciprocate. Under Secretary of Defense Caspar Weinberger, the Pentagon instituted an unparalleled buildup of nuclear forces in order to be able to wage 'protracted nuclear war' – a policy leaked to the *New York Times*, which in 1982 published extracts of Defense Fiscal Guidance documents. The Fiscal Guidance documents were similar to National Security Decision Directive 13, which the President signed in 1981. According to NSDD 13, the aim of US forces would be to 'prevail and be able to force the Soviet Union to seek earliest termination of hostilities on terms favourable to the United States ... even under the condition of a prolonged war'.[77]

This leak, and other pronouncements by members of the Reagan administration, set alarm bells ringing in the USA and Europe. Insiders knew that the real policy of the USA had never been assured destruction; but in the past the articulation of a counter-force doctrine had never been as strident or aggressive as it was now. With new weapons, such as MX, Trident D5, the B1 and B2 bomber, Cruise and Pershing 2, the administration really did seem to countenance the possibility of nuclear war. All told, the Pentagon claimed it would deploy another 17,000 warheads. Moreover, the public comments made about the USSR, the 'evil empire' which Reagan said he hoped to leave on 'the ash heap of history', were deeply troubling. As I argued in Chapter 4, the threat to a modernist conception of war posed by nuclear weapons was offset by a language and taxonomy of precision, control and sober prudence. But now wild and foolish utterances sprang from the mouths of Reagan officials. One such was T. K. Jones, a former engineer at Boeing who had worked for Paul Nitze. Jones, now working in the Pentagon, had given many lectures where he made notorious comments. But arguably he made a rather foolish move in giving his views to the *Los Angeles Times*. Jones was a keen advocate of civil defence. When pressed on how US citizens would survive a nuclear war, he came up with the following extraordinary recommendation: 'Everyone is going to make it if there are enough shovels to go around. The idea is to dig a hole, and cover it over with a couple of doors and then throw three feet of dirt on top. It's the dirt that does it.'[78]

The Reagan administration was full of individuals who, frankly, from the point of view of the scientific establishment, seemed offbeat, perhaps even mad. Michael Krepon captured the situation neatly: 'The Reagan wave of anti-nuclear sentiment ... was a unique product of bizarre declarations by some of Reagan's advisers, his apparent dependency on them and their presumed hidden agendas, the President's clear unfamiliarity with nuclear issues, and the "cowboy" image he fostered.'[79]

The upshot of this was the creation in Europe and the USA of anti-nuclear movements profoundly fearful of US policy. This had been seen before in Europe, but was utterly novel in the USA. In the early 1980s the 'Freeze Movement' captured the new mood of nuclear anxiety. Through 1982 and 1983 the state legislatures of Maine, Connecticut, Minnesota, Kansas, Vermont, Iowa, New York, Oregon, Massachusetts and Wisconsin called on the US Congress to endorse a freeze on the testing, production and deployment of nuclear weapons. Hundreds of towns and cities organized votes which supported the freeze campaign.[80] In June 1982 a million people assembled and marched in Manhattan to protest the new arms buildup. Reagan had succeeded in creating what had previously seemed inconceivable: a mass movement against the central precepts of the USA's nuclear defence policy. The US protests were also mirrored in Europe, where there were demonstrations in Rome, Amsterdam, Brussels, Bonn, Florence and London. From the point of view of those in government, it was easy to construe the new peace movements as the work of activists and extremists. Both Reagan and Caspar Weinberger suggested as much. But the facts said otherwise. A Harris poll conducted in April 1983 in the USA indicated that 83 per cent of the population supported the freeze. Moreover, conservative and mainstream organizations, such as the Lutheran and Catholic Churches, were in favour. In academia the specialist research and teaching of strategy lost its control of the discursive representation of the issues as ethicists and philosophers entered the fray. Holding the line became difficult, nuclear deterrence no longer reassured.

A novel feature of the eruption of interest in nuclear issues in the 1980s was that former and acting senior military personnel came out against the Reagan policy. In the past, proselytizers like Paul Nitze had managed to link nuclear weapons to issues of loyalty and patriotism. As Falk and Lifton argued, to be anti-nuclear was to be anti-American.[81] But when the critics were NATO generals or former Commanders-in-Chief of Pacific Forces (Admiral Noel Gaylor), this tactic was less successful. In the USA several former holders of the office of Secretary of Defense also attacked the new policy.

Throughout societies in the West, many millions of individuals from the whole spectrum of classes and interests spoke out against the new strategic orthodoxy.

Perhaps as important as the serious intellectual output on nuclear war was a new wave of popular interest expressed in films, novels and records by major artists. In 1983 the major American channels screened the TV film *The Day After,* which had an audience of 100 million.[82] The film showed the USA under strategic attack, with graphic images of the destruction of cities, such as Lawrence in Kansas. It pulled no punches, and attempted to depict how people would be vapourized by the heat from nuclear explosions. The American public was deeply traumatized by the screening, and towns and cities provided counselling for their troubled citizens. In Britain the film was run on a Saturday night in November 1984. The following morning an ashen-looking Minister of Defence, Michael Heseltine, appeared on television to reassure the viewing public that 'it was not going to happen'; but the cat was out of the bag. The public was deeply shaken by what it had seen.

The ground-swell of opinion for a freeze led to resolutions in the General Assembly of the UN proposing that the nuclear powers stop the testing and production of nuclear weapons. Thus the governments of NATO countries were on the defensive, not just domestically, but in the whole of the world. There was now a global perception that the nuclear policies of the superpowers were destabilizing and dangerous. In the USA the eminent scientist Carl Sagan published a paper indicating that a nuclear war would lead to the 'nuclear winter'.[83] His model was based on the simple fact that nuclear detonations above a certain power would waft smoke and soot up into the earth's troposphere and stratosphere and block out the sun. It was estimated that the subsequent darkness would last for months, and would lead to a significant cooling of the earth. As a results, survivors of the direct consequences of a nuclear war (heat, blast and radiation) would also be confronted with an extended period of coldness and darkness. In addition, many areas of the Earth which had previously been fertile would now be unable to produce food. Sagan's view was endorsed by the eminent Soviet dissident physicist Andrei Sakharov: 'All-out nuclear war would mean the destruction of contemporary civilization, throw man back centuries, cause the death of millions or billions of people, and, with a certain probability, would cause man to be destroyed as a biological species.'[84]

Many of these themes were taken up in Jonathan Schell's best-selling book *The Fate of the Earth*, published in 1982.[85] With the assistance of a leading US physicist, Schell spelt out in plain language the general effects of nuclear war and the specific effects of a 1 megaton warhead detonating over Manhattan. Amongst other things, what shocked readers about this book was its directness. The majority of strategy books left a profound reality deficit at the point where war was actually described. As Thomas Power once remarked, 'my mind just stops there'. Nuclear war was 'an exchange of cities'; dead civilians were 'collateral damage'; opposing armies suffered 'attrition'; and the nuclear force relationships were expressed in a 'drawdown' curve. But Schell simply stated plainly what would happen to real people in a nuclear war. As with the film *The Day After*, the effect was dramatic, and the book helped to restyle the form of the debate on nuclear weapons. In the previous decades strategists had slipped quietly past the need to speak of moral issues. As insider Bernard Brodie remarked: 'Thus the strategic writer too, will normally regard moral considerations as tiresome impediments to the flow of one's thoughts.'[86] But after Schell's book there was a veritable surge of publications on precisely the moral aspects of nuclear policy. In the USA the prestigious journal *Ethics* devoted a whole special issue to the question in April 1985. In Britain the eminent philosopher and theologian Anthony Kenny provided a devastating critique in his incisive book *The Logic of Deterrence* (1985). Governments already on the defensive on the technical issues of policy were now also in the dock accused of immorality.

COUNTER-OFFENSIVE

In the whole of the post-war period the 1980s produced the greatest challenge to the ideological edifice of state security and the material interests of the high-tech aerospace defence industries of Europe and America. On the surface the policies of politicians such as Thatcher and Reagan produced a cornucopia for such industries, but the loss of legitimation for defence promised difficult times ahead. The truth of all this is difficult to disentangle because, as the peace agenda took hold, the new right claimed it as a victory for its approach to superpower relations. After the fact, the resumption of arms control and the end of the Cold War have been seen as the greatest triumph of the new right in the 1980s. Its policy for dealing with the USSR worked. But this is nonsense. The inclination of many of the key officials in the US government in the early 1980s was to oppose arms control at any cost. Significant people brought into the defence and arms control branch of government, such as Kenneth Adelman and Richard Perle, were overtly hostile to the idea of any deals with the USSR. If we do them the justice of believing that they were sincere, we should take a radically different view of the 1980s from the one which has been bequeathed as common sense. When Adelman took over as head of Reagan's Arms Control and Disarmament Agency, he made the following point about his new job: 'My policy would be to do it for political reasons ... I think it's a sham.'[87] How, then, did the superpowers draw away from the nuclear brink and establish a new détente prior to the real end of the Cold War? More precisely, how did the new cold warriors become the architects of peace?

A PERSONAL INITIATIVE

Ronald Reagan came into the White House committed to an ultra-right agenda. But on strategic issues he lacked any real knowledge or insight. He sought to build up America's strategic forces, and he was briefed on the window of vulnerability issue, which by now had become the vexed question of how to base America's new ICBM, the MX missile. Like millions of other Americans, he did not fully realize that the USA had no effective defences against missile attack. This became clear during a campaign visit Reagan made to the North American Air Defense Command (NORAD) in 1979. While being briefed on how the USA would track incoming Soviet missiles, Reagan asked when they would be shot down. Apparently he was deeply shocked to hear that there was no defence against the missiles, and that all that could be done was to predict their targets and to pass the information on to the National Military Command Centre.[88] He was already a bitter opponent of the ABM treaty, but clearly not an informed one. On his return flight to California, he outlined his anxieties to his campaign manager, and discussed the possibility of putting a commitment to strategic defences in his presidential manifesto.[89]

Ronald Reagan was an outsider. He was not known to the liberal intellectual or scientific establishment. Many of his closest friends and advisers were California businessmen or show business personalities.

His so-called kitchen cabinet comprised business people, such as the brewer Joseph Coors and Karl Bendetsen of Champion Industries. In general he was not interested in deep intellectual questions, which he thought tended to engender a gloomy or serious outlook. He had a 'sunny' outlook, and liked people who were cheerful and optimistic. For Reagan the whole business of deterrence was depressing. The complicated arguments showing that the USA's vulnerability was actually a blessing were anathema to him. After his visit to NORAD, he believed that surely there must be a better answer to the problem of the Soviet threat than that of assured destruction.

The answer was the Strategic Defence Initiative, or Star Wars, as it became known after Ted Kennedy's intervention. In the 1960s, while he was Governor of California, Reagan had met Edward Teller. Teller invited him to visit the Lawrence Livermore Weapons Laboratory near San Francisco. During the visit he told Reagan about the possibility of deploying a defence against Soviet missiles that could be based in space. Teller had been a long-term advocate of ABM, and was a bitter opponent of the technocrats around McNamara at the Pentagon. Reagan was impressed by the idea, but the 1960s was the wrong time to promote an alternative to deterrence.

In the early 1980s strategic defence was being promoted by right-wing think-tanks and institutes such as the Heritage Foundation, the Hertz Foundation, the Hoover Institute and the Citizens Advisory Council on National Space Policy. A new organization, the Marshall Foundation, disbursed funds to those keen to produce studies favourable to a new defence initiative. The aim of these organizations was, to launch a counter-offensive against the establishment's view of deterrence. The Heritage Foundation promoted a high-profile project called 'High Frontier'. In a major report in 1982 High Frontier was launched as an alternative to the 'immoral and bankrupt' doctrine of mutually assured destruction.[90]

In early 1982 Ronald Reagan was briefed on the feasibility of strategic defence by Edward Teller, who was seeking enlarged support for the top-secret 'Project Excalibur' at Lawrence Livermore. Excalibur was under the direction of a protégé of Teller's, Lowell Wood. Wood's O Group, a brilliant cadre of unconventional young scientists, were pursuing work on so-called third-generation nuclear weapons. Their aim was to use small nuclear warheads as the power source for a new form of laser, which could generate a powerful, coherent beam of electromagnetic radiation in the form of X-rays. In the meeting with Reagan, Teller apparently convinced the President that the X-ray laser could be based on battle stations in space or 'popped up' from missiles fired from submarines, and could destroy incoming Soviet missiles. A similar message was given to Reagan by the High Frontier group. But the head of High Frontier, retired Lieutenant-General Daniel O. Graham, told the President that their project could use existing technologies to create an effective shield against nuclear attack.

The President's depressing briefing at NORAD in 1979 had strongly disposed him to this message. Further, he was impressed by the optimism of the supporters of strategic defence. The mentality of the advocates was optimistic, and it resonated with Reagan's own conception of American inventiveness and superiority. As I have indicated above, the triumphalism inherent in the USA's narrative of its own destiny was blunted by nuclear weapons. The modernist underpinning of an American vision of scientific and social progress was also undercut by Soviet H-bombs. In a perverse twist of fate the USA had let its greatest enemy develop the means to destroy it. For those advocating what became known as 'Star Wars', this was the great sin of the liberal establishment, which had betrayed America's future. Star Wars would re-establish US dominance at the next frontier – space. It would also rekindle narrative myths concerning exploration and technological genius. A new drama of exceptionalism could be played out at the final frontier.

Ronald Reagan's interest in strategic defence was unknown to many of his official advisers and to the key actors in the inter-agency process, which monitored the progress of initiatives which might demand serious attention in the National Security Council. In March 1983, when the SDI programme was unveiled in the famous Star Wars speech, it had bypassed the normal agency vetting and evaluation process. To many senior members of the government and their advisers, it came as an extremely unpleasant surprise. Legend has it that officials were keen to leave Washington in order to avoid being questioned about the initiative. Secretary of State George Schultz had a day's notice of the speech, and was given an 'eyes only' copy. The hawks in the Pentagon, including Perle and Weinberger, thought the policy foolish and premature. At the time many commentators expressed astonishment that such a major policy initiative had escaped the normal processes of bureaucratic politics. But with hindsight it seems to me that this move of Reagan's was perhaps his one and only really nimble, astute manoeuvre in office. In scientific terms many of the ideas were so 'whacky' that they were unlikely to survive close scrutiny. Also, as the allies soon pointed out, SDI turned four decades of NATO doctrine on its head. With no consultation, deterrence had been replaced by defence. Thus the particular way that the President brought SDI to the attention of the world was probably the only feasible one. In PR terms he scored a major victory over the strategic liberals. By appealing over the heads of the establishment directly to the people, he made countering his proposal a difficult issue. The public had been told that they could now be defended, and that the curse of nuclear vulnerability could be lifted. It was an irresistible idea. Moreover, it captured a new spirit in popular culture, which, since George Lucas's *Star Wars* trilogy, had been saturated with a new diet of science fiction.

The President's plan to render 'nuclear weapons impotent and obsolete', to counter the 'awesome Soviet missile threat', and to 'intercept and destroy strategic ballistic missiles before they reached our soil' was a piece of pure theatre – although I believe that Reagan himself was sincere about the proposal. In conceptual terms it presupposed a revolution in everything that was known about the history of warfare. SDI envisaged an ending: the new defence would end the nuclear arms race for good. In the past one technology or another had privileged defence over offence, or vice versa. But history showed that the lead was ephemeral. Previous research by the USA in the 1960s had revealed defence to be more expensive than offence in a ratio of 3:1. Regarding SDI, any technologies that worked were likely to be effectively countered. But this was defeatism. The key to SDI was its basis in cultural assumptions and myth. As Zolly Zuckerman noted, an extraordinary feature of the debate, as it developed, was that those lining up to assert its feasibility were individuals utterly unqualified in the disciplines which had the competence to make a considered judgement.[91]

Initially the strategic community failed to see the PR gift inherent in SDI. From the point of view of the beleaguered national security establishment, what Reagan had given them was a counter-offensive against the new movement for peace. SDI profoundly complicated the arguments about nuclear weapons and peace. The establishment was fearful because it was looking at the policy in rationalistic terms. Also NATO country elites wondered what would happen to European security. But in middle America SDI helped to cloud the issue of what the administration's policy meant. The manic Cold War rhetoric was replaced by talk of perpetual peace. In one briefing Reagan even said that the USA might share the technology with the USSR. This was slightly odd as, when SDI came under challenge, some supporters described the USSR's already advanced schemes.

After the initial furore over SDI, many administration officials came round to the President's point of view. Further, organizations and businesses linked to the high-tech side of aerospace saw the possibility of funding for new advanced research. Universities and their sceptical scientists were bought off with massive research grants, often awarded with less than the normal evaluation of project feasibility. In short, SDI was a major boost to high-tech aerospace research. In Europe the allies were bought on-side by promises of a share in the new research funds. But more importantly, as the strategic community learned the truth concerning the project, it came to realize that only a handful of zealots believed that an astrodome defence of the whole United States was possible. If deployed at all, SDI would be a point defence of military assets, such as silos. Deterrence wasn't dead after all. The only problem was that at some point the public might come to believe that it been lied to.

FAREWELL TO ARMS

The second element in the counter-offensive against the peace movement was arms control. In Europe elites were persuaded of SDI's virtues through a promise of sharing research funds; but SDI did not assuage public concern over the Pentagon's new strategy. Particularly in Germany, a deep suspicion remained concerning American policy.

Despite being opposed to arms control, the Reagan administration inherited the machinery of negotiation from the previous administration. In the European theatre, the issues revolved around NATO's 'twin track' decision of the late 1970s to deploy Cruise and Pershing 2 missiles in Europe. The twin track committed NATO to deploy new systems and to negotiate a deal on intermediate-range nuclear forces. The new systems to be deployed were a bargaining chip in the planned negotiations. The ostensible impetus for this Janus-headed policy were SS20 missiles which the USSR had deployed from the mid-1970s and which were targeted on Europe. The public was told that NATO needed a counter to the allegedly mirved triple warhead SS20. But this was nonsense. It was highly likely that the targets allocated for the new NATO systems were already covered by existing NATO deployments. NATO was not short of nuclear weapons.

The real reason for the new NATO systems was actually shrouded in secrecy. In the late 1970s the leaders of West Germany, France and Britain met with the US President in Guadalupe to discuss the SS20 problem. The sensitivity of the meeting was such that not even the Foreign Ministers of the countries involved were in attendance. At the meeting a reluctant Jimmy Carter was persuaded to provide Europe with new systems to 'counter' the SS20. The probable real cause of this baroque manoeuvring was that European NATO members were concerned about the USA's political commitment to Europe's defence. The new systems recoupled the USA to Europe, and gave the USSR a visible sign that war in Europe was *ipso facto* war with the United States. For European leaders, deterrence was enhanced when European deployments directly entailed superpower confrontation.

In the publics of Western Europe the new NATO decision was regarded as highly provocative. The various peace movements pointed out that Cruise and Pershing 2 would mean increased targeting of sites in the countries that would take the new systems. The twin-track policy was the counter to this new anxiety. Nevertheless, the highly visible new systems created a new wave of nuclear fear in Europe. With the arrival of Reagan in the White House, this fear was in danger of unravelling NATO solidarity. Everywhere in Europe in the early 1980s, governments were in crisis over the Cruise and Pershing deployment.

It was in this context that the Reagan administration agreed to begin talks on INF in Geneva in 1981. Its chief negotiator was the now veteran Paul Nitze, who, although on the right, was at least prepared to talk to the Soviets. This was not the position of the new civilian advisers in the Pentagon. As Strobe Talbot has pointed out, an extraordinary feature of the INF talks was that the US administration was at war within itself over whether to negotiate. Individuals at Defense such as Perle, Weinberger and Jones were opposed to any deal.[92] Perle, now Assistant Secretary of Defense for International Security Policy, was apparently determined to wreck the talks, whatever the cost.

In the US State Department those inclined to an Atlanticist position knew that at the very least the appearance of talks was now essential. However, the hawks in the Pentagon had the ear of the President, and were skillful campaigners in the battles now going on in Washington. In reality the talks were doomed. What transpired was that Paul Nitze and his staff were given a brief that was designed precisely so that it would fail. The US side came up with the 'zero option'. This proposed the elimination of all Soviet SS20s in return for the cancellation of NATO's planned deployments. It was an all-or-nothing offer made in the certain knowledge that it would be rejected. The Soviets were to give up a whole class of weapons in return for cancelling a deployment which might not even go ahead as European governments bent under the onslaught of their opponents. Kenneth Adelman was right: arms control was a sham.

History has a habit of mocking man's best-laid plans, and so it turned out with the zero option. In 1985, after the interregnum of Andropov and Chernyenko, the USSR came under the dynamic leadership of Mikhail Gorbachev. The new Soviet leader and his Foreign Minister, Eduard Schevardnaze, promptly launched a highly successful charm offensive in Western Europe, which cemented the now general view of the USA as the new warmongers. A clever mixture of threats and promises further heightened the unease over nuclear war. Gorbachev unveiled a vision of a common European home where security would no longer depend on military strength, but rather would reflect interdependence and co-operation. This was music to Europe's ears, especially in West Germany, where something approaching Gorbymania prevailed. Increasingly, the image of the USSR promoted by Reagan, Weinberger, Perle and others seemed ridiculous. In the cafes and bars of Europe it was Reagan who was now denounced as the great threat to world peace. In short order, Gorbachev and his officials deluged the West with proposals to scrap and eliminate weapons. Indeed, Gorbachev announced his intention to abolish all nuclear weapons by the year 2000, and for good measure threw in a proposal to unilaterally stop nuclear testing. More than any other individual, Gorbachev seemed to sense the mood of anti-nuclearism which had grown up in the Europe of the 1980s.

Because of Gorbachev's initiatives, the ultra-rightists in the Reagan administration were left high and dry. When Gorbachev asked if the zero option was still on the table, Reagan's advisers had their bluff called. As Krepon notes, 'INF changed NATO's position, but by accident. Proponents of the elimination of theatre nuclear weapons did not anticipate success.'[93] Thus an extraordinary turn-around ensued. Proposals made by the right to expose Soviet offers as propaganda rebounded so that NATO had to adopt policies which it really opposed. Former Secretary of State Alexander Haig labelled the INF deal 'absurd', while, privately, Margaret Thatcher expressed bitter opposition. But the die was cast. The West's leaders were now locked into a policy which anticipated a drastic, ongoing series of cuts in nuclear and non-nuclear armaments.

END-GAME

Gorbachev's new foreign policy – new thinking – was complemented at home by the reform programme of *perestroika* and *glasnost.* Since 1982 some of the USSR's leaders had known that the economy was in dire trouble. It was a combination of 'force, waste and bureacracy'. After Brezhnev's death in 1982, reform was delayed because of the interregnum of Andropov and Chernyenko. Andropov had wanted to institute change himself, but was already terminally ill when he took office. His successor was simply not up to the job. Reform began under Gorbachev in 1985.

The aim of Gorbachev was to maintain communism in the USSR, but to liberalize it. He sensed acutely the chronic failure of the Soviet economy and the growing knowledge in the USSR of the level of affluence in the West. He also knew that the achievements of the military industrial complex were not replicated in other sectors of Soviet society. In the 1970s some of these problems were offset by hard currency earned from oil exports. But in 1981 the world price of oil collapsed, with drastic effects for the USSR.

Of necessity, a key element in the new strategy was to reduce arms expenditure. Thus the readiness to negotiate was not simply an act of altruism. Here, though, we encounter the vexed question of SDI. Many of the exotic technologies envisaged in SDI were tens or even hundreds of years away from fruition. Some who claimed that they were feasible at the time have now revealed their endorsement to have been a political manoeuvre. They claim that their real aim was to force the collapse of the USSR. As the USSR did indeed collapse, these far-sighted ones have a perfect *ex-post facto* rationalization for their former perjury on the SDI question. But did SDI force the collapse of the USSR?

The USSR collapsed because the reform programme initiated by Gorbachev proved unpredictable and uncontrollable. As I have already said, the impetus to reform began in the early 1980s, and was predicated on an awareness of economic failure. The Reagan defence buildup increased the pressure for reform, but the USA was not in a position to neutralize the Soviet deterrent. In terms of strategic arms, the USSR was actually outgunned to a far greater degree at the time of the Cuban missile crisis. But SDI did loom large in Soviet calculations. Ironically, both sides were feeling vulnerable and weak in the early 1980s.

In 1982 Soviet technology in the hands of the Syrian Air Force suffered a severe defeat at the hands of the Israeli Air Force in a series of dogfights over Lebanon. The Soviets knew that their aerospace technology was inferior to that of the West. When SDI was launched, Soviet defence analysts were likely to take it seriously. While eminent US scientists poured scorn on the Reagan fantasy, Gorbachev and his advisers were fearful and impressed. Gorbachev did not want another round of the arms race in space. Hence many of the attractive offers made by the Soviet side were conditional on the abandonment of SDI. Thus SDI added to the pressure the USSR felt regarding negotiations. But it did not feed causally into the processes which unravelled the Soviet state.

In 1989 the collapse of East European communism came about in large part because the USSR chose not to intervene. As Ghenadi Gerasimov announced, the 'Brezhnev doctrine' was dead. Gorbachev's failure to act enraged many hard-line Communists who then plotted against him. The result was the bungled *coup* in 1991 which brought the USSR to an end. The Cold War was over, in fact as well as spirit.

In the wake of the end of the Cold War, a virtual euphoria attached to considerations of international security. George Bush proclaimed a new world order. Europe stepped out from the nightmare of nuclear apocalypse. But the Gulf War and the collapse of the former Yugoslavia ushered in a very different era of post-communism to the one that had been expected. As we shall see in Chapter 6, the modernist utopia inherent in the idea of the end of history has not materialized. Having declared that mass war crimes could never again happen in Europe, Western leaders did nothing as untold barbarism unfolded in Bosnia.

6 Aesthetics and Strategic Violence

INTRODUCTION

In contrast to the euphoria of the immediate post-Cold War period, the recent and current state of international politics reveals that a grizzly cycle of violence and lethal conflict continues. Whether in Zaire, Liberia, Rwanda, Angola, Bosnia or Chechnya, the picture seems grim. For a global audience, but particularly for West Europeans and Americans, the international media have provided acute insights into the most appalling atrocities. Bodies pile up against the TV screen; dead and dying lie in the near and far; and pitiful lines of refugees stretch out into the distance. Postmodern theorists have emphasized a one-dimensional response to these events, one in which a bogus sense of pity merely shields Westerners from the need to act.[1] Rather than one of morality, the West's response seems almost to have been aesthetic. We have sat back and been entertained.

This critique appears exaggerated to me, as certain groups and individuals have been clearly distressed and moved by the frightening images these conflicts have generated. Similarly, who can say a priori that the motives of all charitable organizations and individuals are hypocritical and based on a smug sense of superiority, or that the purpose of giving aid is to make us feel superior. This view insults those who feel a moral need to act. While some have shown a disregard for those who suffer, others have not. I believe the postmodern response to Bosnia simplifies what is a very complex process. General theory is attempting to provide analysis better achieved by close empirical research. In my view, Baudrillard and others over-homogenize complex historical and cultural phenomena in order to isolate defining characteristics of Western experience.[2] Paradoxically, deconstruction, which, according to Derrida, is now simply 'the case',[3] often results in intellectual edifices more monumental and iconoclastic than anything thrown up by modernity. I seek to suggest in this chapter that there has been, again in Derrida's words, a 'quasi-nihilistic abdication', but that this is not a symptom of the era of the triumph of liberal democracy or postmodernity, and that it does not signify that we live in the age merely of 'assorted victimhoods'.[4] Victimhood has been a constant in international politics, with the forces of modernity able to create more victims and more devastation than would have been remotely conceivable in previous eras. Victimhood is now more palpable, because our gaze is not riveted on the prospect of nuclear war. As I argued in Chapter 1, Hegel was right to see something utterly new at the Battle of Jena, but wrong to believe that it was symptomatic of spiritual progress.[5]

ABDICATION

The recent hypocrisy over Bosnia and the failure to act to stop the genocide is nothing new. Western states, which bathed in the reflective glory of their own theories of enlightenment in the guise of the project of modernity, have long since shown that their real value systems were often characterized mainly by xenophobic nationalism, imperialism and racism. Even the much vaunted beacon of democracy is very much a feature of the post-1945 period, and had virtually nothing to do with the political creeds set out at the beginning of the modern period. The dominant self-consciousness of the modern period has always been one which denied the authentic being of the 'other', whether they were Africans, Amerindians, Asians or large sections of domestic society – although, as I implied above, not all groups and individuals are tarred with the same brush. Regarding Bosnia, we should remember that Western Europe's contempt for the Balkans is so long-standing that the term has come in itself to signify a political negative; the word radiates images of confusion and quagmire. Hence I reiterate, there is nothing new about the recent reaction to events in Africa and southern Europe; they do not signify that we are in the era of postmodernity.

Despite its familiarity, much of the West's reaction to the Bosnian crisis has, of course, been depressing. As Meštrović has passionately argued, many sat back and watched genocide on their television screens while doing little to prevent it.[6] A typical response to Bosnia simply led to feelings of despair; the catalogue of violence resulted in a shrug of the shoulders. It seemed that the problems were intractable; these environments were the terrain of unreason. In particular, in the Bosnian case a realist analysis led to a concept of exclusion; Bosnia was a nasty little civil war which raised no real security issues for the West. Cognitively and socially, it was located in the far beyond; chronologically, it was a throw-back to a time which modernity had long since vanquished. The barbarity was depicted as typical of a pattern of Balkan behaviour which results from the tableaux of ancient tribal hatreds. This reality was and is, of course, counterposed to a different political and moral framework in Western countries. It secured a sense of identity conducive to the retention of a model of lofty superiority. The catastrophe, out there, occurred in the realm of the unreason of outside: a dimension from which civilized, law-governed behaviour was absent.

It can be argued that this framework for dealing with the seemingly barbaric was extremely useful on a number of levels. It absolved us of moral responsibility, because the agents did not qualify as agents in our sense. It also relieved us of the pressure for any practical action, because unreason cannot be moulded to rational purposes. For some it represented an aesthetic spectacle; disengagement and distance allowed the objective appraisal of the consequences of a collapsed state. Finally, it reinforced the view some have of the West as the site of a unique development in human rationality. Western states have transcended the dark pits of tribalism and brutalism. The heart of darkness lies elsewhere.[7]

The process of exclusion whereby the outside is the 'other', something primitive and untamed, is, as I have already implied, coterminous with the whole trajectory of Western development. In the modern period the process of imperial conquest was often conducted with a self-understanding of bearing a beacon of reason. Western practices in the legal, economic and political spheres were inscribed on the global stage through colonization. The results of this process varied from absorption, at one end of a continuum, to extermination, at the other. Frequently, indigenous peoples were simply swept aside or subject to genocide. As we have seen, in Leopold II's reign the population of the Belgian Congo was reduced from 20 to 8 million in a policy of 'administrative massacres'.[8] The African 'other' was excluded, and then removed from the scene by the use of modern instruments of war. The people were no more important than the jungle or bush that had to be cleared for 'modernization'. Little critical reflection penetrated these events as territorial imperialism was complemented by cultural imperialism. The process of domination was set down in textual form by Westerners in Western categories. Hegel described Africans as 'a people without history',[9] while Weber spoke of them as *Kulturlos.*[10]

As Coker notes, 'Africa became everything Europe was not – a continent singularly lacking in civic or moral virtue.'[11] According to Edward Said, this has been critical in the sphere of legitimation, because Western discourse opens the dimensions of domination up to a merely managerial framework. In a recent study Said suggests that the discourse of Africanism, as manifested in the writings of authors such as Conrad, is chiefly a way of dealing with Africa for the West. Tribalism, primitivism and vitalism serve to preclude any serious investigation of indigenous culture and traditions.[12] Of course, it is not just in Africa that indigenous culture was denied authenticity. The European conquest of the Americas obliterated the historicity of the Amerindians.[13] In his seminal study *The Conquest of America* Tordorov asserts that the Spanish regarded the Indians as 'culturally virgin', a *tabula rasa* awaiting the 'Christian inscription'.[14] In the Spanish case David Campbell believes that the 'other' was essentially defined as pagan, but as capable of conversion to Christianity. However, the English attitude to the Indians of North America he describes as based on the duality of civilized/barbarian. In this instance the exclusion was total, with massacres and extermination an entirely routine affair. Some calculations estimate that 3 million Amerindians died in massacres, forced marches and re-settlement,[15] a process which was paralleled in Australia, where 'culls' of Aboriginals still occurred in the 1920s.

WAR AND CULTURAL SELF-IMAGES

The process of exclusion, the total denial of the social space of other human beings, and their destruction have an explicitly aesthetic dimension. In the process of colonization, forms of behaviour could be engaged in against Africans and Amerindians which were vigorously censored in the realm of civil society. As Engelhardt expresses it, 'For the European released into this periphery, the first American "freedom" was from captivity to certain norms. It was the freedom to organize a bloodletting that could be justified in a land of invasive savages and threatening subhumans.'[16] A second aesthetic dimension existed in the realm of entertainment. The story of the destruction of the 'other', and later, its cinematic depiction formed a centre-piece within the narrative of (in this specific case) the transformation of America from wilderness into a utopian civilization. The destruction of Indians was a social good. 'From the seventeenth century on, Americans were repeatedly shown the slaughter of Indians as a form of entertainment; and audiences invariably cheered, or were cheered by what they read, heard or saw.'[17]

Nothing new is being said here, but the memory of these events has been largely suppressed. In her novel *Beloved*, Toni Morrison argues for the need to engage in 'memory work' to reconstruct the history of slavery in the USA.[18] I contend here that such a strategy is needed with respect to racism and imperialism in the consciousness of mainstream political science. We should grasp that the story of the transparent racism of the history of imperialism is routine. As Sartre pointed out, 'There is nothing more consistent than a racist humanism, since the European has only been able to become a man through creating slaves and monsters.'[19] This is true in a material sense; but it is also true in a cultural sense.[20] The mastery has been woven into the central narratives of Western culture, and has been reproduced endlessly in the fabric of popular culture. Today, at the borderlands of culture, the hegemony of Western narratives is challenged, as the victims of domination promote their own textual retaliation. But this is at the margins of mass culture, and is challenged by the globalization of Western cultural practises through a universal media enterprise which saturates the developing world with images of Western life-styles and practices. In addition, it is now clear that in many cases the dominated accept and copy the values of the dominant.[21] In consequence, many indigenous peoples become strangers in their own culture. Thus, while Western intellectuals absorb the shock waves of a critical post-colonial narrative, Western transnational media organs bombard the globe with our images of sport, aesthetics, music and art – since the end of the Cold War a process resisted only by Islamic fundamentalism. One African novelist sees the problem in these terms:

> But the biggest weapon wielded and actually daily unleashed by imperialism against collective defiance (of the oppressed and exploited) is the cultural bomb. The effect of the cultural bomb is to annihilate people's belief in their names, in their languages, in their environment, in their heritage of struggle, in their unity, in their capacities and ultimately in themselves.[22]

In intellectual circles it is fashionable today to see the power of the West as declining. It is argued that although the Cold War is won, the European Union and the USA face severe economic challenges from a variety of Asian capitalist countries, not least from China. But this view is locked into a national model of power articulation. The transmission of Western cultural values is essentially the province of the transnational media corporations. Therefore it is these organizations which seek to universalize key elements of Western culture. What I wish to challenge here is the notion of a progressive and liberal popular culture which is compatible with ideas of global pluralism. On the contrary, I wish to assert that an imperialist legacy is apparent in the globalization of Western values and culture. This culture reflects the West's constant struggle with world forces which are inimical to modernization. One could say that others are now doing our work for us as the project of modernity becomes truly globalized. Although the Western state may be much less important than it used to be in the further intensification of global capitalism, this does not mean the decline of the West. The West is now able to globalize itself using many non-state actors and non-Western states. Even the suppression of rogue elements such as Saddam Hussein is now better achieved by a coalition than by individual Western countries. The West planned and executed the Gulf War, but persuaded others to pay the bill.

What the Gulf War also showed is that we can still erect a culture of propaganda, or, as I call it, a 'strategic anthropology', a vision of struggle between rival nations and peoples. This serves to articulate a sense of threat, and it seeks to justify forms of acute violence against putative enemies. Its potential is awesome; it has allowed the use of atomic bombs against innocent civilians. It can justify bombing countries back into the Stone Age. It also drives strategic formulations, because it articulates ways and means of dealing with different threats.

During the Cold War, Western strategic anthropology was virtually a mono-culture. The threat inflation centred more or less exclusively on the USSR and the menace of world communism. The central locus of this mono-culture was the USA, and as Campbell asserts, American identity was constructed around the presentation of communism as a threat to core American values and global order.[23] However, Campbell believes that the framing of a discourse of danger in terms of Soviet malfeasance was merely one instance of a historical need rooted in the ambiguities and uncertainties of American identity. The binary relation of self and 'other' constructs identity. As Kammen notes, 'Only in a country where it is so unclear what is American do people worry so much about the threat of things "un-American".'[24] On this view, identity is created chiefly through the reaction to the danger of what must be excluded. But as Campbell notes, danger is not an objective characteristic of objects and events. Danger presupposes a reading, an interpretation which galvanizes attention and fear. In American history the rendering of danger has often taken a dramatic, eschatological form: 'the apocalyptic mode – in which a discourse of danger functions as providence and foretells a threat that prompts renewal has been conspicuous in the catalog of American statecraft'.[25] In addition, the framework has been replete with bodily metaphors in which exclusion is critical to health: 'the ability to represent things as alien, subversive, dirty or sick has been pivotal to the articulation of danger in the American experience'.[26]

In recent works by Coker and Bauman, use has been made of a distinction drawn by Lévi-Strauss between anthrophagic and anthropoemic strategies for dealing with what is strange or alien. According to Lévi-Strauss pre-modern and non-modern societies deal with what is alien or strange by absorbing it. To the extent that strangers may be deemed to possess exotic or magical powers, the advantage of this is that these qualities are ingested. Anthropoemic strategies, which Lévi-Strauss suggests are characteristic of modern societies, exclude or literally vomit out the strange and alien.[27] The latter strategy fits well with the sentiment of modernity to deny authenticity to social forms which stand in the way of modernization. Anthropoemic strategies are also compatible with cultural self-images which frame insider/outsider distinctions and which have been central in the realm of international conflicts in which 'others' have felt the power of Western military might. The culture of exclusion and danger has been part of a persuasive discourse of war propaganda which has sought to legitimize brutal forms of military statecraft. It is now a cliché of peace and conflict studies that democracies do not make war on each other; however, this misses the point. Western democracies have been constantly at war with non-Western states in both colonial and non-colonial settings. After the Congress of Vienna, it is commonly thought that European states constructed a period of unparalleled peace. However, European armies were continually fighting colonial campaigns in the nineteenth century, with the British substantially involved in colonial wars between 1863 and 1901.[28] As Coker observes, these conflicts were the precursors of twentieth-century warfare. 'Many of the phenomena that were to form part of the twentieth-century style of warfare – genocide as a tactic of war, the use of technology at the expense of tactics ... were practiced systematically, and consciously, in Africa after 1870.'[29]

In the twentieth century the period of the Cold War, when bipolarity and nuclear deterrence had brought 'stability', saw 127 wars with 22 million fatalities.[30] According to Irving Louis Horowitz, NATO armies were responsible for 4 million deaths in the first two decades after 1945.[31] Thus, however one views it, the question of warfare and Western states is somewhat more complex than the issue of intra-democracy conflict.

The continual involvement in warfare necessitates a war culture and justifications for the slaughter of other peoples. It is central to war that we create the enemy. Before the conflict comes the image. With modern technologies, the process of killing is increasingly abstract and remote, with legitimation made easier by the physical and cognitive distance of the victim from the perpetrators. Air power introduced a new aesthetic into the process, as the machines themselves have often been viewed as instruments of aesthetic beauty. The symmetry and power of the war-plane demands our adulation. In the twentieth century totalitarian states have engaged in massive land campaigns in which millions have perished as huge land armies fought protracted engagements. However, the chosen method of annihilation in the Western democracies has usually been air power. As we saw in Chapter 3, in the Second World War it was the democracies which waged strategic air warfare and which exterminated several hundred thousand civilians by means of strategic bombing.

In case after case the victims of Western military power have been the peoples of less developed countries, where the level of military sophistication has been inferior to that of the West. As both France and the USA found in South-east Asia, this does not always guarantee success; but it means utter devastation for the enemy. In the Gulf War these historical anomalies have been put right; America had its revenge for Vietnam. Hyper-destruction guaranteed rapid victory. Said sees recent events as typical of a continuing pattern in Western behaviour. As he puts it, 'Arabs are only an attenuated recent example of Others who have incurred the wrath of a stern White Man.'[32] This process reveals the way in which the cultural articulation of 'others' as inferior, as a threat and as enemies undercuts professions of moral universalism. Thus universalism is tainted by the production of narratives of moral particularity and their embeddedness in the cultural practices of the powerful. Moreover, these particularities are not attractive. As Bauman argues, 'contrary to the widely shared view of modernity as the first universal civilization, this is a civilization singularly unfit for univerzalization'.[33]

CONSTRUCTING EXCLUSION: THE CULTURE INDUSTRY

Before the age of mass literacy, the shared assumptions of cultural domination existed in textual form for elites, but were not available in written form for the mass population. However, the advent of mass literacy and cheap printing techniques allowed a generalized promulgation of in-group/out-group culture in the form of nationalism, as well, of course, as forms of opposition in the realm of class politics. But as the First World War revealed, the class-based internationalist pretensions of European socialism were weaker than the ideology of imperialist nationalism. In bellicose nationalism the persuasive discourse of war culture has been an enormously powerful instrument in the realm of identity formation, where the moral rights of the 'other' are swept to one side. Thus it should come as no surprise that the grandest narrative schemes of Western moral discourse, beginning with the French Enlightenment, which emphasized universal rights, have not seemed able to constrain the empirical acts of transparent immorality which have characterized the behaviour of Western states. My contention is that moral schematics have not paid sufficient attention to the cultural practices which reproduce moral particularism and which deny authenticity to the victims of Western power. This is not surprising, for as Meštrović points out, the Enlightenment saw itself as the end of tradition and culture, and as the critical weapon wielded against traditions and cultures that were doomed.[34] As the particularity of the West's drive to modernization destroyed the prevailing *Gemeinschaft*, this was seen as the price to be paid for unleashing reason. This is a difficult point to grasp; but Bauman puts it well:

> With one stone of rationality, modernity killed two birds. It managed to recast as inferior and doomed all those forms of life which did not harness their own plans to the chariot of reason. And it obtained a safe conduct for the pains it was about to inflict itself ... They made the rule-governed house which modernity built hospitable to cruelty, which presented itself as superior ethics.[35]

In this chapter I follow the lead given by Toynbee and Baudrillard in viewing the USA as the state which most perfectly articulates the essence of modernity.[36] Thus I believe that the tendency to see the destruction of the 'other' as beneficial to civilization has been most pronounced in the USA. As Theodore Roosevelt remarked in 1896, 'The most righteous of all wars is war with savages.'[37] This super-confidence in the project of modernity has been underscored by a popular culture which saluted the USA's crusade against its enemies. Thus different cultural traditions have produced output which consolidated American identity and located threats to American interests. Almost isomorphically, this production followed the path of 'others' who the American state had defined as enemies. From the late 1880s a genre of fiction emerged in the United States which celebrated core American values and highlighted the likely struggles America would face to protect its privileged position in the world, and, in effect, a concocted notion of US identity. The image of America which was presented centred on American genius, the frontier, individualism, race and democracy. Repeatedly this literature depicted the USA engaging in heroic struggles to extinguish unwelcome challenges to US supremacy. Historically, it emerged when the business of subduing indigenous peoples had been completed and when US power was aiming towards a global reach. It also corresponds to the period when the USA became a metropolitan manufacturing nation and was experiencing large waves of immigration.[38]

A number of studies have traced the emergence of a popular war culture in the United States manifested in novels, films and television.[39] They identify a process of glorification of core beliefs which have been used to justify violence against other peoples. According to Franklin, this process began in the late nineteenth century. He writes:

Between 1880 and America's entry into World War I, novels and stories imagining future wars became an influential part of popular culture. Projecting the causes, forms and consequences of wars fought years or centuries hence, the literature expressed and helped to shape the apocalyptic ideology prominent in America's wars from 1898 through the waning years of the twentieth century. In this popular fiction, the emerging faith in American technological genius wedded the older faith in America's messianic destiny, engendering a cult of made-in-America superweapons and ecstatic visions of America defeating evil empires, waging wars to end all wars, and making the world eternally safe for democracy.[40]

The themes in the novels and stories which Franklin has in mind, by authors such as King Wallace, Jack London, J. H. Palmer and Park Benjamin, are varied. However, they, and scores of others, range across the following: race *angst*, especially in relation to Asians; notions of technological supremacy; fear of invasion by colonial countries; anxiety concerning rivalry from European powers; anti-populism; and eschatological visions of new orders created from the debris of wars. As I indicated above, the process of cultural production is tightly coupled to historical developments. At the turn of the century, Roosevelt's East Asia policy brought in large numbers of Asian immigrants, with 100,000 from China in 1900 alone. Perceptions of this immigration led to considerable race *angst*, and were manifested culturally in a 'yellow peril' syndrome. After 1905 and the Russo-Japanese War, anti-Japanese racism emerged as a category in itself, and it is significant that in California in 1906 Japanese school children were segregated.[41] The period after the Russo-Japanese War saw an increase in novels and stories in which Japan was the enemy and where the USA was subject to invasion. As we saw in Chapter 2, the best known of these was Homer Lea's *The Valour of Ignorance*, published in 1909. Lea's book presents Japan as a powerful threat to the USA, particularly because Japan is a racially pure country. The book also picks out targets in domestic society which constitute an enemy within. Particular attention is paid to feminists, the problem of Negroes and commercialism.[42]

The popular culture of enmity has nearly always had racial overtones in the United States. However, the First World War saw attention, as in Britain, riveted upon Germany. The 'munitions of the mind', as Taylor has called them, had an anti-German focus: 'all of America's earlier imagined enemies virtually disappeared beneath torrents of anti-German images'.[43]

CULTURAL PLURALISM?

In a totalitarian state the fit between historical exigencies of state policy and propaganda culture simply reflects the output of state organs. Thus Eisenstein can be legitimate in Stalin's Russia at one moment, and beyond the pale the next. But what of this fit in liberal societies? The dominant narratives of liberalism have bequeathed powerful assumptions positing a separate state and civil society. In this image morality and culture exist in spaces which are deliberately constructed as free and spontaneous. In the ideological battle with communism, the post-1945 version of these assumptions celebrated pluralism as the critical normative principal of Western practice. However, as studies of power have revealed, pluralist conclusions derived essentially from a pluralist methodology.[44] Also, dominant paradigms in media studies have concentrated on the notion of the individual as receiver and decoder of cultural output.[45] However, focus on the output of cultural production reveals the endless repetition and homogeneity of mass culture. The dominant liberal discourse emphasizes the overt, factual separation between the state and private enterprises, but fails to theorize the covert connections between private constellations of power and state institutions and the homogenization of the values of private corporate capital. Indeed, pluralism has been reluctant to theorize the state at all.

During the Second World War the Western allies absorbed the culture industry into the state. In America, Hollywood came under the direction of the Bureau of Motion Pictures headed by Elmer Davis.[46] In reality, this was a subdivision of the Office of War Information.[47] The purpose of the bureau was to control the output of movies about Japan; the key issue was whether a film would help win the Pacific War. The output was unrelentingly crude.[48] A series of racist documentary films portrayed the Japanese as a people devoid of individuality: herd-like and fanatical.[49] In terms of mobilizing the populace and the armed forces against the Japanese people, these films and other output were remarkably successful. At the end of the war, nearly a quarter of Americans favoured the use of more atomic bombs against the Japanese. To restate Keen's argument, mass killing was culturally prefigured. The use of a horrific technology became justifiable because its victims were dehumanized. This is the ultimate form of moral exclusion, as the 'other' is denied the ontological status of a subject. Earlier in the conflict, incendiary raids on major Japanese cities were excused in army and air force circles because of an explicit racism which had long been guiding military thinking with regard to anti-Japanese strategy. As Michael Sherry notes, 'in misjudging their enemy America also drew on a tradition of casual racism which made air-war against Japan easy and shallow'.[50]

In addition to documentary films, such as Capras's *Know Your Enemy – Japan*,[51] academics weighed in with more 'serious' accounts of Japanese personality. Geoffrey Gorer believed that drastic toilet training was to blame; Margaret Mead claimed that Japanese culture was 'childish and pathological'; while Frank Tannenbaum noted 28 points of similarity between the Japanese and American gangsters.[52]

While it may seem obvious that a state will disseminate cultural propaganda during a war, it should be remembered that this process continued during the confrontation with the USSR. During the Second World War Hollywood made scores of films which showed the Russians in a good light. However, in the late 1940s, with treason and treachery as pervasive political issues, these films were an embarrassment. Hollywood promptly reversed policy, and directed by Sam Wood's Motion Picture Alliance, many pro-Russian films were withdrawn and not shown again for 20 years. Moreover, a more appropriate output was produced. As Coppes and Black remark, 'The studios atoned profusely for their pro-Russian films with some fifty anti-communist pictures in the late 1940s and early 1950s.'[53]

The films of the Second World War were nothing new as regards the real and celluloid dehumanization of other peoples. In 1929 Capra's film *Flight* depicted the heroism of marine pilots who bombed towns in Nicaragua; the victims of the bombing were not considered at all. This film reflects very well the developing use of air power in the politics of imperialism, and also its aesthetic appeal. In France the use of bombers against African and Arab peoples led to the open use of the term 'Type Coloniale' for the plane which was used. In Britain the RAF under Trenchard routinely bombed Pathan tribesmen on the North-west frontier under a policy known as 'Control without Occupation'.[54]

THE AESTHETICS OF MASS DESTRUCTION

The use of modernist instruments of violence against the vulnerable and less technologically sophisticated was not confined to the democracies. In Spain the new *Luftwaffe* practised its art against the Republicans, while Mussolini unleashed air war against Abyssinia. However, as Sherry has shown, it was the democracies which built huge air forces for the purpose of strategic bombing. Building on the diet of cultural racism which I have described above, the USA approached the war with Japan with the explicit aim of bombing the Japanese into submission.[55] This was no idle boast, as America's air power did exactly what US strategists had promised. By June 1945 all the major cities of Japan had been destroyed except for four which were on a special target list. In some raids whole cities were reduced to an inferno, in which everything perished. These raids also indicated a worrying aesthetic dimension to air warfare. The scale of the destruction, the huge fireballs, and the colours of burning materials provided a vast and awesome spectacle which many witnesses found fascinating and beautiful. On the night of 10 March 1945 the 20th Army Air Force destroyed much of the centre of Tokyo in an incendiary raid which probably killed more than 100,000 people. Yet a priest who was watching could write that the explosions 'appeared translucid, unreal, light as fantastic dragonflies'.[56] As M47 napalm bombs and M69 magnesium cluster bombs turned Tokyo into an inferno, air crews spoke of the city as 'illuminated like a forest of brightly lighted christmas trees'.[57] Some victims applauded as the planes flew over. Many since have spoken of their delight in seeing napalm ignite, of loving its 'silent power'. What is apparent here is not just the psychological distance which I have mentioned above, but also a scale and intensity of horror which transcend normal experience altogether. This allows a distanced appreciation of the manifestation of pure power, a celebration of the creativity of destruction. It represents, as Susan Mansfield comments, 'the appeal of transcendental power and awesomeness as opposed to that of design, regularity and grace'.[58]

After-the-fact ethical reflection on the Pacific War has focused on the atomic raids, but the moral threshold of killing innocents had long been passed in the conventional raids in which more people died than at Hiroshima and Nagasaki. Indeed, more Japanese military personnel perished in the war than did civilians. In America the culture industry bombarded the US public with films which fantasized the real events. In Disney's *Victory through Airpower* (1943) planes are seen attacking cities which are empty. The aesthetic was not touched by real images of dead and dying people. In general these films ignored the fate of the victims, and played on major Western prejudices about non-white peoples. In the case of the Pacific War the terrain itself symbolized Western anxieties about the primitive and uncivilized. To use a contemporary idiom, the war was at the borderlands, the margin of civilization. As Coppes and Black note, 'the Pacific War ... took place in the wilderness, much of it a particularly frightening wilderness: the jungle. There is a long tradition in the West of identifying the wilderness with the absence of civilization – indeed, as a place of evil.'[59] Thus jungle imagery helped justify the technological brutalism which was manifested in air attacks, but was also misrepresented in domestic presentations: 'The symbolism of the World War Two movies, by excluding pertinent truths about their subjects and framing issues in misleading ways was thus ... dangerously manipulative.'[60] In particular, as Franklin has argued, the suffering of victims was ignored, and the effects of the military technology trivialized.[61]

Strictly speaking, the orchestration of cultural output by the state after the Second World War loosened. But, in reality, the Cold War engendered such a degree of conformism in the culture industry that direct control was not necessary. In the 1950s US culture succumbed to the near total exclusion of themes and characterizations which did not fit the ideological needs of the confrontation with the USSR or the dominant image of domestic society. As is widely recognized, Hollywood acted to cleanse itself of elements that were not sound on the issue of anti-communism. However, because of the USSR's nuclear arsenal, the cultural presentation of the military confrontation was a difficult issue. As Franklin shows, many of the films of the 1950s concentrated on either the men who operated America's nuclear deterrent, or the actual machines which it comprised. In three major films, *Strategic Air Command* (1955), *Bombers B-52* (1957) and *Above and Beyond* (1952) there is no serious account of the real function of the weapons. These films glorify the technology, and present the airmen in charge as sober and rational custodians of the nation's fate. It was possible to control the output of Hollywood in these films because USAF and SAC would only allow their hardware to be used in return for supportive scripts and action.[62] In consequence, mainstream output was highly conducive to the ideological needs of the nuclear state.[63] This is not to say that there were not critical films and novels. A case in point was Neville Shute's novel *On The Beach* (1955), which was made into a film by Stanley Kramer. But this film, which Eisenhower considered suppressing, depicts personal human tragedies in the face of global forces (war) which have gone out of control.[64] Other movies in the 1950s transmuted the nuclear theme into science fiction, where beasts and monsters were created through exposure to radiation. Invariably the monsters were defeated by the US's high-tech weapons, which meant the vicarious defeat of nuclear war.[65]

In the nuclear contest with the USSR, exclusion was problematic because of the risks to American society. The 'other' could pay back in kind. Moreover, hydrogen weapons meant the complete extermination of the rival society, and left scant room for notions of heroism or individual virtues. In military discourse the problem of justifying the wholesale extermination of societies was overcome by reproducing the nuclear problematic in a language devoid of reference to pain and suffering. In the classical texts of nuclear strategy the destruction of whole cities often appears more akin to events in a game of chess. As S. Collins observes: 'Nuclear strategists often describe nuclear attacks, in which millions would be killed and wounded, as though they were great chess games with cities, aircraft carriers, great industrial areas, and other sources of national power as the pieces.'[66]

In academic publications on strategy, the political problem was partly resolved, because most of what was being theorized was actually speculation. As Robert Jervis has argued, a key characteristic of nuclear strategic theory has been a lack of empirical evidence. Often it was possible to manipulate the desired conclusion. From the point of view of some critics, this meant that arrant nonsense was merely disguised behind a façade of scientific rigour.[67] What I am suggesting here is that assumptions about recovery after nuclear war or the viability of deterrence, not to mention policies for winning nuclear war, could be fashioned from the imagination of strategists unencumbered by the intrusion of facts. Morover, the overall cohesion of America in the 1950s meant that a troubled consensus on nuclear war was possible. In the 1980s, with the renewal of nuclear anxiety in the wider society, this form of consensus was unattainable. In 1983, when 100 million Americans watched the film *The Day After*, there was grave concern in the USA about nuclear war, with the scientific community split on issues such as the nuclear winter and the feasibility of the SDI project.

FROM EXCLUSION TO EXTERMINATION

After the Second World War the Nuremberg War Crimes Tribunal symbolized the guilt of totalitarian regimes regarding offences concerning issues of human rights. In 1945 the sins of the Nazi state were all too apparent in the Holocaust. Soon it was also politically possible, and then essential, to highlight the grievous sins of Stalinism. But there was little official reflection on some of the obvious misdemeanours of the Allies. Despite the ready-made justification for Hiroshima and Nagasaki – which is so powerful that many academics and authors articulate it even though they haven't a clue about the facts – the extinguishing of so many innocent lives was controversial, as was the decision to proceed and build a huge armoury of nuclear munitions. In 1950 this inventory of might was enhanced again by the secret decision to proceed with the H-bomb, or the 'super', as its devotees called it. All this went largely uncriticized. Some, such as John Hersey, called attention to the dilemmas of the Hiroshima attack, but the majority of Americans thought the nuclear attacks were justified.[68] In the early 1950s *Scientific American* attempted to publish articles criticizing nuclear policy, but the Atomic Energy Commision forced them to halt and had other articles burned.[69] Thus a policy of potential extermination, through the use of large numbers of hydrogen weapons against Russia, became acceptable. By the end of the 1950s American policy was based on the possible use of several thousand atomic weapons against Russia and her allies, with likely casualties in the range of several hundred million.[70] In the mainstream academic accounts of this process, its reality was hidden beneath a welter of technical detail and through the emotional distance which theorists put between themselves and the likely facts of nuclear war.

It should be mentioned here as well that behind the Iron Curtain, where another version of modernity had developed, albeit in Marxist-Leninist form, the USSR had also constructed a doomsday apparatus. Here it is difficult to criticize what was written about the bomb, because virtually nothing was written or said about it. But it should be emphasized that both sides in the 'Great Contest' were prepared to risk the rest of humanity in their search for victory.

As I have tried to show above, the advent of nuclear weapons created constraints as regards a triumphalist discourse of Western cultural domination. But whereas the problem of exterminism was mutual between East and West, the domination of the West over the rest of the planet was not inhibited by fear of retaliation. In the post-1945 period decolonization was complicated by the Cold War and the fear that Western retreat would open up opportunities for international communism. Moreover, only some colonies were given up without a fight. The result was that Western powers were constantly at war with non-white peoples in the post-war period. In Africa it was the French, the Belgians, the Portuguese and the British, with the French, British and Dutch heavily involved in Asia. But contrary to its professed anti-colonialism, it was the USA that was now the real policeman. According to Richard Barnett, US military intervention occurred every year in the Third World from 1945 to 1967, with the key event the escalating involvement in Vietnam.[71] With regard to

Vietnam there has of course been a huge academic and media output, much of it critical. However, as a handful of authors, notably Chomsky and Engelhardt, have illustrated, the 'liberal' critique of Vietnam emphasized the damage done to American society: the social fissures caused by the war, the 59,000 dead, the drug addiction, the broken marriages, the fact that the war was lost, and the foolish reasons for going into Vietnam in the first place. To quote Hélé Béji, this was 'the singeing contrition of defeat'.[72] But little attention was paid to the damage which the USA had inflicted on a Third World country, damage so severe that as well as ecological destruction the genetic development of the Vietnamese people has been affected. No undisputed figures for casualties for Vietnam exist, but estimates range from 1 million to 2.6 million, including 600,000 children. Here then was the archetypal war of modernity. The most powerful state in the world had been engaged in a policy of nihilism through the means of a war of attrition against a poor Asian country. In Washington Secretary of Defense McNamara and his advisers conceived the conflict in cold, abstract/scientific terms, with the utilitarian calculus based on the body count. The bodies were supposed to be VC, but as everyone now knows, target discrimination in Vietnam was illusory. The firepower used was a totally blunt instrument. Coker notes that at Khe Sanh in 1967 US B52s dropped 75,000 tons of ordnance in nine weeks – that is, the equivalent of five Hiroshima-sized bombs.[73] After the war the normal procedure of exchanging information about the location of mines and other unexploded munitions was rejected by the United States, and in consequence thousands have been killed or injured since. Moreover, the USA continued to bear a grudge, because there was an engrained belief that thousands of MIAs were rotting in prison camps in South-east Asia. The facts were rather different. While American forces had 3,000 men missing in action, the Vietnamese had to come to terms with a figure of 300,000.

In Western popular culture there has been virtually no representation of these facts. Repeatedly, films and novels in the 1980s revealed the daring exploits of Special Forces Units in South-east Asia, or the failure of veterans to readjust to domestic life. American police and private-eye series invariably depict a veteran who has dark memories of active service which cause psychological problems. I have no objection to this; my point is that the reality of the war has been utterly distorted. The nihilistic destruction of a developing country, neatly encapsulated in Ronald Reagan's advice 'to flatten it and pave it over', has not penetrated into general American consciousness. Even more problematically anecdotal evidence suggests that contemporary US practice works against the storage of significant historical facts in any forms of collective awareness. Weart cites data that suggests that little is known of the Second World War: 'Many American high school students in the 1980s did not even know that the United States had once dropped atomic bombs on Japan.'[74] Edward Said is making a similar point when he reveals that, 'a recent poll showed that 89 per cent of high school juniors believed that Toronto was in Italy'.[75] Said maintains that US culture has little interest in the social practices of other societies, unless they represent a problem for the United States: 'The history of other cultures is non-existent until it erupts in confrontation with the United States.'[76]

CONTEMPORARY EXCLUSIONS

Recent and contemporary popular culture in the West reveals the enduring fascination of destructive fabrications of other societies. In the 1980s American cinema-goers were treated to a diet of right-wing revenge movies seeking to set the story straight on Vietnam. US consciousness needed little pushing in this direction, as two important myths had already been established: first, that the USA had lost the war because the political elite had tied the military's hands behind their backs, and secondly, that the main enemy in Vietnam was the American media. Since then the ethnicity and the geography have changed, but not the plot. Today Arabs and Latins are the culprits; the more violent media revel in depictions of Western heroes dealing decisively with Latin American drug traffickers or Arab terrorists. Today there is a standard media diet of alleged information about non-Western societies. In Western media consciousness one of the most persistent images is of the terrorist, the scourge of Western tourists, diplomats and servicemen. In the mind's eye the terrorist is invariably an Arab, a fundamentalist dressed in fatigues with the face covered by a scarf. This construct is now an ever present demon, and current narratives emphasize that he has friends and supporters in the growing Muslim populations of the West. In America perhaps the greatest shock of the tragedy of the Oklahoma City bombing was that the alleged perpetrator turned out to be a white US citizen. Another profound surprise has been that a black male can be found not guilty of the murder of a white woman. But despite these counter-factuals, the Arab is the most plausible symbol of evil on the scene today. Even elite members of states which are loyal allies of the USA, such as the Saudi ambassador, feel moved to complain: 'The United States prides itself on being open-minded and believing in pluralism. Yet the media and many in your (USA) political elite abound in stereotypes and the most elementary misunderstanding about Islam.'[77]

The construct of the Arab terrorist is a cliché, yet it is a recognizable image from our TV screens. Moreover, it has a serious element, because many in the West who are searching for a new enemy now see Islam as the likeliest candidate. What seems missing from our purview is any image of ordinary Arab civil or family life, particularly if their country has any association with fundamentalism. Because of the threat of terrorism, and also as a legacy of the Gulf War, the Arab has been demonized as the antithesis of Western civility and decency. In 1986 American planes bombed Tripoli, killing men, women and children. Indeed, a fourteen-month-old girl was killed who was Qaddafi's step-daughter. But these images do not break through; our view of terrorism remains opaque. In 1993 US cruise missiles struck Baghdad, killing two receptionists at the Al Rashid hotel. But this transparently criminal act was promptly forgotten. Here I believe is a parable about the West's moral awareness. The 'other', who should be our partner in moral discourse, is now so remote that we barely sense his or her existence. Also, as Lévinas has argued, the 'other' is weak and vulnerable, and certainly cannot pay back what is done to them.[78] Those who bear the brunt of our technology, and especially military technology, are so distant that we can no longer visualize the consequences of our actions. Thus we have slipped from a concrete form of exclusion, based on xenophobia and racism, to an abstract form based on distance and invisibility.

In 'telecity', to use Henning Beck's term, we experience a decontextualized media-created world in which certain images take hold and grow in power and plausibility, while others perish virtually before they are ever articulated. A global network of communications now 'knits the world together' for us. According to media-imperialist theorists such as Schiller, the world news media are now in the hands of a small number of mainly private corporations who bombard the globe with their versions of the truth as regards news and Western values as regards social, economic and cultural affairs. Thus, for example, what the world knew about the Gulf War was information supplied mainly by CNN, CBS, NBC and ABC. This coverage prefigured later analysis, as it supplied the initial working assumptions for journalists and other commentators. As Kellner argues, 'In a sense television now writes the first draft of history that was previously the province of the press.'[79] I am not articulating here the view that the message is necessarily always believed, or that it represents a conspiracy. But the homogeneity of the message and the hegemony it represents are significant factors in global politics. It is a conceit of much Western thinking that aspects of Western thought and culture are universal. This has been said of Beethoven's music and Chaplin's humour. But, as Tomlinson has pointed out, this may only reflect power: 'one reason why Chaplin's humour can plausibly be seen to be universal is that it is universally present'.[80] Said sees a global network of meaning creation which can portray highly misleading images and accounts of critical events:

> this world system, articulating and producing culture, economics and political power along with their military and demographic coefficients, has a tendency to produce out-of-scale transnational images that are now reorienting social discourse and process ... they are fearful images that lack discriminate contents or definition, but they signify moral power and approval for whoever uses them, moral defensiveness and criminalisation for whomever they designate.[81]

NEW ENEMIES AND NEW AESTHETICS

Not the least remarkable aspect of the Persian Gulf War is the way it has faded into history. With the utilitarian aspects of the task completed, the events have promptly been forgotten. Of course, they have not been forgotten in Iraq, where millions of children face starvation and illness because of food shortages and lack of medicines. Nor will the War have become history for the Marsh Arabs and Kurds who were encouraged to rise up against Saddam. The neglect of reflection has also extended to a lack of concern for the casualties. In an aesthetically nuanced presentation of the air attacks against Iraq, the Western media articulated the wholesale destruction of large areas of the country as a geo-political video game where the key issue was the thrill of the sight of the miraculous technology which destroyed only military targets. As Kellner notes, 'TV presented the Gulf War primarily as entertainment complete with dramatic titles, graphics and music.'[82] He continues: 'The images of precision, coordination, effectiveness and cleanness of the war were relayed day after day.'[83]

Much of this was false. In particular, the claim that Iraq was attacked primarily with precision munitions was an utter fabrication, which was vigorously promoted by the Western media. At a briefing on 15 March 1991 Air Force Chief of Staff General Merrill McPeak admitted that of 88,500 tons of bombs used, only 6,520 were precision-guided. McPeak claimed that of these 90 per cent hit their target; but other informed commentators, such as former Navy Secretary John Lehman, suggested a success rate of around 60 per cent. Contrary to popular perception, much of the accuracy of the early raids resulted from homing devices which had been placed on the ground by special forces. As Bosnia has shown, the problems of precision bombing are much greater than the media presentation of the Gulf War indicated. In consequence, many more civilians died in Iraq than was generally recognized. This fact has been reported by specialist agencies and noted by some journalists; but it emphatically has not penetrated into mainstream media consciousness. As in Vietnam, the precise number of fatalities in Iraq will never be known. The CIA estimated between 100,000 and 250,000; Greenpeace estimated more than 150,000 dead, with up to 15,000 civilian fatalities. In an interview with David Frost, Norman Schwarzkopf showed that it didn't really matter anyway: '50,000 or 100,000 or 150,000 or whatever of them to be killed'.[84] But the point is that this was a massive loss of life, presented on Western TV screens virtually as entertainment. The American media in particular seemed to become utterly obsessed with the video material shown at briefings, which revealed laser-guided bombs seeking out their targets. This fantasy was already situated in many minds precisely because the latest buzz in the entertainment industry was violent video and computer games. The images presented made it seem as if ordinary Iraqis were going about their business while only the military components of their infrastructure were being destroyed. In fact, the whole infrastructure of Iraq – its sewerage systems, water systems, power systems, communications network and industrial base – was being destroyed in an air offensive which lasted more than forty days.[85] A moment's reflection reveals that this was not just a war against

Saddam Hussein; it was war against the civilian population which was bound to cause major suffering for a long period after the fighting stopped, as indeed it has.

Fabrications, though, were not just confined to the myths about the precision bombing. Prior to the conflict, the Pentagon fed the American media a continual diet of stories about the size and formidable nature of Iraq's forces with their elite units of Republican Guards. In the desert hundreds of thousands of troops were supposedly dug into massive fortifications. In addition, these forces were equipped with chemical and biological weapons which they would not hesitate to use. But this was largely false; many of the units in the desert were of Kurdish and Shiite conscripts who were unwilling participants in the conflict. As the US war machine approached, many simply ran away as tanks equipped with earth-moving equipment buried their colleagues alive in trenches which became mass graves. How could it have been otherwise? Can anyone believe that a real war took place in which one side lost a few hundred men, many from 'friendly fire', and the opposition suffered losses in the hundred thousands. All military history shows that this is inconceivable unless something extraordinary has occurred. The extraordinary was the scale of the lie that indicated that the Iraqis were a formidable force.

A truer picture of the war emerges in the extensive casualties that were inflicted as Iraqi units were fleeing from Kuwait in a convoy heading to Basra. At Al-Jahra and Mutlah Gap the Iraqis were hit by wave after wave of US war-planes using cluster and compression bombs. The scene at the end of the slaughter was unprecedented. For as far as the eye could see, burnt-out vehicles stretched to the horizon. An American officer at the scene described it as Armageddon; journalists said they were standing in a river of blood which flowed along the highway. This really was high-tech warfare, and some of the images did penetrate into Western media presentations. However, the most graphic video-tape was never shown in the West: material which revealed lines of headless, mutilated corpses. The abiding image in Western countries was of an endless line of destroyed vehicles, but no corpses. But this was the 'party' that Powell and Schwarzkopf had promised.[86] In the lead-up to the conflict, General Powell had spoken of the 'tools' in the 'toolbox' which the Pentagon had available. Al-Jahra showed what the tools could do. A beaten army was systematically annihilated from the air by a technologically superior force engaged in mass killing. According to Philip Taylor, US Navy pilots were so keen to return to the battle that, in order to rearm, they would take any munitions they could get.[87] As one American said, it was a 'turkey shoot'; the Iraqis were like 'cockroaches' that you crush under your foot.

This slaughter and the damage done to Iraq has been quickly forgotten. However, at the time there was a frenzied celebration in America of the triumph of US high-tech warfare. The benefits to the US political elite were obvious. A clear lesson was sent out to the Third World concerning threats to US interests. All threats to US oil supplies would be dealt with in decisive terms. The US military had regained its credibility, and the vast sums of money spent in the 1980s, ostensibly to meet the Soviet threat, could be justified. Also the legacy of Vietnam had been vanquished; the USA had had its revenge. But how were ordinary people seduced into celebrating an orgy of killing that seemed to challenge all codes of moral decency? The reality is that in the USA an extremely ugly war psychosis set in, which was substantially created by the mainstream media. After reporting the propaganda about the emerging conflict spread by the Bush administration, the media collaborated in the erection of a massive framework of cultural misinformation which demonized the Iraqis and created a Hitler image around the personality of Saddam Hussein, whose name was pronounced by members of the administration in a way to invoke the phonetics of sodomy and satanism. In the US print media there were no fewer than 1,170 references linking Saddam to Hitler; American discourse was also heavily racist and sexist. It constantly spoke of 'dark chaos', 'the law of the jungle' and 'rape' and 'penetration' in relation to Kuwait. According to Kellner and Engelhardt, these images have a long history in US narratives concerning captivity and the violation of white women by natives and Indians. Significant here was the infamous story of the baby incubator which Iraqi forces had allegedly switched off after putting 15 babies on the floor to die. President Bush mentioned this story eight times over a 44-day period, but it was a fabrication. In October 1990 a teenage girl testified to the House Human Rights Caucus that she had witnessed the murder of these babies. Her identity was not revealed; but in fact, she was the daughter of the Kuwaiti ambassador to the USA. Before the hearing she was coached by the public relations firm Hill and Knowlton, on which the Kuwaitis spent 5.6 million dollars between August and November 1990. In this period Hill and Knowlton, which was run by former Bush aides, put out 30 video reports which were seen by 30 million people.[88] On

17 January 1991 ABC revealed that a doctor who claimed
to have buried the babies was a liar and also not a doctor. But
these factual rectifications were irrelevant against the unrelenting
propaganda about Saddam and the Iraqis. Insider/outsider
rhetoric framed Iraq perfectly as the locus of the barbarian. As
Kellner notes, 'Throughout the crisis, the dichotomy between
foreign and uncivilised Arabs and civilised Westerners was drawn
upon.'[89] In consequence, it is not surprising that the USA appeared
to be in the grip of a kind of war psychosis. Robert Lifton found
it deeply troubling:

> We cannot long postpone the questions we are now avoiding: is
> this responsible behaviour on the part of a country claiming to be
> a humane democracy; could we not have avoided much of the
> slaughter by ending the war much earlier ... we became quickly
> dominated by an ugly pattern of war psychology that justifies the
> killing of large numbers of defenceless people. Our hi-tech
> weapons eased the process by enabling us to remain numbed to it
> and disassociated from it.[90]

CONCLUSIONS

The realities of the Gulf War demand more space than is available
here. However, I believe I can make my central point. The West, in
the guise of the culture of modernity, has a long history of present-
ing others in a subhuman and demonized form. These articulations
have served to justify imperialism and genocide, and are a general
part of the pattern of war propaganda. In the past the power of these
images reflected the material power of Europe and the United
States. The conquerors wrote the history of the conquered in their
language, usually English, Spanish, French or German. These narratives were aesthetically pleasing, because they confirmed Western
self-images of superiority. This discourse is now challenged by the
work of intellectuals from former colonies, and metropolitan intellectuals now encounter many rival discourses to those from the West.
However, as the Gulf War revealed, the decline in the material inventory of Western power is not matched by a decline in cultural power.
Both in domestic society and transnationally, Western media enterprises now have vast potential to shape and define global agendas.
The logic of this process flows from the continuing globalization of

capitalism. Now that the Cold War is over, the obvious focus of opposition has been removed. Thus, while the power of specific capitalist countries may have declined, the overall path of transnational capital has been smoothed. Thus the potential exists today for a tremendous homogenization of global culture as the media industry lays down the advance aesthetic pathways for the nuts and bolts of capitalist practice. As a result of what Foucault termed 'discourse and practise', the victims of modernization now speak its language. In this process America stands at the centre. Although the lives of many of its own citizens no longer correspond to the American dream, US media enterprises now have the capacity to globalize the image. As Edward Said suggests, 'rarely before in human history has there been so strong an intervention from one culture to another as there is today from America to the rest of the world'.[91] Discourses, texts and narratives which are not commensurate with this culture are excluded. Moral practices of a highly dubious character are sanctioned not by argument, but by sheer empirical weight of presentation. The Gulf War showed that the potential today for information management is enormous; led by CNN, the world's media gave an utterly distorted account of the conflict choreographed by the Pentagon.

A major problem which derives from the situation I have described above is that cultural imperialism can spark repressive and xenophobic nationalism in developing countries. It is a remarkable achievement to pursue policies which prompt support for a dictator such as Saddam Hussein. But, as Said points out, the USA has never supported any progressive regimes or movements in the Middle East. For the Arab masses Saddam was a hero precisely because he pitted himself against the USA, which has long been associated with injustice and repression in the region. As militants in Egypt today attack Western tourists, we should perhaps ponder how their mind-set has reached this impasse, instead of simply imagining that the people involved are deranged. What is it about the image of the West which engenders such antagonism? Could it be the slaughter of the Iraqi people? Could it be Western support for one-party states and dictatorships? Could it be the staggering level of inequality, and the fact that millions of poor Arabs wander the region in search of work? Or is it the virtually unconditional support for Israel, even when its actions clearly violate international law? What is certain is that we will not get honest answers to any of these questions from transnational media which trivialize, decontextualize and sometimes lie. As Baudrillard asserts, there is today an all-pervasive hyper-reality projected by the media. But wrongly, as Norris shows,[92] Baudrillard rejects the other reality: one of struggle, one of suffering, one of hope for millions that things will improve and that assistance will come. As Bosnia showed, hope and despair can mingle in complex ways; to be moral, we must recognize the 'other' as a partner in moral discourse. We must also realize that the power of technology today makes us remote from those whose lives we affect for good or ill. To say that we live in a new age of assorted victimhoods is false. There have always been victims; but today there are fewer plausible alibis for exclusion and violence.

Notes

Introduction

1. Zygmund Bauman, *Postmodern Ethics*, Oxford, 1993, p. 28.
2. Tom Engelhardt, *The End of Victory Culture*, New York, 1995, pp. 1–3.
3. David Campbell, *Writing Security*, Manchester, 1992, p. 20.

Chapter 1   Enlightenment, Modernity and War

1. Stejpan G. Meštrović, *The Balkanization of the West*, London, 1994, ch. 1.
2. Bauman, *Postmodern Ethics*, p. 215.
3. See Christopher Norris, *Uncritical Theory: Postmodern Intellectuals and the Gulf War*, London, 1992, p. 13.
4. Bogdan Denitch, *Ethnic Nationalism*, Minneapolis, 1994, p. 17.
5. Christopher Coker, *War and the Twentieth Century*, London, 1994, p. 2.
6. Ibid., p. 3.
7. See Dante Germino, *Modern Western Political Thought*, New York, 1972, p. 117.
8. Ibid.
9. Roberto M. Unger, *Knowledge and Politics*, New York, 1975, p. 51.
10. Quoted, A. P. d'Entrèves, *The Notion of the State*, Oxford, 1967, p. 50.
11. Ibid., ch. 6.
12. G. Sabine and T. L. Thorson, *A History of Political Thought*, New York, 1978, p. 425.
13. See Meštrović, *Balkanization of the West*, ch. 1.
14. Bauman, *Postmodern Ethics*, p. 26.
15. William Connolly, *Political Theory and Modernity*, Oxford, 1988, p. 1.
16. Unger, *Knowledge and Politics*, p. 5.
17. Quoted, Jürgen Habermas, *Theory and Practice*, London, 1974, p. 257.
18. Germino, *Modern Western Political Thought*, p. 58.
19. Quoted, F. Chalk and K. Jonassohn, *The History and Sociology of Genocide*, New Haven, 1990, p. 151.
20. Coker, *War and the Twentieth Century*, p. 3.
21. Jacques Domenech, *L'Éthique des Lumières: les fondements de la morale dans le philosophie française de XVIII siecle*, Paris, 1989, p. 9.
22. See Bauman, *Postmodern Ethics*, p. 26.
23. Quoted, ibid.
24. Ibid. pp. 27–8.
25. Ibid., p. 26.
26. Anthony Giddens, *The Nation State and Violence*, Cambridge, 1985, p. 5.
27. See Johannes Fabian, *Time and the Other: How Anthropology Makes its Object*, New York, 1983.
28. Quoted, Jürgen Habermas, *The Theory of Communicative Action*, Boston, 1984, p. 146.
29. K. Kumar, *Prophecy and Progress*, Harmondsworth, 1986, p. 105.

30. Ibid., p. 104.
31. Quoted, Germino, *Modern Western Political Thought*, p. 223.
32. W. B. Gallie, *Understanding War*, London, 1991, p. 42.
33. Manuel de Landa, *War in the Age of Intelligent Machines*, New York, 1991, p. 66.
34. Ibid.
35. H. W. Koch, *The Rise of Modern Warfare*, London, 1981, p. 153.
36. Theodore Ropp, *War and the Modern World*, New York, 1959, p. 99.
37. Ibid.
38. Ibid., p. 100.
39. De Landa, *War in the Age of Intelligent Machines*, p. 31.
40. Ropp, *War in the Modern World*, p. 101.
41. Ibid.
42. See Bruce H. Franklin, *War Stars*, Oxford and New York, 1988, p. 11.
43. Ropp, *War in the Modern World*, p. 102.
44. Ibid., p. 104.
45. Quoted, Koch, *Rise of Modern Warfare*, p. 229.
46. Quoted, Ropp, *War in the Modern World*, p. 109.
47. Quoted, ibid.
48. Coker, *War and the Twentieth Century*, p. 3.
49. Koch, *Rise of Modern Warfare*, p. 229.
50. Ibid., p. 221.
51. Ropp, *War in the Modern World*, p. 137.
52. Peter Paret, 'Clausewitz', in Peter Paret, (ed.), *Makers of Modern Strategy: From Machiavelli to the Nuclear Age*, Princeton, 1986, p. 188.
53. Ropp, *War in the Modern World*, p. 137.
54. See John Shy, 'Jomini', in Paret (ed.), *Makers of Modern Strategy*, p. 181.
55. Quoted, Ibid.
56. John Keegan, *A History of Warfare*, London, 1993, p. 354.
57. Ibid.
58. Shy, 'Jomini', p. 180.
59. Paret, 'Clausewitz', p. 196.
60. Ropp, *War in the Modern World*, p. 158.
61. Shy, 'Jomini', p. 177.
62. Ibid.
63. Ibid., p. 144.
64. Quoted, ibid., p. 146.
65. De Landa, *War in the Age of Intelligent Machines*, p. 89.
66. Shy, 'Jomini', p. 146.
67. De Landa, *War in the Age of Intelligent Machines*, p. 102.
68. See Bradley Klein, *Strategic Studies and World Order*, Cambridge, 1994, p. 48.
69. Paret, 'Clausewitz', p. 191.
70. Ibid., p. 197.
71. Ibid.
72. Ibid., p. 212.
73. Carl von Clausewitz, *On War*, ed. and trans. Michael Howard and Peter Paret, Princeton, 1976, pp. 583–4.
74. Keegan, *History of Warfare*, pp. 372–3.

75. Ropp, *War in the Modern World*, p. 141.
76. Ibid.
77. Ibid., p. 163.
78. Franklin, *War Stars*, pp. 15–17.
79. Ibid., pp. 3–19.
80. Ibid., pp. 3–5.
81. See the argument in Meštrović, *Balkanization of the West*, p. 62.
82. Quoted, Chalk and Jonassohn, *History and Sociology of Genocide*, p. 202.
83. Franklin, *War Stars*, p. 5.
84. Ibid.
85. Merrit Roe Smith, 'Army Ordnance and the "American System" of Manufacture', in Merrit Roe Smith (ed.), *Military Enterprise and Technological Change*, Cambridge, Mass., 1987, p. 41.
86. De Landa, *War in the Age of Intelligent Machines*, p. 32.
87. Ropp, *War in the Modern World*, p. 193.
88. Ibid.
89. Quoted, ibid., p. 179.
90. Martin van Creveld, *Command in War*, Cambridge, Mass., 1985, p. 269.
91. Trevor Dupuy, *Understanding War*, New York, 1987, p. 201.
92. Ropp, *War in the Modern World*, p. 181.
93. Ibid., p. 182.
94. Quoted, Daniel Pick, *War Machine*, New Haven, 1993, p. 53.
95. Giddens, *Nation State and Violence*, p. 226.
96. Pick, *War Machine*, p. 49.
97. Ropp, *War in the Modern World*, p. 143.
98. Pick, *War Machine*, p. 23.
99. Kenneth Waltz, *Man, the State and War*, New York, 1959, p. 85.
100. Giddens, *Nation State and Violence*, p. 223.
101. Ibid.
102. Ropp, *War in the Modern World*, p. 146.
103. Coker, *War and the Twentieth Century*, p. 99.
104. Ibid., p. 227.
105. Klein, *Strategic Studies and World Order*, p. 15.
106. Giddens, *Nation State and Violence*, p. 227.
107. Bauman, *Postmodern Ethics*, p. 227.
108. Ibid., p. 219.
109. Coker, *War and the Twentieth Century*, p. 15.
110. Engelhardt, *End of Victory Culture*, pp. 5–6.
111. Ibid., p. 5.
112. Coker, *War and the Twentieth Century*, p. 227.
113. Keegan, *History of Warfare*, p. 312.
114. Ibid., p. 132.
115. Franklin, *War Stars*, p. 5.

Chapter 2   Rumours of War

1. See Franklin, *War Stars*, ch. 1.
2. Sam Keen, *Faces of the Enemy*, New York, 1986, p. 10.

3. Gallie, *Understanding War*, p. 5.
4. Coker, *War and the Twentieth Century*, p. 239.
5. V. G. Kiernan, *The Lords of Human Kind*, London, 1988, p. 311.
6. See Pick, *War Machine*, p. 1.
7. See G. F. R. Henderson, *The Science of War*, London, 1913, pp. 401–7.
8. Pick, *War Machine*, ch. 9.
9. Coker, *War and the Twentieth Century*, p. 231.
10. Pick, *War Machine*, p. 75.
11. Karl Pearson, *The Scope and Importance to the State of the Science of National Eugenics*, London, 1911, p. 10.
12. Quoted, Pick, *War Machine*, p. 75.
13. Quoted, Coker, *War and the Twentieth Century*, p. 9.
14. Friederich von Bernhardi, *Germany and the Next War*, New York, 1914, p. 37.
15. Ropp, *War in the Modern World*, p. 200.
16. See Karl D. Bracher, *The German Dictatorship*, Harmondsworth, 1973, ch. 1.
17. Pick, *War Machine*, p. 88.
18. Ibid., p. 90.
19. Ibid., p. 147.
20. Quoted, ibid., pp. 148–9.
21. Ibid., p. 133.
22. Quoted, Ropp, *War in the Modern World*, p. 218.
23. Ibid., p. 205.
24. Franklin, *War Stars*, ch. 1.
25. Ibid., p. 41.
26. Ibid., p. 42.
27. Quoted Richard Hofstadter, *Social Darwinism in American Thought*, Boston, 1944, p. 170.
28. Quoted, ibid., p. 170.
29. Ibid., p. 189.
30. Engelhardt, *End of Victory Culture*, pp. 1–6.
31. Ibid., p. 5.
32. Ibid.
33. A. T. Mahan, *The Influence of Sea Power on History*, Boston, 1895.
34. Klein, *Strategic Studies and World Order*, p. 87.
35. Ropp, *War in the Modern World*, p. 210.
36. Hofstadter, *Social Darwinism in American Thought*, p. 170.
37. Mahan, *Influence of Sea Power on History*, p. 83.
38. Klein, *Strategic Studies and World Order*, p. 89.
39. Holly Maze-Carter, *The Asian Dilemma in U.S. Foreign Policy: National Interest versus State Planning*, London and New York, 1989, p. 10.
40. Franklin, *War Stars*, p. 41.
41. Ibid., p. 45.
42. Pick, *War Machine*, p. 115.
43. Ibid., p. 118.
44. Klein, *Strategic Studies and World Order*, p. 81.
45. Ibid., p. 91.

46. William Connolly, 'The Dilemma of Legitimacy', in Connolly (ed.), *Legitimacy and the State*, p. 226.
47. Quoted in Ropp, *War in the Modern World*, p. 203 (emphasis in original).
48. Colin McInnes, *Men, Machines and the Emergence of Modern Warfare*, Strategic and Combat Studies Institute, London, 1992, p. 7.
49. Quoted, ibid., p. 8; emphasis added.
50. See Ivan S. Bloch, *The Future of War*, Boston, 1903, p. xxxi.
51. Ropp, *War in the Modern World*, p. 219.
52. Quoted, ibid.
53. Ibid., p. 220.
54. Ibid., p. 239.
55. Quoted in Thomas Allen, *War Games*, New York, 1987, p. 67.
56. De Landa, *War in the Age of Intelligent Machines*, p. 91.
57. Quoted, Keegan, *History of Warfare*, p. 359.
58. McInnes, *Men, Machines and the Emergence of Modern War*, p. 21.
59. Keegan, *History of Warfare*, p. 365.
60. Coker, *War and the Twentieth Century*, p. 24.
61. Quoted, Ropp, *War in the Modern World*, p. 239.
62. Coker, *War and the Twentieth Century*, p. 126.
63. Ropp, *War in the Modern World*, p. 180.
64. Ibid., p. 250.
65. Ibid.
66. Henry Williamson, *The Wet Flanders Plain*, London, 1929, pp. 14–16.
67. Coker, *War and the Twentieth Century*, p. 132.
68. Quoted, ibid.
69. Pick, *War Machine*, pp. 201–2.
70. Coker, *War and the Twentieth Century*, p. 126.
71. Quoted, ibid., p. 161.
72. See A. Giddens (ed.), *Durkheim, Selected Writings*, Cambridge, 1972, pp. 1–50.
73. Quoted, Coker, *War and the Twentieth Century*, p. 120.
74. See Peter Berger et al., *The Homeless Mind*, Harmondsworth, 1972.

Chapter 3   The Enchantment of War in the Air

1. Alfred N. Whitehead, *Science and the Modern World*, New York, 1948, p. 362.
2. Keegan, *History of Warfare*, p. 362.
3. See Michael S. Sherry, *The Rise of American Air Power*, New Haven, 1987, p. 23.
4. Ibid., p. 3.
5. Lee Kennett, *A History of Strategic Bombing*, New York, 1982, p. 2.
6. Ibid., p. 5.
7. Ibid.
8. Ibid., pp. 7–8.
9. See Franklin, *War Stars*, ch. 1, and Spencer Weart, *Nuclear Fear*, Cambridge, Mass., 1988, pp. 5–8.

10. Sherry, *Rise of American Air Power*, pp. 8–10.
11. Ibid., p. 10.
12. Quoted, ibid.
13. Kennett, *History of Strategic Bombing*, p. 8.
14. Franklin, *War Stars*, p. 67.
15. Ibid., p. 70.
16. Kennett, *History of Strategic Bombing*, p. 12.
17. Franklin, *War Stars*, p. 86.
18. See Sherry, *Rise of American Air Power*, p. 14.
19. Ibid., p. 65.
20. Kennett, *History of Strategic Bombing*, p. 19.
21. Sherry, *Rise of American Air Power*, p. 15.
22. Ibid., p. 14.
23. Kennett, *History of Strategic Bombing*, p. 33.
24. Keith Hayward, *The British Aircraft Industry*, Manchester, 1989, p. 10.
25. Ibid., p. 11.
26. William E. Leuchtenberg, *The Perils of Prosperity*, Chicago, 1958, p. 29.
27. Ibid., p. 44.
28. Sherry, *Rise of American Air Power*, p. 20.
29. Ibid.
30. William Mitchell, *Winged Defense: The Development and Possibilities of Modern Air War*, New York, 1925, p. 15.
31. Ibid., p. 16.
32. Coker, *War and the Twentieth Century*, p. 32.
33. Lawrence Freedman, *The Evolution of Nuclear Strategy*, London, 1981, p. 48.
34. Guilio Douhet, *Command of the Air*, New York, 1942, p. 22.
35. Ibid., p. 122.
36. Ibid., p. 25.
37. See Fred Kaplan, *The Wizards of Armageddon*, New York, 1983, p. 269.
38. Basil Liddell-Hart, *Paris, or the Future of War*, London, 1925, p. 43.
39. Sherry, *Rise of American Air Power*, p. 25.
40. Ibid., p. 24.
41. Ibid., p. 27.
42. C. G. Grey, *Bombers*, London, 1942, p. 41.
43. Robert B. Asprey, *War in the Shadows*, London, 1994, p. 277.
44. Ibid.
45. Ibid., p. 279.
46. Ibid.
47. Quoted, ibid., p. 280.
48. Franklin, *War Stars*, p. 95.
49. Hayward, *British Aircraft Industry*, p. 20.
50. Quoted in Franklin, *War Stars*, p. 95.
51. Cited in Sherry, *Rise of American Air Power*, p. 59.
52. Ibid., p. 55.
53. Hayward, *British Aircraft Industry*, p. 20.
54. Sherry, *Rise of American Air Power*, p. 72.
55. Ibid., p. 71.
56. Keegan, *History of Warfare*, p. 370.

57. Quoted, John Newhouse, *The Nuclear Age*, London, 1989, pp. 9–10.
58. Joachim Fest, *Hitler*, Harmondsworth, 1981, chs 4–5.
59. Quoted, Sherry, *Rise of American Air Power*, p. 76.
60. Ibid., p. 69.
61. Ibid., p. 88.
62. Ibid., p. 90.
63. Ibid.
64. Asprey, *War in the Shadows*, p. 280.
65. Sherry, *Rise of American Air Power*, p. 93.
66. See Keegan, *History of Warfare*, p. 374.
67. Franklin, *War Stars*, p. 106.
68. Ibid.
69. Ibid.
70. Ibid.
71. Sherry, *Rise of American Air Power*, p. 260.
72. Franklin, *War Stars*, p. 113.
73. Sherry, *Rise of American Air Power*, pp. 256–60.
74. Franklin, *War Stars*, p. 113.
75. Robert Higham, *Air Power: A Concise History*, New York, 1972, p. 130.
76. Sherry, *Rise of American Air Power*, p. 114.
77. Quoted, ibid., p. 109.
78. Franklin, p. 109.
79. Ibid., p. 110.
80. Keegan, *History of Warfare*, p. 376.
81. Engelhardt, *End of Victory Culture*, p. 4.
82. Keegan, *History of Warfare*, p. 379.
83. Quoted in Engelhardt, *End of Victory Culture*, p. 3.
84. David Campbell, *Writing Security*, 1992, p. 110.
85. Keegan, *History of Warfare*, p. 377.
86. Asprey, *War in the Shadows*, p. 482.
87. Engelhardt, *End of Victory Culture*, p. 6.
88. Ibid.
89. John Schaar, *Legitimacy in the Modern State*, New York, 1981, p. 21.

Chapter 4   Intellectuals and Strategic Discourse

1. Paul Kennedy, *The Rise and Fall of the Great Powers*, London, 1988, p. 358.
2. Bruce Blair, *Strategic Command and Control*, Washington, 1985, p. 24.
3. W. Kincade, 'American National Style and Strategic Culture', in C. Jacobsen (ed.), *Strategic Power: USA/USSR*, London, 1990, p. 13.
4. Robert Rothstein, 'On the Costs of Realism', *Political Science Quarterly*, 87, no. 3, 1972, pp. 347–62.
5. M. Banks, 'The Evolution of International Relations Theory', in M. Banks (ed.), *Conflict in World Society*, Brighton, 1988, p. 9.
6. Engelhardt, *End of Victory Culture*, p. 7.
7. Philip K. Lawrence, *Preparing for Armageddon*, Brighton, 1988, p. 35.
8. Weart, *Nuclear Fear*, p. 234.
9. Kaplan, *Wizards of Armageddon*, p. 170.

10. Weart, *Nuclear Fear*, p. 157.
11. Michael C. MccGwire, 'The Dilemmas and Delusions of Deterrence', in G. Prins (ed.), *The Choice: Nuclear Weapons Versus Security*, London, 1994, pp. 81–2.
12. Colin S. Gray, 'Through a Missile Tube Darkly: New Thinking about Nuclear Strategy', *Political Studies*, 41, no. 4, 1993, p. 668.
13. Franz Neumann, 'The Intelligentsia in Exile', in P. Connerton (ed.), *Critical Sociology*, Harmondsworth, 1976, p. 429.
14. Ibid.
15. Quoted in Theodore Roszak, 'On Academic Delinquency', in T. Roszak (ed.), *The Dissenting Academy*, Harmondsworth, 1969, p. 12.
16. Ibid., p. 5.
17. Ibid., p. 17.
18. Colin Gray, *Strategic Studies*, New York, 1982, p. iii.
19. Ibid., p. 9.
20. Ibid., p. 7.
21. Gray, 'Through a Missile Tube Darkly', p. 661.
22. Charles Reynolds, *The Politics of War*, Brighton, 1989, p. 117.
23. Gray, *Strategic Studies*, p. 28.
24. Ibid., p. 21.
25. Gray, 'Through a Missile Tube Darkly' p. 664.
26. Ibid.
27. Irene Gendzier, *Managing Social Change: Social Scientists and the Third World*, Boulder, Colo., 1985, p. 9.
28. Quoted in M. Windmuller, 'The New American Mandarins', in Roszak (ed.), *Dissenting Academy*, p. 112.
29. Quoted, ibid.
30. See Kaplan, *Wizards of Armageddon*, and Gregg Herken, *Counsels of War*, New York, 1985.
31. De Landa, *War in the Age of Intelligent Machines*.
32. Ibid., p. 102.
33. Bernard Brodie, *The Absolute Weapon*, New York, 1946.
34. Herken, *Counsels of War*, p. 6.
35. Kaplan, *Wizards of Armageddon*, p. 78.
36. Campbell, *Writing Security*, ch. 1.
37. Herken, *Counsels of War*, p. xiv.
38. Quoted, ibid., p. 83.
39. B. Klein, 'Hegemony and Strategic Culture', *Review of International Studies*, vol. 14, no. 2, 1988, p. 139.
40. Weart, *Nuclear Fear*, p. 234.
41. Published as W. Kaufman, *Military Policy and National Security*, Princeton, 1956.
42. See Kaplan, *Wizards of Armageddon*, p. 226.
43. Coker, *War and the Twentieth Century*, p. 216.
44. Kaplan, *Wizards of Armageddon*, p. 223.
45. Quoted in Chomsky, p. 241.
46. Ibid. pp. 241–2.
47. Quoted, Kaplan, *Wizards of Armageddon*, p. 226.
48. Franklin, *War Stars*, p. 116.

49. Henry Kissinger, *Nuclear Weapons and Foreign Policy*, New York, 1957.
50. Ibid., p. 114.
51. D. Wise and T. B. Ross, *Invisible Government*, New York, 1974, p. 244.
52. Kaplan, *Wizards of Armageddon*, p. 256.
53. Ibid., p. 269.
54. Quoted, ibid., p. 270.
55. Ibid., p. 255.
56. Quoted, Weart, *Nuclear Fear*, p. 235.
57. Stephen Ambrose, *American Foreign Policy: The Rise to Globalism*, Harmondsworth, 1978, p. 205.
58. See also D. Halberstam, *The Best and the Brightest*, New York, 1972, p. 193.
59. Ibid., p. 193.
60. Wise and Ross, *Invisible Government*, p. 244.
61. Ambrose, *American Foreign Policy*, p. 208.
62. Ibid., p. 208.
63. Ibid., p. 207.
64. Bernard Fall, *The Two Vietnams*, London, 1963, p. 373.
65. W. Corson, *The Betrayal*, New York, 1969, p. 48.
66. Halberstam, *Best and Brightest*, pp. 628–40.
67. Ambrose, *American Foreign Policy*, p. 215.
68. Franklin, *War Stars*, p. 118.
69. Gendzier, *Managing Social Change*, p. 15.
70. R. Nisbet, *Tradition and Revolt*, New York, 1970, pp. 250–3.
71. Ibid., p. 252.
72. R. Engler, 'Social Science and Social Consciousness', in Roszak (ed.), *Dissenting Academy*, p. 181.
73. Windmuller, 'New American Mandarins', p. 113.
74. W. J. Crockett, 'Two-Way Communication with the Educational Community', *Department of State Bulletin*, vol. 55, 1966, pp. 73–4.
75. Hannah Arendt, 'Lying in Politics' in H. Arendt, *The Crisis of the Republic*, Harmondsworth, 1973.
76. Ibid., p. 15.
77. Ibid., p. 38.
78. Cited in Nisbet, *Tradition and Revolt*, p. 250.
79. Quoted, Halberstam, *Best and Brightest*, p. 197.
80. Quoted, Chomsky, 'Responsibility of Intellectuals', p. 240.
81. Engler, 'Social Science and Social Consciousness', pp. 111–12.
82. Edward Said, *Culture and Imperialism*, London, 1992, p. 366.

Chapter 5   The Rise and Fall of Nuclear Culture

1. Quoted, Freedman, *Evolution of Nuclear Strategy*, p. 51.
2. Weart, *Nuclear Fear*, p. 121.
3. Ibid.
4. Quoted, Robert Junck, *Brighter than a Thousand Suns*, Harmondsworth, 1960, p. 249.
5. See Coker, *War and the Twentieth Century*, ch. 7.
6. Weart, *Nuclear Fear*, p. 121.

7. Seymour M. Lipset, 'The End of Ideology', in C. Waxman (ed.), *The End of Ideology Debate*, New York, 1968, p. 57.

8. See Charles Wright-Mills, *The Power Elite*, Oxford and New York, 1956.

9. Engelhardt, *End of Victory Culture*, p. 78.

10. Ernest May, 'The U.S. Government: A Legacy of the Cold War', in Michael J. Hogan (ed.), *The End of the Cold War: Its Meaning and Implications*, Cambridge, 1992, p. 218.

11. Ibid., p. 226.

12. Engelhardt, *End of Victory Culture*, p. 75.

13. Ibid.

14. See Hans Morgenthau, *Politics among Nations*, New York, 1946.

15. Campbell, *Writing Security*, pp. 25–7.

16. See Steven Longstaff, 'European Intellectuals and the Cultural Cold War', in Philip K. Lawrence (ed.), *Knowledge and Power: The Changing Role of European Intellectuals*, Aldershot, 1996, pp. 138–50.

17. See Alfred Grosser, *The Western Alliance*, London, 1980, pp. 52–4.

18. Ibid., p. 71.

19. See Thomas Braden, 'I'm Glad the CIA is Immoral', *Saturday Evening Post*, 20 May 1967, p. 10.

20. Longstaff, 'European Intellectuals', p. 138.

21. Ibid., p. 139.

22. Ibid., p. 140.

23. Ibid., p. 142.

24. Ibid., p. 144.

25. Grosser, *Western Alliance*, p. 36.

26. Longstaff, 'European Intellectuals', p. 141.

27. Ibid.

28. Grosser, *Western Alliance*, p. 73.

29. Richard Falk and Robert J. Lifton, *Indefensible Weapons*, New York, 1982, p. 158.

30. Herken, *Counsels of War*, p. 27.

31. Freedman, *Evolution of Nuclear Strategy*, p. 35.

32. Quoted, ibid., p. 75.

33. Ibid., p. 66.

34. See David P. Conradt, 'Political Culture, Legitimacy and Participation', *West European Politics*, 4, no. 2, 1981, pp. 1–2.

35. Freedman, *Evolution of Nuclear Strategy*, p. 149.

36. Ibid.

37. Ibid.

38. Bernard Brodie, *Strategy in the Missile Age*, Princeton, 1959, p. 213.

39. Freedman, *Evolution of Nuclear Strategy*, p. 230.

40. Paul Bracken, *Command and Control of Nuclear Forces*, Cambridge, Mass., 1983, p. 164.

41. Ibid.

42. See BBC, *Panorama*, 20 March 1994.

43. Franklin, *War Stars*, p. 182.

44. Ibid., p. 158.

45. Weart, *Nuclear Fear*, p. 148.

46. Ibid., p. 251.

47. Quoted, ibid., p. 133.
48. Franklin, *War Stars*, p. 180.
49. See Trevor Findlay, *Nuclear Dynamite*, Rushcutters Bay, New South Wales, 1990.
50. Weart, *Nuclear Fear*, p. 204.
51. Ibid., p. 204.
52. Kaplan, *Wizards of Armageddon*, p. 141.
53. Franklin, *War Stars*, pp. 170–4.
54. See Peter Biskind, *Seeing is Believing*, New York, 1983, p. 102.
55. Ibid., p. 102.
56. See Ira Chernos, *Dr Strangegod*, New York, 1986.
57. Quoted, Coker, *War and the Twentieth Century*, p. 199.
58. Quoted, ibid., p. 203.
59. Ibid., p. 103.
60. See Weart, *Nuclear Fear*, p. 192.
61. Ibid., p. 224.
62. Franklin, *War Stars*, p. 174.
63. Ibid., p. 183.
64. Weart, *Nuclear Fear*, p. 254.
65. Coker, *War and the Twentieth Century*, p. 203.
66. Weart, *Nuclear Fear*, p. 259.
67. Quoted, ibid., p. 268.
68. Newhouse, *Nuclear Age*, p. 233.
69. Ibid., p. 233.
70. Ibid.
71. See Edward Luttwak, *The Grand Strategy of the Soviet Union*, London, 1983.
72. See Philip K. Lawrence, 'Strategic Studies and Political Theory: A Critical Assessment', *Review of International Studies*, 11, no. 1, 1985.
73. Quoted, Union of Concerned Scientists, *Beyond the Freeze*, Boston, 1982, p. 38.
74. Quoted, Michael Sheehan, *The Arms Race*, Oxford, 1983, p. 35.
75. Kaplan, *Wizards of Armageddon*, p. 389.
76. Newhouse, *Nuclear Age*, p. 297.
77. Quoted, Kaplan, *Wizards of Armageddon*, p. 386.
78. Quoted, Newhouse, *Nuclear Age*, p. 295.
79. Michael J. Krepon, 'The Changing American Strategic Environment', in Jacobsen (ed.), *Strategic Power*, p. 429.
80. Franklin, *War Stars*, p. 197.
81. Falk and Lifton, *Indefensible Weapons*, p. 156.
82. Engelhardt, *End of Victory Culture*, p. 271.
83. Carl Sagan, 'Nuclear War and Climatic Catastrophe', in Fred Holroyd (ed.), *Thinking about Nuclear Weapons*, London, 1985, p. 28.
84. Quoted, ibid., p. 22.
85. Jonathan Schell, *The Fate of the Earth*, New York, 1982.
86. Bernard Brodie, *War and Politics*, London, 1973, p. 47.
87. Quoted, Jeff MacMahan, *Reagan and the World*, London, 1984, p. 52.
88. Sanford Laycoff and Herbert York, *A Shield in Space*, Berkeley, 1989, p. 9.
89. Ibid, p. 91.

90. Sidney Blumenthal, *The Rise of the Counter-Establishment*, New York, 1986, p. 306.
91. Lord Zolly Zuckerman, 'The Strange Case of SDI', *New York Review of Books*, 33, no. 1, 1986, p. 10.
92. Strobe Talbot, *Deadly Gambits*, London, 1984, pp. 14–16.
93. Krepon, 'Changing American Strategic Environment', p. 421.

Chapter 6   Aesthetics and Strategic Violence

1. Jean Baudrillard, 'Pas de pitié pour Sarajevo', *Liberation*, 17 January 1994, pp. 5–6. (I am grateful to Ann Pilaud for a translation of this article.)
2. Ibid., p. 6.
3. Jacques Derrida, 'Some Statements and Truisms about Neologisms, Newisms, Postisms, Parasitisms, and Other Small Seismisms', in David Caroll (ed.), *The States of 'Theory', History, Art and Critical Discourse*, Stanford, Calif., 1990, p. 85.
4. Baudrillard, 'Pas de pitié pour Sarajevo', p. 6.
5. This is discussed in Coker, *War and the Twentieth Century*, p. 3.
6. Meštrović, *Balkanization of the West*, p. vii.
7. Former British Foreign Secretary Douglas Hurd frequently referred to Rwanda as a 'true heart of darkness'.
8. Coker, *War and the Twentieth Century*, p. 227.
9. Ibid.
10. Ibid.
11. Ibid.
12. Said, *Culture of Imperialism*, p. 233.
13. Cited in Campbell, *Writing Security*, pp. 111–12.
14. Ibid., p. 111.
15. Coker, *War and the Twentieth Century*, p. 15.
16. Engelhardt, *End of Victory Culture*, p. 25.
17. Ibid., p. 5.
18. See Catherine Hall, 'The Ruinous Ghost of Empire Past', *Times Higher Education Supplement*, 8 March 1996, pp. 18–19.
19. Quoted, Said, *Culture of Imperialism*, p. 237.
20. Ibid., p. 233.
21. Bauman, *Postmodern Ethics*, p. 216.
22. Quoted, Herbert Schiller, *Culture Inc*, Oxford, 1989, p. 134.
23. Campbell, *Writing Security*, p. 34.
24. Quoted, ibid., p. 105.
25. Ibid.
26. Ibid., p. 2.
27. See Bauman, *Postmodern Ethics*, p. 163, and Coker, *War and the Twentieth Century*, p. 24.
28. Giddens, *Nation State and Violence*, p. 223.
29. Coker, *War and the Twentieth Century*, p. 226.
30. Paul Ekins, *New World Order: Grass Roots Movements for Social Change*, London, 1991, p. 15.

31. I. L. Horowitz, *Imperialism and Revolution*, Harmondsworth, 1969, p. 232.
32. Said, *Culture of Imperialism*, p. 357.
33. Bauman, *Postmodern Ethics*, p. 215.
34. Meštrović, *Balkanization of the West*, pp. 64–5.
35. Bauman, *Postmodern Ethics*, p. 226.
36. See Meštrović, *Balkanization of the West*, p. 62.
37. Quoted, Coker, *War and the Twentieth Century*, p. 226.
38. W. Kincade, 'American National Style and Strategic culture', in C. Jacobsen (ed.), *Strategic Power: USA/USSR*, p. 15.
39. Franklin, *War Stars*, p. 20.
40. Ibid., p. 40.
41. Maze-Carter, *Asian Dilemma in US Foreign Policy*, p. 3.
42. Franklin, *War Stars*, p. 40.
43. Ibid., p. 45.
44. See my *Democracy and the Liberal State*, Aldershot, 1990, ch. 3.
45. Schiller, *Culture Inc.*, p. 137.
46. G. D. Coppes and C. Black, *Hollywood Goes to War*, New York, 1987, p. 82.
47. Ibid.
48. Ibid., p. 252.
49. Ibid., p. 250.
50. M. Sherry, *The Rise of American Air Power*, 1987, p. 250.
51. Coppes and Black, *Hollywood Goes to War*, p. 252.
52. Ibid.
53. Ibid., p. 250.
54. Kennett, *History of Strategic Bombing*, p. 67.
55. Sherry, *Rise of American Air Power*, p. 109.
56. Quoted, ibid., p. 273.
57. Ibid., p. 276.
58. Quoted, Coker, *War and the Twentieth Century*, p. 165.
59. Coppes and Black, *Hollywood Goes to War*, p. 253.
60. Ibid., p. 235.
61. Franklin, *War Stars*, p. 113.
62. Ibid., p. 114.
63. Ibid., p. 116.
64. Weart, *Nuclear Fear*, p. 217.
65. Ibid., p. 194.
66. A. S. Collins, 'Current Nato Strategy: A Recipe for Disaster', in Prins (ed.), *The Choice, Nuclear Weapons versus Security*, London 1984, p. 32.
67. Chomsky 'Responsibility of Intellectuals', pp. 251–2.
68. Weart, *Nuclear Fear*, p. 107.
69. Ibid., p. 180.
70. See Kaplan, *Wizards of Armageddon*, p. 269.
71. Cited, Said, *Culture of Imperialism*, p. 346.
72. Quoted, Bauman, *Postmodern Ethics*, p. 227.
73. Coker, *War and the Twentieth Century*, p. 244.
74. Weart, *Nuclear Fear*, p. 379.
75. Said, *Culture of Imperialism*, p. 391.
76. Ibid.

77. Quoted, Meštrović, *Balkanization of the West*, p. 7.
78. Cited, Bauman, *Postmodern Ethics*, p. 219.
79. Douglas Kellner, *The Persian Gulf TV War*, Boulder, Colo., 1992, p. 4.
80. John Tomlinson, *Cultural Imperialism*, London, 1991, p. 53.
81. Said, *Culture of Imperialism*, p. 375.
82. Kellner, *Persian Gulf TV War*, p. 113.
83. Ibid., p. 11.
84. Quoted, A. G. Frank, 'A Third World War', in Howard Mowlana et al., *Triumph of the Image*, Boulder, Colo., 1992, p. 11.
85. Ibid., p. 13.
86. Kellner, *Persian Gulf TV War*, p. 204.
87. Philip Taylor, *War and the Media*, Manchester, 1992, p. 252.
88. Kellner, *Persian Gulf TV War*, p. 67.
89. Ibid., p. 63.
90. R. J. Lifton, *The Guardian*, 3 March 1991, p. 23.
91. Said, *Culture of Imperialism*, p. 387.
92. Norris, *Uncritical Theory*, London, 1992, chs 1 and 2.

Select Bibliography

Articles and essays

Arendt, Hannah, 'Lying in Politics', in H. Arendt, *The Crisis of the Republic*, Harmondsworth, 1973.

Chomsky, Noam, 'On the Responsibility of Intellectuals', in T. Roszak (ed.), *The Dissenting Academy*, Harmondsworth, 1969.

Conradt, David P., 'Political Culture, Legitimacy and Participation', *West European Politics*, 4, no. 2, 1981.

Gray, Colin S., 'Through a Missile Tube Darkly: New Thinking about Nuclear Strategy', *Political Studies*, 41, no. 4, 1993.

Habermas, Jürgen, 'Modernity versus Postmodernity', in J. Alexander and S. Steadman (eds), *Culture and Society*, Cambridge, 1990.

Hall, Catherine, 'The Ruinous Ghost of Empire Past', *Times Higher Education Supplement*, 8 March 96.

Krepon, Michael J., 'The Changing American Strategic Environment', in Carl C. Jacobsen (ed.), *Strategic Power: USA/USSR*, London, 1990.

Lawrence, Philip K., 'Strategic Studies and Political Theory: A Critical Assessment', *Review of International Studies*, 11, no. 1, 1985.

Lawrence, Philip K., 'Strategy, the State and the Weberian Legacy', *Review of International Studies*, 13, no. 4, 1987.

Lawrence, Philip K., 'Strategy, Imagery and Mythology', in R. Little and S. Smith (eds), *Belief Systems and International Politics*, Oxford, 1988.

Lawrence, Philip K., 'Ideology, Rationality and the United States's Strategic Policy', *Australian Journal of Politics and History*, 39, no. 1, 1993.

Lawrence, Philip K., 'Strategy, Hegemony and Ideology: The Role of Intellectuals', *Political Studies*, 44, no. 1, 1996.

Longstaff, Steven, 'European Intellectuals and the Cultural Cold War', in Philip K. Lawrence (ed.), *Knowledge and Power: The Changing Role of European Intellectuals*, Aldershot, 1996.

May, Ernest, 'The U.S. Government: A Legacy of the Cold War', in Michael J. Hogan (ed.), *The End of the Cold War*, Cambridge, 1992.

MccGwire, Michael C., 'The Dilemmas and Delusions of Deterrence', in Gwyn Prins (ed.), *The Choice: Nuclear Weapons Versus Security*, London, 1994.

Paret, Peter, 'Clausewitz', in Peter Paret (ed.), *Makers of Modern Strategy: From Machiavelli to the Nuclear Age*, Princeton, 1986.

Rothstein, Robert, 'On the Costs of Realism', *Political Science Quarterly*, 87, no. 1, 1972.

Roszak, Theodore, 'On Academic Delinquency', in T. Roszak (ed.), *The Dissenting Academy*, Harmondsworth, 1969.

Shy, John, 'Jomini', in Peter Paret, (ed.), *Makers of Modern Strategy: From Machiavelli to the Nuclear Age*, Princeton, 1986.

Snyder, Jack, 'The Concept of Strategic Culture', in Carl C. Jacobsen (ed.), *Strategic Power: USA/USSR*, London, 1990.

Zuckerman, Lord Zolly, 'The Strange Story of SDI', *New York Review of Books*, 33, no. 1, 1986.

Books

Aldridge, Robert C., *First Strike! The Pentagon's Strategy for Nuclear War*, London, 1983.

Allen, Thomas, *War Games*, New York, 1987.

Ambrose, Steven, *American Foreign Policy: The Rise to Globalism*, Harmondsworth, 1978.

Asprey, Robert B., *War in the Shadows*, London, 1994.

Bauman, Zygmund, *Postmodern Ethics*, Oxford, 1993.

Berger, Peter, et al., *The Homeless Mind*, Harmondsworth, 1972.

Bernhardi, Friederich von, *Germany and the Next War*, New York, 1914.

Biskind, Peter, *Seeing is Believing*, New York, 1983.

Black, G. D., and Coppes, C. R., *Hollywood Goes to War*, New York, 1987.

Blair, Bruce, *Strategic Command and Control*, Washington, 1985.

Bloch, Ivan S., *The Future of War*, Boston, 1903.

Bracher, Karl D., *The German Dictatorship*, Harmondsworth, 1973.

Bracken, Paul, *Command and Control of Nuclear Forces*, Cambridge, Mass., 1983.

Broad, William, *Star Warriors*, London, 1987.

Brodie, Bernard, *The Absolute Weapon*, New York, 1946.

Brodie, Bernard, *Strategy in the Missile Age*, Princeton, 1959.

Brodie, Bernard, *War and Politics*, London, 1973.

Campbell, David, *Writing Security*, Manchester, 1992.

Chalk, F., and Jonassohn, K., *The History and Sociology of Genocide*, New Haven, 1990.

Charlton, W., *Aesthetics*, London, 1970.

Chernos, Ira, *Dr Strangegod*, New York, 1986.

Clausewitz, Carl von, *On War*, ed. and trans. Michael Howard and Peter Paret, Princeton, 1976.

Coker, Christopher, *War and the Twentieth Century*, London, 1994.

Connolly, William, *Political Theory and Modernity*, Oxford, 1988.

Creveld, Martin van, *Command in War*, Cambridge, Mass., 1985.

Denitch, Bogdan, *Ethnic Nationalism*, Minneapolis, 1994.

Douhet, Guilio, *Command of the Air*, New York, 1942.

Dupuy, Trevor, *Understanding War*, New York, 1987.

Engelhardt, Tom, *The End of Victory Culture*, New York, 1995.

d'Entrèves, A. P., *The Notion of the State*, Oxford, 1967.

Fabian, Johannes, *Time and the Other: How Anthropology Makes its Object*, New York, 1983.

Falk, Richard, and Lifton, Robert J., *Indefensible Weapons*, New York, 1982.

Fall, Bernard, *The Two Vietnams*, London, 1963.

Farrar, I. L. L., (ed.), *War: A Historical, Political and Social Study*, Santa Barbara, Calif., 1978.

Fest, Joachim, *Hitler*, Harmondsworth, 1981.

Findlay, Trevor, *Nuclear Dynamite*, Rushcutters Bay, New South Wales, 1990.

Franklin, Bruce H., *War Stars*, Oxford and New York, 1988.

Freedman, Lawrence, *The Evolution of Nuclear Strategy*, London, 1981.

Gallie, W. B., *Understanding War*, London, 1990.
Gendzier, Irene, *Managing Social Change: Social Scientists and the Third World*, Boulder, Colo. 1985.
Germino,, Dante, *Modern Western Political Thought*, New York, 1972.
Giddens, Anthony, *The Nation State and Violence*, Cambridge, 1985.
Gray, Colin, *Strategic Studies*, New York, 1982.
Grey, C. G., *Bombers*, London, 1942.
Grosser, Alfred, *The Western Alliance*, London, 1980.
Habermas, Jürgen, *Theory and Practice*, London, 1974.
Habermas, Jürgen, *The Theory of Communicative Action*, Boston, 1984.
Halberstam, David, *The Best and the Brightest*, New York, 1972.
Hayward, Keith, *The British Aircraft Industry*, Manchester, 1989.
Henderson, G. F. R., *The Science of War*, London, 1913.
Herken, Gregg, *Counsels of War*, New York, 1985.
Higham, Robert, *Air Power: A Concise History*, New York, 1972.
Hofstadter, Richard, *Social Darwinism in American Thought*, Boston, 1944.
Junck, Robert, *Brighter than a Thousand Suns*, Harmondsworth, 1960.
Kaplan, Fred, *The Wizards of Armageddon*, New York, 1983.
Keegan, John, *A History of Warfare*, London, 1993.
Keen, Sam, *Faces of the Enemy*, New York, 1986.
Kellner, Douglas, *The Persian Gulf TV War*, Boulder, Colo., 1992.
Kennedy, Paul, *The Rise and Fall of the Great Powers*, London, 1988.
Kennett, Lee, *A History of Strategic Bombing*, New York, 1982.
Kenny, Anthony, *The Logic of Deterrence*, London, 1985.
Kiernan, V. G., *The Lords of Human Kind*, London, 1988.
Klein, B., *Strategic Studies and World Order*, Cambridge, 1994.
Koch, H. W., *The Rise of Modern Warfare*, London, 1981.
Kumar, K., *Prophecy and Progress*, Harmondsworth, 1986.
Landa, Manuel De, *War in the Age of Intelligent Machines*, New York, 1991.
Lawrence, Philip K., *Preparing for Armageddon*, Brighton, 1988.
Laycoff, Sanford, and York, Herbert, *A Shield in Space*, Berkeley, 1989.
Lee, Christopher, *War in Space*, London, 1988.
Leuchtenberg, William E., *The Perils of Prosperity*, Chicago, 1958.
Liddell-Hart, Basil, *Paris, or the Future of War*, London, 1925.
Luttwak, Edward, *The Grand Strategy of the Soviet Union*, London, 1983.
MacMahan, Jeff, *Reagan and the World*, London, 1984.
Meštrović, Stejpan G., *The Balkanization of the West*, London, 1994.
Mowlana, Howard, et al. *Triumph of the Image*, Boulder, Colo., 1992.
John, Newhouse, *The Nuclear Age*, London, 1989.
Robert, Nisbet, *Tradition and Revolt*, New York, 1970.
Norris, Christopher, *Uncritical Theory: Postmodern Intellectuals and the Gulf War*, London, 1992.
Pearson, Karl, *The Scope and Importance to the State of the Science of National Eugenics*, London, 1911.
Pick, Daniel, *War Machine*, New Haven, 1993.
Reynolds, Charles, *The Politics of War*, Brighton, 1989.
Ropp, Theodore, *War in the Modern World*, New York, 1959.
Said, Edward, *Culture and Imperialism*, London, 1992.

Schell, Jonathan, *The Fate of the Earth*, New York, 1982.

Schiller, Herbert, *Culture Inc.*, Oxford, 1989.

Sheehan, Michael, *The Arms Race*, Oxford, 1983.

Sherry, Michael S., *The Rise of American Air Power*, New Haven, 1987.

Smith, Meritt Roe, (ed.), *Military Enterprise and Technological Change*, Cambridge, Mass., 1987.

Tomlinson, John, *Cultural Imperialism*, London, 1991.

Unger, Roberto M., *Knowledge and Politics*, New York, 1975.

Waltz, Kenneth, *Man, the State and War*, New York, 1959.

Weart, Spencer, *Nuclear Fear*, Cambridge, Mass., 1988.

Index